AF809793

THE LOWER CRIMINAL COURTS

This book explores misdemeanor courts in the United States by focusing on the processing of misdemeanor crimes and the resultant consequences of conviction, such as loss of employment and housing, the imposition of significant fines, and loss of liberty—all amounting to the criminalization of poverty that happens in many U.S. misdemeanor courts. A major concern is the lack of due process employed in lower courts. Although the seminal case of *Gideon v. Wainwright* required the appointment of counsel to individuals too poor to hire counsel in felony cases, it was not until 1967, when the President's Commission on Law Enforcement and Administration of Justice found a crisis in the lower courts, that the Supreme Court extended the right to counsel to some (though not all) prosecutions of misdemeanor offenses.

The first step to improving our understanding of the lower courts is a concerted effort by scholars to focus on the processing and outcomes of misdemeanor cases. This collection begins to fill the void by providing a comprehensive review of the scholarly work on the lower courts in the United States. Collecting analysis from key academics engaged in work in this area today, the book reviews the varying specialized lower criminal courts, including specialty courts that have emerged in just the last couple of decades, along with discussions of the history, legal challenges, operation, primary actors (judges, prosecutors, defense counsel, and defendants), and current research on these courts. The book explores the profound consequences misdemeanor processing has for defendants and discusses the future of the lower criminal courts and offers best practices to improve them.

The Lower Criminal Courts is essential for scholars and undergraduate and graduate students in criminology, sociology, justice studies, pre-law/legal studies, political science, and social work, and it is also useful as a resource providing legal practitioners with important information, highlighting the significance of consequences of misdemeanor arrests, detentions, and adjudications.

Alisa Smith is an Associate Professor and the Chair of the Department of Legal Studies at the University of Central Florida. She holds a PhD in Criminology and Criminal Justice, and a JD from the Florida State University. She practiced law for 29 years, mostly in the area of criminal defense and appeals. She has authored more than 20 peer-reviewed and law journal articles, reports, and book chapters, and she has authored two previous books. Her research has appeared in the *Journal of Criminal Justice, Florida Law Review,* and *American Journal of Criminal Law.*

Sean Maddan is Associate Professor and Chair of the Department of Social Sciences at Texas A&M International University. Dr. Maddan has authored over a dozen articles, which have appeared in many outlets, including *Justice Quarterly, Crime and Delinquency, Journal of Criminal Justice,* and the *American Journal of Criminal Justice.* Dr. Maddan has also authored/co-authored several books. His most recent book is the fifth edition of his statistics book.

The Lower Criminal Courts is a timely and meaningful addition to the literature on courts and criminal justice. The authors focus much-needed attention on an understudied and misunderstood, but extremely important aspect of the criminal justice system. This is must-read material for anyone interested in how the criminal courts provide (or fail to provide) justice.

Craig Hemmens, JD, PhD, Department of Criminal Justice and Criminology, Washington State University

Although misdemeanors represent the vast majority of American criminal cases, they have historically received inadequate academic attention. This thorough and serious survey, with its wide range of scholarly offerings, helps to fill that void. For students, the book provides an effective introduction to the enormous and complex lower court landscape. For scholars and policymakers, it offers careful and useful analyses. Overall, it deepens the current conversation about misdemeanors and their centrality to our criminal justice system.

Alexandra Natapoff, author of Punishment Without Crime: How Our Massive Misdemeanor System Traps the Innocent and Makes America More Unequal

Every year millions of people are charged with misdemeanor offenses, an event that can have surprising impact on life and livelihood. Yet much remains unknown about the inner workings of what, in many courts, can only charitably be called the misdemeanor "system." The chapters in this book shine a bright light on the way the various criminal justice players through an array of common court practices actually work to shape due process—for better and for worse. This book takes a deep and candid look at the actions of police, prosecutors, defense attorneys, and judges, and is highly recommended for those with an interest in the challenges facing misdemeanor courts and the possibility of reform.

Brian J. Ostrom, PhD, National Center for State Courts

In the United States more than 13 million individuals are prosecuted for misdemeanor crimes annually. Yet, *The Lower Criminal Courts* provides irrefutable evidence that "the vast majority of these defendants are deprived of their fundamental rights to counsel and jury trial." Professors Alisa Smith and Sean Maddan have compiled a tour de force that fully explores the history of the nation's misdemeanor courts and how they have become one of the most powerful engines of assembly line injustice ever devised. An impressive array of authors present the research and findings that prove the magnitude of this injustice, and analyze the many factors that contributed to this blight on the American notions of fairness and justice. As importantly, in identifying potential reforms, the compilation offers a cautionary tale about the dangers of overreliance on seemingly simplistic panaceas, such as dubious policing practices, and the need to embrace innovation at all stages of the criminal justice process. *The Lower Criminal Courts* is an essential resource for anyone who wants to understand the disgraceful state of the nation's misdemeanor courts and intelligently pursue meaningful and effective reform.

Norman L. Reimer, Executive Director of the National Association of Criminal Defense Lawyers

THE LOWER CRIMINAL COURTS

Edited by Alisa Smith and Sean Maddan

Routledge
Taylor & Francis Group
NEW YORK AND LONDON

First published 2019
by Routledge
52 Vanderbilt Avenue, New York, NY 10017

and by Routledge
2 Park Square, Milton Park, Abingdon, Oxon, OX14 4RN

Routledge is an imprint of the Taylor & Francis Group, an informa business

© 2019 Taylor & Francis

The right of Alisa Smith and Sean Maddan to be identified as the authors of the editorial material, and of the authors for their individual chapters, has been asserted in accordance with sections 77 and 78 of the Copyright, Designs and Patents Act 1988.

All rights reserved. No part of this book may be reprinted or reproduced or utilised in any form or by any electronic, mechanical, or other means, now known or hereafter invented, including photocopying and recording, or in any information storage or retrieval system, without permission in writing from the publishers.

Trademark notice: Product or corporate names may be trademarks or registered trademarks, and are used only for identification and explanation without intent to infringe.

Library of Congress Cataloging-in-Publication Data
A catalog record for this title has been requested

ISBN: 978-0-367-21929-1 (hbk)
ISBN: 978-0-367-21930-7 (pbk)
ISBN: 978-0-429-26881-6 (ebk)

Typeset in Bembo
by codeMantra

AMS: This book is dedicated to my husband, G. Jeffrey Klepfer, and our children, Ann Marie Klepfer, Skyler Ramos, and Alec Ramos.

SM: This book is dedicated to my parents, Richard and Janice Maddan.

CONTENTS

CONTRIBUTORS

Julian Adler is the director of policy and research at the Center for Court Innovation. He leads the Center's work on a range of national criminal justice reform projects, and he is the co-author of *Start Here: A Road Map To Reducing Mass Incarceration* (The New Press, 2018). He was previously the director of the Red Hook Community Justice Center in Brooklyn, New York, and the lead planner of Brooklyn Justice Initiatives. He was also part of a small planning team that launched Newark Community Solutions, the first community court in New Jersey. He is a New York State licensed clinical social worker and attorney.

Sierra Bell is a Master's student in the Department of Criminology at the University of West Georgia. Her areas of research interest include the misdemeanor courts, serial killers, gangs, and public opinions of crime. She has presented her research at national and regional conferences. Ms. Bell is currently completing several projects on serial murder.

Alyssa M. Clark is a PhD student in the School of Criminal Justice at the University at Albany, State University of New York; she earned her MA from the University at Albany. Her research interests pertain to rural criminal justice, local courts and their legal cultures, and qualitative methods. She is a member of the research staff at the New York State Office of Indigent Legal Services and has worked on the implementation of indigent defense reforms across that state.

Amanda P. Cook is an Assistant Professor of Criminology in the Department of Arts and Sciences at Mississippi State University-Meridian. She received her Ph.D. from Mississippi State University in Sociology in 2015. She has conducted research focusing on a wide range of topics such as deterrence, community and prison capital, punishment, and recidivism. She is currently working as a researcher for the Meridian, Mississippi partner site of the Research Network on Misdemeanor Justice.

Sherene Crawford, a former Assistant District Attorney in the New York County District Attorney's Office, is the project director of the Midtown Community Court, an operating program of the Center for Court Innovation. Prior to joining the Center, she served as the Deputy Director of the Institute for Innovation in Prosecution at John Jay College of Criminal Justice and as part of the leadership team at the Mayor's Office to Combat Domestic Violence at the Brooklyn Family Justice Center. She received her JD from New York Law School and her BA in Women's Studies from the University of Minnesota.

Andrew Davies is Director of Research at the New York State Office of Indigent Legal Services and post-doctoral fellow at the State University of New York (SUNY) Albany School of Criminal Justice. His job is to track data on the provision of legal services around the state and to push a research agenda for their improvement. He earned a PhD in criminal justice in 2012 from SUNY Albany and has published research on public defense in a variety of books, academic journals, and law reviews. His work has been funded by the National Institute of Justice, the National Science Foundation, and the Bureau of Justice Statistics. Prior to coming to the Office of Indigent Legal Services, he also worked for several years as a researcher for the New York State Defender Association and spent a short but formative time as an intern gathering mitigation evidence in capital cases in Atlanta, Georgia.

Amy Dezember is a doctoral student in Criminology, Law and Society at George Mason University. Her research interests include plea bargaining, *Alford* pleas, legal decision-making, juvenile transfer, and other court procedures and processes. She currently works as a Graduate Research Assistant with Dr. Allison D. Redlich on a project looking at youth and adult engagement in the plea-bargaining process.

Jennifer Earl is a Professor of Sociology and (by courtesy) Government and Public Policy at the University of Arizona. She is Director Emeritus of the Center for Information Technology and Society and Director Emeritus of the Technology and Society PhD Emphasis, both at University of California, Santa Barbara. Her research focuses on social movements, information technologies, and the sociology of law, with research emphases on Internet activism, social movement repression, youth activism, and legal change. She is the recipient of a National Science Foundation CAREER Award for research from 2006 to 2011 on Web activism, was a member of the MacArthur Research Network on Youth and Participatory Politics, and co-authored with Katrina Kimport, *Digitally Enabled Social Change.*

Jacinta M. Gau, PhD, is an associate professor in the Department of Criminal Justice at the University of Central Florida. Her areas of expertise are policing, race, and quantitative methods. She also teaches and researches court practices. Dr. Gau's research has been published in numerous peer-reviewed journals, and she has written the books *Criminal Justice Policy: Origins and Effectiveness* (Oxford University Press) and *Statistics for Criminology and Criminal Justice* (Sage Publications). She is also the editor-in-chief of the peer-reviewed journal *Race and Justice.*

Richard D. Hartley is Professor in the Department of Criminal Justice at the University of Texas at San Antonio. He received his PhD from the School of Criminology and Criminal Justice at the University of Nebraska. His research interests include decision-making practices for criminal court outcomes, race, ethnicity, criminal justice, and process and outcome evaluation. His most recent research has appeared in *Justice Quarterly, Criminal Justice Policy Review,* and *Drug Court Review.* His research has been funded by the National Institute of Justice, the American Statistical Association, and the Bureau of Justice Statistics.

Samantha Luna is a doctoral student in Criminology, Law and Society at George Mason University. Her research interests include wrongful convictions, plea bargaining, and specialty courts.

She currently works as a Graduate Research Assistant with Dr. Allison D. Redlich on projects looking at the impact of discovery policies and access to discovery on legal decision making.

Sean Maddan is an Associate Professor and Chair of the Department of Social Sciences at Texas A&M International University. He has authored over a dozen articles, which have appeared in many outlets, including *Justice Quarterly, Crime and Delinquency, Journal of Criminal Justice*, and the *American Journal of Criminal Justice*. He has also authored/co-authored several books. His most recent book is the fifth edition of his statistics book.

Kirstin A. Morgan is an Assistant Professor in the Department of Government and Justice Studies at Appalachian State University. Her research interests are juvenile justice, perceptions of criminal justice, criminal court culture and reform, policy and program evaluation, responses to youth street gangs, and research methods and design.

Mai E. Naito is an Assistant Professor at the University of West Georgia in the Department of Criminology since earning her Ph.D. in Criminal Justice & Criminology from Sam Houston State University in 2014. Dr. Naito's research interests include legal issues in criminal justice, wrongful convictions, and sentencing. Her publications appear in *Journal of Criminal Justice & Law, The Criminal Law Bulletin*, and *Silliman Law Journal*.

Nicholas Paul is currently a criminal justice doctoral student at the University of Central Florida. He holds a bachelor's and a master's degree in criminal justice from the University of Central Florida. Nicholas also has several years of law enforcement experience. He was employed as a deputy sheriff in Orlando, Florida, for approximately ten years, where he served in various units to include uniformed patrol, the Problem-Oriented Policing squad, the Gang Enforcement Unit, and the Special Weapons and Tactics (SWAT) team. Nicholas also served in the United States Marine Corps as a military police officer for four years from 2001–2005.

Tia Pooler is the deputy director of Data Analytics and Applied Research at the Center for Court Innovation. She conducts and oversees data management, data analysis, and on-site research at the Center's operating projects and initiatives, including Supervised Release—a pretrial alternative to bail program. She is currently leading a mixed-methods evaluation of Brooklyn's Young Adult Court. Previously, at the Center, she served as the Research and Data Associate for the Midtown Community Court, Harlem Community Justice Center, and Bronx Community Solutions. Recent research projects include a needs-assessment survey of costumed workers in Time Square, an evaluation of the Harlem Parole Reentry Court, and an impact evaluation of the Bronx Mental Health Initiative. She holds a BA in Economics from Boston University and an MSc in Criminal Justice Policy and an MSc in Social Research Methods, both from the London School of Economics.

Allison D. Redlich is a Professor of Criminology, Law and Society at George Mason University. Her research focuses on miscarriages of justice, including wrongful convictions (false confessions and false guilty pleas) and violations of due process (factors influencing knowing, intelligent, and voluntary legal decision-making). In addition, she has a separate line of research on mental health courts.

Michael Rempel is director of jail reform at the Center for Court Innovation, overseeing projects that involve reducing the jail population in New York City. He previously served for 16 years as the Center's research director. He has long been interested in bridging the gap between the worlds of research and practice, and joins with his co-authors in the embrace of transformative change in our criminal justice system in ways that thoughtfully harness lessons gained from rigorous scientific inquiry.

Reveka V. Shteynberg is an Assistant Professor in the Department of Criminal Justice at the California State University San Bernardino. She received her Ph.D. and Master's degree in Criminal Justice from the University at Albany, SUNY, and her Bachelor's degree in Criminology, Law and Society from the University of California, Irvine. Her research and published work addresses citizens' access to justice and issues surrounding criminal justice decision-making policies and practices, including court and legal reforms, pretrial justice, plea bargaining and sentencing, indigent defense systems, juvenile justice, gender differences in the legal system, law enforcement, and program implementation and evaluation.

Alisa Smith is an Associate Professor and the Chair of the Department of Legal Studies at the University of Central Florida. She holds a PhD in Criminology and Criminal Justice, and a JD from the Florida State University. She practiced law for 29 years, mostly in the area of criminal defense and appeals. Her scholarly research interests focus on the access to justice in the misdemeanor courts, empirical legal studies, and the use of social science by the courts. She has authored more than 20 peer-reviewed and law journal articles, reports, and book chapters, and she has authored two previous books. Her research has appeared in the *Journal of Criminal Justice, Florida Law Review,* and *American Journal of Criminal Law.*

Rachel Swaner is the research director at the Center for Court Innovation. She has led local and national research and evaluation projects related to procedural justice, community courts, violence prevention, the commercial sex trade, and youth development. Prior to joining the Center, she was a researcher at the Harlem Children's Zone, where she evaluated social, educational, and health programs for children and youth. Dr. Swaner received her Bachelor of Science and Masters of Public Administration from New York University and her PhD in Sociology from the College University of New York (CUNY) Graduate Center. She teaches at New York University's (NYU) Wagner School of Public Service and is a board member for the Participatory Budgeting Project.

Alissa Pollitz Worden is on the faculty of the School of Criminal Justice at the University at Albany, State University of New York (SUNY). Her research addresses questions about decision making, defendants' and victims' rights, and policy reform in the criminal courts; several of her projects have been funded by the National Institute of Justice. Her current work focuses on the provision of indigent defense, both at initial appearances and bail hearings, and throughout adjudication; the impact of counsel on case outcomes; and the causes of inequities in local and state funding for public defender offices.

FOREWORD

As the author of books on misdemeanor courts and court reform published in the late 1970s and early 1980s, I was delighted to have an advance opportunity to read the chapters in this volume. They reveal a renewed interest in misdemeanor justice and bring the study of misdemeanor justice and related reform efforts up to date by assessing recent research in current context. I would like to use my limited space here to reflect on the themes and findings highlighted in this volume in light of the themes and findings in my work of 40 years ago. There are both changes and continuities. This volume is one of several recent books and many articles by social scientists that assess the state of misdemeanor justice in the face of plummeting rates of index crimes, declining felony arrests, and the beginnings of what may be a marked decline in imprisonment. Ironically, misdemeanor arrests have not followed this trend, at least as far as we can tell. (Since there are no nationwide data on misdemeanors, and what counts as a misdemeanor varies widely by state, it is hard to tell.) Still, in a world of Broken Windows, quality-of-life policing, and "random" auto stops that inform current police practices in many communities, misdemeanors compared to felonies do not appear to have declined nationwide, and certainly not or not much in some of our big cities. Perhaps the rate of misdemeanor *convictions* has declined, but the nuisance of arrests, decisions about pretrial release, weekends in jail, and the like—the "process costs" associated with arrests for low-level offenses—have not. Misdemeanor *arrests* have always served useful social control functions, whether or not they resulted in convictions. The arrest itself is used to diffuse a troublesome situation and to mark and manage troublesome people. Conviction is often incidental to the process. With the continued emphasis on quality-of-life policing, and with the secondary consequences of arrest and conviction increasing (loss of jobs, possible deportation, loss of benefits, court-imposed fees, and the like), both arrests and convictions are likely to have more severe and lasting effects today than they did 40 or 100 years ago.

Some changes are even more retrograde. Broken Windows policing and racial profiling have dramatically enhanced the powers and policy making of "street level bureaucrats." Police probably have more unchecked discretion than they did 40 years ago, and new massive surveillance policies may lead to more racial discrimination than they did 40 years ago. Increased arrests and ironically checks on sentencing through guidelines may have transferred even more powers from judges to prosecutors. Actuarial thinking coupled with vastly greater capacities for systematically assessing (or appearing to systematically assess) big data have turned misdemeanor courts into institutions to manage the underclass, even as they make attempts to locate the few dangerous offenders among the rabble. These new programs are enhanced by a new set of silver bullets promoted by big foundations and supported by those on the left and the right; they promise to use big data and algorithms to rationalize the criminal justice system—to "get smart on crime," to save money, and to enhance deterrence. But, as the studies in this volume reveal, these new technologies remain as unfilled promises and, as I have suggested, make things massively worse. What is certain is that new strategies of misdemeanor crime control have increased the numbers of black and Hispanic individuals in the criminal process.

In the past 40 years, private contractors have also emerged as important innovators, entrepreneurs who promote bold new alternatives and form public-private partnerships designed to increase the efficiency and efficacy of criminal justice institutions, and hence the development of private jails and fee-for-service custodial and probation programs. Private contractors have taken the lead in promoting electronic monitoring as an alternative to custody with claims of being much cheaper and more effective. Yet research—including much that is reported in this volume—reveals that electronic monitoring almost always is an add-on to probation or pretrial release, and only occasionally redirects someone from jail or prison into the community. Contractors promote the cost savings of electronic monitoring, but once they have the contracts, risk averse officials direct them to low hanging fruit, individuals earmarked for probation, or pretrial release. Private contractors both market and manage electronic monitoring, turning it over to the police when the red light starts to flash. It is a huge expansion of both net widening and private engagement in the criminal process. The next step, already underway in fact, is the development of private criminal courts that by-pass public police and courts altogether.

Furthermore, increasingly cash strapped municipalities and counties have come to rely on higher fines. And they have begun to levy an array of new fees that are reminiscent of the nineteenth century's system of writs and fees to cover basic expenses for municipal services. Even a new normative theory of courts has emerged that shifts attention away from adjudication, guilt, and punishment to "problem solving." On the surface, this appears to be a good idea, and in many cases, it clearly is. In many situations, it makes sense to address "underlying" problems rather than narrowly focus only on manifestations of them. But, as David Rothman has reminded us, conscience is easily thwarted by convenience. Accordingly, "problem solving" can deteriorate into "rabble management" in short order.

The contributors to this volume are experts on these and related topics. They are familiar with the latest research, able to locate their particular concerns in context, and skilled in sophisticated techniques and methodologies. Each chapter focuses on a particular feature of misdemeanor courts; reviews the literature; assesses its context; and offers insights into the nature and function of America's lower courts, and by extension America's social policy toward some of its most vulnerable citizens. From the first chapter to the last, the authors consider a host of cherished ideals in the administration of justice, fairness, evenhandedness, right to counsel, right to bail, proportionality, fair hearing, probation, diversion, and the like, and subject them to the harsh light of social science research. They reveal the uncomfortable truths of dashed hopes due to carelessness, caprice, error, class, and racism, and compounded by misperceptions, fragmentation, and under-administration. A collective portrait that shames us all.

This volume reinforces my belief that when assessed in cross-national comparison, the United States criminal process should be compared not with the countries of Northern Europe but with South America. Comparing our practices with Brazil or Argentina may be more insightful and useful than comparisons with Great Britain or the Netherlands or Germany. Like Brazil and Argentina, and unlike Great Britain, the Netherlands, and Germany, American state governments do not have a monopoly over the control of lethal violence. Neither do they have strong administration, ministries of justice, and centralized justice systems. They are all characterized by decentralization and hyper-fragmentation in funding, oversight, and administration. Indeed, it is amazing that the United States, itself a woefully underdeveloped country, does not have even greater problems of the sort experienced by South American countries.

The contributors to this volume do much more than contrast lofty aspirations with squalid reality. Each chapter assesses a vast body of research, and like good social scientists, their authors look for variation and seek to account for it. They proffer hypotheses and examine them, identify and explore patterns and trends, and account for them as best they can. The authors adopt different frameworks and theories, but each addresses a substantively important issue, engages with important data, and embraces a time honored social science framework. The result is an impressive set of essays. This book should become a standard text in courses on the administration of criminal justice, social welfare policies, criminal procedure, and race and social class in the United States.

Indeed, there is something in this book for just about every type of reader. It should appeal to any civic-minded person who is curious about how lower criminal courts operate and why. It should also be of particular value to students. Undergraduates will be treated to smart essays that identify major issues in the administration of criminal justice and then review the best of the recent research on these issues, allowing them ample detail to ponder both crucial policy questions and research agendas. This volume should be a success in the classroom and attentive students cannot help but come away as better-informed citizens. Research-minded undergraduates will also receive insight into how to interpret data and conduct research.

Increasingly, social science work is being incorporated into law school training, and increasingly, criminal law professors have social science training. So, this book should be a useful supplement in law school courses on criminal procedure as well as in more specialized courses on police and prosecutors. Certainly, it would be a welcome addition in doctrine-based courses, and it might lead reform-oriented students and their professors to move beyond their traditional calls for expanded constitutional rights and turn their attention to organization theory and structure, and issues of administration and management.

Graduate students in criminal justice, sociology, and political science will be treated to cogent essays that review the best of recent research, assess it, and draw important conclusions—findings, controversies, and implications—from it. Individually, these chapters should provide wonderful resources for graduate students; they can use them as launching pads for their own masters and PhD theses. At a minimum, this volume should be valuable reading for graduate students preparing for field exams. Individual chapters are models of smart literature reviews.

Senior scholars can also profit from this volume. The essays bring readers up to date; they are smart, methodologically sophisticated, and chock full of insights.

It is a rare book that provides significant value to readers from such a variety of levels—informed citizens, undergraduates, law students, graduate students, and specialized researchers. This is one of those rare books. Such consistent high quality in an edited volume is remarkable. The editors are to be congratulated.

Malcolm Feeley
Claire Sanders Clements Dean's Professor Emeritus
Jurisprudence and Social Policy Program
School of Law
University of California at Berkeley

ACKNOWLEDGMENT

We would like to acknowledge the thorough and helpful reviews by the anonymous reviewers who helped us to structure and focus this book. We are also indebted, of course, to the contributors, who provided timely, thorough, and engaging chapters as well as Ellen Boyne, Francesca Hearn, Esther Saks and the behind-the-scene staff at Taylor & Francis for working to produce this text. We owe gratitude for the assistance of Dr. Jeff Klepfer, who copy-edited several of the chapters, and Alisa Smith is thankful for the support of Dean Pamela "Sissi" Carroll, who allowed her the freedom to work on this book while serving in her administrative role.

SECTION 1

Introduction to the Legal and Empirical History of the Lower Courts

1

INTRODUCTION—WHY MISDEMEANOR COURTS MATTER

Alisa Smith

Few books start with describing why they were written or why their topic is worthy of study. We do so here because scholarly work on misdemeanor courts, until recently, has been understudied. Yet its study is significant in the sheer volume of cases that are processed in these courts every year. Over the last 60 years, scholars have attempted to draw attention to these important, yet understudied, cases, with three waves of interest, beginning in the 1950s. The first two waves were significant but sputtered and flattened. The third wave of study began with Amy Bach's 2010 exposé, in *Ordinary Injustice*, which highlighted "minor" crimes processed with little fanfare in an assembly-line fashion but resulted in important injustices to defendants and victims from the lack of due process. Bach's book ignited an interdisciplinary burst of research on misdemeanor arrests, court processing, and sentencing outcomes. The interest in misdemeanors now has become entrenched with a groundswell of research showing no signs of abating. But why study misdemeanor cases?

Misdemeanors Dominate the Courts and Cause Real Harm

While scholarly literature and legal practitioners focus on felonies and the felony courts, misdemeanors dominate the criminal justice system with an estimated 13.2 million cases prosecuted annually, that is, three times as many felonies as misdemeanors prosecuted every year (Roberts, 2011; Stevenson & Mayson, 2018). Most people who interact with the criminal justice system are arrested for misdemeanor crimes (Natapoff, 2015), and simply by the number of ordinary people impacted by misdemeanor arrests and prosecutions, they warrant study. Yet, unlike felonies, there is no national clearinghouse that gathers data on misdemeanor arrests, filings, or dispositions (Boruchowitz, Brink, & Dimino, 2009; Measures for Justice, n.d.; Stevenson & Mayson, 2018).

We know a great deal about felonies and the felony courts. The United States Sentencing Commission (n.d.) provides insight into federal felony case processing; the Uniform Crime Report (UCR) by the Federal Bureau of Investigation (n.d.) gathers arrest data on violent and nonviolent felonies; and the Bureau of Justice Statistics, National Crime Victimization Survey (n.d.) focuses on felony victimizations. None systematically analyzes or reports data on misdemeanor offenses, not even on the most basic of information or national statistics (Natapoff, 2015;

Stevenson & Mayson, 2018). Stevenson and Mayson (2018) provide the most comprehensive estimate of national data on misdemeanor criminal justice statistics, and they gathered their information by cobbling together information on misdemeanors from the National Center for State Courts (NCSC) and UCR data.

The NCSC is "an independent, nonprofit court improvement organization founded at the urging of Chief of the Supreme Court Warren E. Burger" (National Center for State Court, n.d.). The NCSC provides "research, information services, education, [and] consulting" to assist courts (National Center for State Courts, n.d.). States electronically submit caseload data to NCSC, and it began collecting misdemeanor caseload information in 2012 (NCSC, n.d.; Stevenson & Mayson, 2018). "From 2012 to 2016, the number of states that reported annual misdemeanor caseload numbers ranged from twenty-eight to thirty-four" (Stevenson & Mayson, 2018, p. 741). Even with weaknesses in data collection—mostly related to varying state definitions and methods of counting offenses—the NCSC has reported a "stable ratio of felony-to-misdemeanor cases over the past decade," which allowed Stevenson and Mayson to infer trends in misdemeanor caseloads (2018, p. 731).

Stevenson and Mayson (2018) further used the UCR by the Federal Bureau of Investigation (n.d.) as the best available data to estimate misdemeanor arrests. Relying on voluntary reporting from police agencies, the Federal Bureau of Investigation (FBI) gathers data from information from over 18,000 agencies and covers more than 95 percent of the United States (2018; Uniform Crime Reporting, n.d.). Stevenson and Mayson relied on the traditional Summary Reporting Program arrest data, focusing on Part II of the report, which includes the less serious felony and misdemeanor crimes (Uniform Crime Reporting, n.d.). Using this data, Stevenson and Mayson "constructed two 'proxy' measures comprised of those offenses most likely to be classified as misdemeanors" and drew inferences about misdemeanor arrest rates (2018, p. 743).

Using these data sources, Stevenson and Mayson (2018) estimated that there were 13.2 million misdemeanor cases filed in the United States in 2016, and after peaking in 1982, arrest rates remained flat until 1990 and then began to steadily decline. There was some variation in state reporting, but they found no patterns in these variations. Stevenson and Mayson (2018) revealed that states with "large minority populations and lower levels of income and education tended to have higher misdemeanor case-filing rates" (p. 745); the correlations, however, were not strong.

Falling rates of misdemeanor arrests are consistent with declining numbers of arrests for serious crimes (Natapoff, 2015; Stevenson & Mayson, 2018). A variety of reasons for the declining rate of felony arrests have been suggested, including "changes in policing, higher incarceration rates, greater access to abortion, reductions in toxic lead exposure, improved technologies for crime-prevention, and shifts in age demographics, among others" (Stevenson & Mayson, 2018, p. 765, citing Zimring, 2008; Ford, 2016). Whether the same factors are causing the decline in misdemeanor arrests is open to question.

On the other hand, misdemeanors are not merely "mini-felonies" (Natapoff, 2015; Stevenson & Mayson, 2018, p. 766). Although they result in real consequences (discussed more later), research has demonstrated that police and prosecutors wield more discretion in the processing of misdemeanor cases (Natapoff, 2015; Roberts, 2013), and less due process is afforded to misdemeanor defendants (Boruchowitz, et al., 2009; Roberts, 2011; Smith & Maddan, 2011). Few defendants are represented by counsel, some misdemeanor defendants are prosecuted by courts presided over by nonlawyer judges, and most misdemeanor defendants' cases are resolved quickly with little care for advising defendants of their rights or the consequences of misdemeanor convictions (Boruchowitz et al., 2009; Roberts, 2011; Smith & Maddan, 2011; Smith, Maddan, Price, & Tvedt, 2017). Compared to those in felony prosecutions, misdemeanor defendants are far less likely to be represented by counsel, and despite calls for standards by scholars, little attention has been dedicated to what qualifies as adequate or effective defense representation, what are appropriate caseload limits, or whether due process is afforded to misdemeanor defendants (Roberts, 2011).

Even if misdemeanor sanctions are less punitive than felonies, misdemeanor prosecutions and convictions are not inconsequential (Natapoff, 2012b; 2015). These consequences range from deportation and losing employment to crushing debt (Natapoff, 2012a; Roberts, 2011). Misdemeanor defendants, who are poor and unable to post bail, remain incarcerated for relatively minor crimes, resulting in loss of job, housing, and other benefits (Baughman, 2018; Natapoff, 2012a; Roberts, 2011). Mass misdemeanor arrests, incarcerations, and convictions impact families and neighborhoods (Joe, 2018).

Misdemeanor crimes are typically defined as those that carry no more than one year in jail, but a recent study has demonstrated that that is not always the case. In one state, some misdemeanor crimes may result in maximum sentences of ten years in prison (Stevenson & Mayson, 2018). This is not the only variability that plagues misdemeanors; misdemeanor crimes are defined differently in each state. Possession of marijuana, for example, may be a felony in one state, a misdemeanor in another, or legal in a third (Stevenson & Mayson, 2018). In some states, misdemeanors may be enhanced to felonies on a third or fourth conviction. The number of misdemeanor defendants charged with crimes, subject to pretrial detention, and jail terms has caused at least one scholar to characterize the "current criminal justice crisis" as "one of mass misdemeanor processing" (Roberts, 2013). Misdemeanors are consequential for defendants but also for society and the legal system.

Since most individuals interact with the legal system through the misdemeanor courts, their perception of justice is gleaned from these experiences. The legitimacy of the courts hangs in the balance as these courts operate with a fast pace and a lack of due process or even dignity (Natapoff, 2012b). The study of misdemeanors, the system, and its impact on society are worthy of study, and scholars have begun the tedious work of parsing the data that does exist, creating a national database, conducting comparative studies on misdemeanor arrests and case processing, holding scholarly conferences that focus on misdemeanors, and advancing recommendations to restore legitimacy to the courts.

A Brief History of Misdemeanor Courts[1]

Most of Europe moved to professional judges between the 1300s and 1789, but not England, which preserved its reliance on lay justices (Ashman & Lee, 1977; Dawson, 1960). During colonization, transportation was poor, and few were educated lawyers, so the tradition of lay justices in the early lower courts in Colonial America transferred from England (Ashman & Lee, 1977; Langbein, 2003). Many of these early courts were called justices of the peace, and "like other colonial institutions, [justices of the peace] soon evolved away from its English counterpart" (Ashman & Lee, 1977, p. 567).

With little guidance from England, misdemeanor or lay courts began to change in how they were created, their titles, and even their roles in society (Surrency, 1967). The local courts varied widely one from the other (Surrency, 1967). Each colony adopted their own types of courts, jurisdiction, and operation (Surrency, 1967). At the time, "the most important courts in America were those held by the justices of the peace, whose jurisdiction was limited" (Surrency, 1967). American justices of the peace, unlike their English counterparts, heard civil cases; they began to be paid, and some were popularly elected (Ashman & Lee, 1977). "[T]he position 'came to be filled by people of humble calling and scant education'" (Ashman & Lee, 1977, p. 567). These justices presided over many local matters as wide ranging as supervising the building of roads and issuing licenses, resolving misdemeanor criminal and minor civil disputes, and presiding over slave courts (Surrency, 1967). In the criminal context, these courts were the courts of last resort: "[N]o appeal was possible in a criminal case in the colonial period" (Surrency, 1967, p. 270).

As early as the late 1600s and early 1700s, "[t]he administration of justice in the British North American colonies was a source of constant complaint to the Home Government" (Surrency, 1967, p. 254). The registered and documented complaints included those of "irregular procedure," "delays in holding sessions," and attacks on the "character and ability of the judges" (Surrency, 1967, p. 254). Some citizens complained about the numbers of these courts (Surrency, 1967). For example, with a population of only 291 males, Charleston had 14 annual court sessions, with additional sessions held by a variety of other lower courts, called the mayor's courts, courts of common pleas, and court of sessions (Surrency, 1967). Despite the complaints, no changes were made (Surrency, 1967).

By the 1800s, society became "more complex and its legal system more sophisticated, the administration of the law by those lacking any formal legal education was increasingly questioned" (Ashman & Lee, 1977, p. 567). Nineteenth-century critics chastised justices of the peace for abusing their position and power (Newton, Welch, & Hamilton, 2012). These courts were perceived as having too much discretion and too little oversight, and being incompetent (Newton et al., 2012; Steele, 1981)

Criticism grew in the 1900s, with lawyers and organizations calling for the dismantling of the justices of the peace or, at a minimum, requiring that justices have legal training. These minor courts (much like today) are the courts the citizenry most likely encounter, and as such, ineptitude, delay, and abuse were undermining the administration of justice and its perceived legitimacy (Smith, 1927). Roscoe Pound, in a stinging critique, referred to nonlawyer judges as "a humiliating anachronism" (Pound, 1920, p. 146). In 1906, reformists had their first success with Chicago abolishing its justice courts; other cities followed their lead, dismantling these courts into the 1920s (Alfini, 1981; Newton, et al., 2012). These early reformists, including Pound, remained critical of nonlawyer judges, viewing them as out of step with modern society (Alfini, 1981; Pound, 1913).

In 1932, reformists received support from the Wickersham Commission report, which characterized misdemeanor courts as "the least satisfactory part of our judicial system" (National Commission on Law Observance and Enforcement, 1932). The report advocated for improved selection, tenure, and compensation of trained judges. By the 1960s, "[n]early every major study or group that looked at the justice of the peace system either 'explicitly or implicitly sought the abolition of justices of the peace'" (Gazell, 1975, p. 800; Newton et al., 2012, p. 35).

Not much improved over the next 30 years. In the 1950s, Professor Caleb Foote observed police-court proceedings (some early lower courts were called police courts and were presided over by lay magistrate judges) in Philadelphia. He described justice in these courts as lacking due process, with inequitable and questionable sentences meted out by lay justices, and with few appeals to higher courts for review (Foote, 1956; 1970). More than ten years later, the President's Commission on Law Enforcement and Administration of Justice Report, in 1967, similarly reported inequity, indignity, and ineffectiveness in the lower courts, and concluded that these courts were in crisis, with little in the process that was likely to instill respect for the system of criminal justice in defendants, witnesses, or observers (Katzenbach, 1967).

Another 50 years later, the lower courts—much like their predecessors—hear most cases, presiding over many local matters, including misdemeanor prosecutions (Dolan & Fenton, 1969; Furr, 1966; Johnson, Chapman, Clifton, & Field, 1966; Surrency, 1967). They also remain subject to much criticism for their lack of due process and oversight.

Overview of the Book

This book focuses on the lower or misdemeanor courts and capitalizes on the interdisciplinary research conducted on and about these courts. We have assembled notable scholars from varying fields, including the law, criminal justice, psychology, and social work, to contribute their expertise on research concerning the processing of misdemeanors by the lower criminal courts. Their research sheds light on the importance of this work separate from the study of felonies, and as previously noted, misdemeanors are not merely "mini-felonies" (Natapoff, 2015; Stevenson & Mayson, 2018, p. 766).

The book is organized around three themes. The first introduces the misdemeanor courts by focusing on their legal history through the decisions by the Supreme Court of the United States and the seminal work of Malcolm Feeley, who undertook the first systematic study of how the lower courts actually work. The second section summarizes and discusses the state of the research in the lower courts today, ranging from the impact of quality-of-life policing to the courtroom workgroup to specialized courts. In the final section of the book, top-notch scholars and practitioners will make practical recommendations to improve the processing of cases, defendants' satisfaction with the courts, and the perceived legitimacy of the lower courts.

In the aftermath of the previously mentioned President's Commission Report, in 1967, the Supreme Court rendered several important decisions on misdemeanor cases. The Court's decision was intended to impact due process and fairness in misdemeanor court proceedings, including the right to counsel for some misdemeanor defendants, in *Argersinger v. Hamlin* (1972)—but as described by **Alisa Smith, in Chapter 2**, the Court has fallen short of that mark. Not all misdemeanor defendants have the right to counsel, the right to a jury trial, or the right to a presiding attorney judge. This chapter provides an overview of the legal history of the misdemeanor courts, which suggests a gap between the law on the books and the law in practice that is highlighted by the authors of the remaining chapters of the text.

During this first wave of empirical study, Malcolm Feeley (1979) produced his seminal work, *The Process is the Punishment*, which provided the first systematic study of misdemeanor case processing. For this study, Feeley conducted a comprehensive review of misdemeanor cases in the Court of Common Pleas in New Haven, Connecticut. He found most cases were resolved by dismissal or plea, and with a focus on courtroom workgroup relationships, plea bargaining, and swiftness in case processing. He concluded that it was not the punishment, but the process itself that was most punitive in the disposition of these minor cases. In **Chapter 3**, **Jennifer Earl** looks back on the 40-year history of Feeley's work and extends it to understand today's criminal justice system, including the lower courts, particularly focusing on the impact of pretrial processes in the age of mass incarceration and the influence of actors, not considered by Feeley's arguments about the open system model, on misdemeanor outcomes.

The seven chapters in **Section II** of the text explore recent research that has been conducted on the misdemeanor courts since the Supreme Court decision in *Argersinger v. Hamlin* (1972) and the research by Malcolm Feeley (1979). As noted earlier, research that studies misdemeanors and the misdemeanor courts are important due to their sheer volume. Over 13 million misdemeanor cases are filed each year, amounting to 75 percent of all criminal cases. Recent study has suggested that in spite of this overwhelming number of cases, misdemeanor arrests and prosecutions are actually declining in most jurisdictions (Stevenson & Mayson, 2018) but not all (Kohler-Hausmann, 2018). Even if the numbers have declined over the last two decades—beginning in the late 1990s—the disparity between the prosecution of misdemeanors to felonies, which is 3:1, has remained consistent (Stevenson & Mayson, 2018).

One explanation for this growth and disparity may be rooted in changing police practices, in particular, the impact of the quality-of-life or broken-windows policing approach. In 1982, Wilson and Kelling wrote an article, in *The Atlantic*, asserting—with no empirical support—that vigilant enforcement of minor crimes would reduce more serious criminality. **Jacinta M. Gau and her colleague, Nicholas Paul, in Chapter 4**, discuss the implications of broken-windows policing on the lower courts, which must deal with the swollen number of misdemeanor arrests. They discuss the consequences of this approach to due process and the potential consequences for deterrence when lower courts are so burdened that they cannot devote adequate resources to individual cases.

The large number of cases processed in the court has been found to affect due process in these courts. An overarching finding by contemporary scholars has been that misdemeanor defendants are rarely afforded counsel in the lower courts. **Andrew Davies and Kirstin A. Morgan, in Chapter 5,** look beyond the numbers to describe the four categorical barriers that obstruct misdemeanor defendants' access to counsel. These are: (1) systemic obstacles, (2) logistical impediments, (3) procedural weaknesses, and (4) individual factors. The chapter covers the significance of uncounseled defendants for the individual and its potential impact on perceptions of court legitimacy, and closes with recommendations to improve access in the future.

Misdemeanor courts are local, and how they operate varies by their location. **Alissa Pollitz Worden and Alyssa M. Clark, in Chapter 6,** discuss the diversity of the lower courts by investigating the varying protocols, pace, and outcomes in the courts across the states, particularly focusing on how courthouse cultures influence case processing in rural communities. They conclude that it is unlikely the rural lower courts will be replaced, so they recommend potential adaptations to reform and advance these courts to improve service for rural constituents.

Although varying widely, one common theme among misdemeanor (and felony) courts is that most are resolved by plea: 97 percent of criminal cases are resolved through the plea-bargaining process. Ironically, little research has explored the validity of defendants' decisions to enter into these pleas. For pleas to be valid, defendants must forfeit their right to trial knowingly, intelligently, and voluntarily. Also, defendants must be factually guilty. Trial judges are responsible for ensuring the validity of defendants' pleas and the factual basis for those pleas. **Samantha Luna, Amy Dezember, and Allison D. Redlich, in Chapter 7,** review the literature that has studied the validity of pleas with a particular focus on defendants' (1) knowledge and intelligence with respect to the decision, (2) volition in entering the plea, and (3) factual guilt. With a focus on misdemeanor plea bargaining, the authors identify the potential consequences if pleas are invalid or not properly evaluated, and they suggest future research to address these concerns.

Research on the influence of race dominates research on felony sentencing, but like plea bargaining, little scholarly attention has focused on the influence of race on misdemeanor outcomes. **Amanda P. Cook, in Chapter 8,** provides an overview of the research that does exist on the impact of race in the misdemeanor courts and compares those findings to felony court research. In addition to race, Dr. Cook touches upon the intersection and impact of gender and age on these outcomes. She concludes by recommending research on these under-explored influences on misdemeanor court outcomes to develop a more robust theoretical understanding of misdemeanor sentencing.

Misdemeanor defendants who are convicted are most often sentenced by the imposition of financial obligations. **Sean Maddan and Sierra Bell, in Chapter 9**, provide a brief history and the empirical research that has examined the most common monetary sanctions imposed in the misdemeanor courts: fines, court costs, and restitution. These financial obligations burden misdemeanor defendants with debt that, in most instances, they cannot afford. The financial obligations result in direct and indirect costs to misdemeanor defendants. Although fines were instituted as an alternative to incarceration, the compounding debt has led to counter-intuitive outcomes, like increasing recidivism and, for some, incarceration.

Another alternative to traditional criminal court processes has been the inception of specialized courts. Beginning with drug courts in the late 1980s, problem-solving courts have rapidly expanded across the United States. **Richard D. Hartley, in Chapter 10**, provides an overview of problem-solving courts, also referred to as specialty courts, which operate to serve misdemeanor defendants under the philosophy of therapeutic jurisprudence and focusing on the underlying causes of criminal behavior and rehabilitation, rather than punishment. His historical and empirical review highlights the most common specialty courts: Drug Courts, Mental Health Courts, and Domestic Violence Courts.

Section III comprises five chapters that discuss reform efforts that have been or should be undertaken to improve due process and fairness in the lower courts. With 75 percent of criminal cases prosecuted in the lower criminal courts and an understanding that misdemeanor courts are not "mini-felony" courts (Natapoff, 2015; Stevenson & Mayson, 2018, p. 766), an appreciation for how prosecutors interact with public defenders and judges to do their jobs is important and the focus of **Chapter 11 by Julian Adler, Sherene Crawford, and Tia Pooler**. First, they take note that there is tremendous variation in the judge-prosecutor-defender dynamic in the lower criminal courts. As noted previously in Chapter 6, these courts are different from felony courts, and they are themselves diverse. Adler and his colleagues summarize what is known about the courtroom workgroup in the lower courts and against this backdrop outline suggestions for prosecutors to rethink how business is conducted in the lower courts and propose reforms to reduce the use of incarceration for misdemeanants as well as to lower recidivism rates.

Research has identified short- and long-term consequences associated with pretrial detention and bail. Misdemeanor defendants who are poor and unable to post bond are detained long enough to lose their jobs and housing. Many states are in their third wave of bail reform since the early 1960s, and drawing on this history and research, **Reveka V. Shteynberg and Alissa Pollitz Worden, in Chapter 12,** discuss public and private policy initiatives at the local, state, and federal levels, highlighting the political and commercial contexts in which proposed reforms are debated and the challenges of reform that face the lower courts.

A seemingly simple approach to improving the courts and reducing recidivism is to treat criminal defendants with respect and decency. **Julian Adler, Rachel Swaner, and Michael Rempel, in Chapter 13,** review the growing body of research on how this simple idea, which has evolved from principles of procedural justice and the use of problem-solving and community courts, has improved defendant and victim satisfaction while simultaneously reducing repeat offending.

As discussed in Chapter 10, specialty courts have grown in number and focus. In **Chapter 14, Mai E. Naito** extends the discussion of specialty courts, with a focus on the future of these courts and the importance of admission, policy, and treatment standards in courts that include substance disorders, veteran-defendants, and homelessness and crime. Based on empirical study and the bridging of research and policy, these specialty courts hold the promise of transforming courts from the quintessential adversarial approach to a therapeutic model yielding lower recidivism rates and reducing the pressing misdemeanor caseloads.

Chapter 15 by Sean Maddan concludes by commenting on the state of knowledge, the policy implications, and recommendations for future research on the misdemeanor courts. This chapter explores the future of misdemeanor courts, including how misdemeanor courts operate, possibilities for easier access to quality legal representation, reform to the bail system, a de-emphasis of financial sanctions, a more robust plea process, and the need for expanded use of specialty courts. Finally, the chapter identifies the need for more aggressive and expansive research, and scholarly work on the study of misdemeanor courts.

Note

1 With permission, this section was taken liberally from a forthcoming article, by the chapter author, in the *Law Journal for Social Justice at Arizona State University*, Beyond the impressionistic analysis: An empirical evaluation of 21st century nonlawyer courts.

References

Alfini, J. (1981). Understanding misdemeanor courts: A review of the literature and recent case law. In J. Alfini (Ed.), *Misdemeanor courts: Policy concerns and research perspectives* (pp. 1–28). Washington, DC: U.S. Department of Justice.

Ashman, A., & Lee, D.L. (1977). Non-lawyer judges: The long road North. *Chicago-Kent Law Review, 53*, 565–595.

Bach, A. (2010). *Ordinary injustice: How America holds court*. New York, NY: Henry Holt and Company.

Baughman, S.B. (2018). The history of misdemeanor bail. *Boston University Law Review, 98*, 837–883.

Boruchowitz, R.C., Brink, M.N., & Dimino, M. (2009). *Minor crimes, massive waster: The terrible toll of America's broken misdemeanor courts*. Washington, DC: National Association of Criminal Defense Attorneys.

Bureau of Justice Statistics, National Crime Victimization Survey (n.d.). Retrieved from www.bjs.gov/index.cfm?ty=dcdetail&iid=245

Dawson, J. (1960). *A history of lay judges*. Cambridge, MA: Harvard University Press.

Dolan, R.J., & Fenton, W.B. (1969). The justice of the peace in Nebraska. *Nebraska Law Review, 48*, 457–487.

Feeley, M. (1979). *The process is the punishment: Handling cases in a lower criminal court*. New York, NY: Russell Sage Foundation.

Foote, C. (1956). Vagrancy-type law and its administration. *University of Pennsylvania Law Review, 104*, 603–650.

Foote, C. (1970). Comments on preventive detention. *Journal of Legal Education, 23*, 48–53.

Ford, M. (2016, April 15). What caused the great crime decline in the U.S.? *The Atlantic*. Retrieved from www.theatlantic.com/politics/archive/2016/04/what-caused-the-crime-decline/477408/

Furr, W.R. (1966). The justice of the peace in Virginia, A neglected aspect of the judiciary. *Virginia Law Review, 52*, 151–188.

Gazell, J.A. (1975). A national perspective on justice of the peace and their future: Time for an Epitaph? *Mississippi Law Journal, 46*, 800–813.

Joe, I.O. (2018). The prosecutor's client problem. *Boston University Law Review, 98*, 885–913.

Johnson, R., Chapman, M., Clifton, J., & Field, J.W. (1973–1974). Justice courts in Oregon. *Oregon Law Review, 53, 411–420.*

Katzenbach, N. (1967). *United States President's commission on law enforcement and administration of justice*. Washington, DC: U.S. Government Printing Office.

Kohler-Hausmann, I. (2018). *Misdemeanorland*. Princeton, NJ: Princeton University Press.

Langbein, J. (2003). *The origins of adversary criminal trial*. New York, NY: Oxford University Press.

Measures for Justice (n.d.). https://measuresforjustice.org

Natapoff, A. (2012a, April 27). Why misdemeanors aren't so minor. *Slate*. Retrieved from https://slate.com/news-and-politics/2012/04/misdemeanors-can-have-major-consequences-for-the-people-charged.html

Natapoff, A. (2012b). Misdemeanors. *Southern California Law Review, 85*, 1313–1375.

Natapoff, A. (2015). Misdemeanor decriminalization. *Vanderbilt Law Review, 68*, 1055–1116.

National Center for State Courts (n.d.). Retrieved from www.ncsc.org/About-us.aspx

National Commission on Law Observance and Enforcement (Wickersham Commission) (1931). *Report on criminal procedure*.

Newton, S.P., Welch, T.L., & Hamilton, N.G. (2012). No justice in Utah's justice courts: Constitutional issues, systemic problems, and the failure to protect defendants in Utah's infamous local courts. *Utah Law Review Online, 1*, 27–72.

Pound, R. (1913). The administration of justice in the modern city. *Harvard Law Review, 26*, 302.

Pound, R. (1920). Anachronisms in law. *Journal of the American Judicature Society*, 3, 142–148.
Roberts, J. (2011). Why misdemeanors matter. *University of California, Davis, 45*, 277–372.
Roberts, J. (2013). Crashing the misdemeanor system. *Washington and Lee Law Review, 70*, 1089–1131.
Smith, A., & Maddan, S. (2011). *Three-minute justice: Haste and waste in Florida's misdemeanor courts.* Washington, DC: National Association of Criminal Defense Lawyers.
Smith, A., Maddan, S., Price, D. D., & Tvedt, C. (2017). *Rush to judgment: How South Carolina's summary courts fail to protect constitutional rights.* Washington, DC: National Association of Defense Lawyers.
Smith, C. H. (1927). The justice of the peace system in the United States. *California Law Review, 15*, 118–141.
Surrency, E. C. (1967). The courts in American colonies. *The American Journal of Legal History, 11*(3), 253–276.
Steele, E. H. (1981). The historical context of small claims courts. *American Bar Foundation Research Journal, 293*, 329–343.
Stevenson, M., & Mayson, S. (2018). The scale of misdemeanor justice. *Boston University Law Review, 98*, 731–777.
Uniform Crime Reporting, Federal Bureau of Investigation, U.S. Department of Justice. Retrieved from www.fbi.gov/services/cjis/ucr
United States Sentencing Commission (n.d.). Retrieved from www.ussc.gov/research/datafiles/commission-datafiles
Wilson, J.Q., & Kelling, G. L. (1982, March). Broken windows: The police and neighborhood safety. *The Atlantic.* Washington DC: Hayley Romer.
Zimring, F. (2008). *The great American crime decline.* New York, NY: Oxford University Press.

2

LEGAL HISTORY OF MISDEMEANOR COURTS

Alisa Smith

The United States Constitution was signed on September 17, 1787. Article III of the Constitution provided that "the trial of all crimes, except cases of impeachment, shall be by jury." The first ten amendments to the Constitution, which conveyed fundamental rights to individuals, were adopted on December 15, 1791. These ten amendments, known as the Bill of Rights, include the Fifth and the Sixth Amendments, which protect the right to due process of law and that "in all criminal prosecutions the accused shall enjoy the right to a speedy and public trial, by impartial jury … and have the Assistance of Counsel for his defence."

Despite this seemingly plain language, *all* criminal defendants do not enjoy these rights. From the 1800s, the Supreme Court interpreted "crimes" and "criminal prosecutions" narrowly, which meant that not all prosecutions for criminal offenses had to be tried by a jury and not all defendants were entitled to counsel (*Callan v. Wilson*, 1888). Over 100 years later, this remains the case—not all criminal defendants enjoy the right to trial by jury or the right to counsel. This chapter provides an overview of the history of these rights, particularly focusing on the right to jury trial, the right to counsel, the right to appeal, and the right to be heard by an attorney-judge in misdemeanor cases.

Misdemeanors and the Right to Jury Trial

At the time the Constitution was adopted, nonlawyer judges were common, and these courts were called justices of the peace or police magistrate courts. Cases heard in these courts concerned local matters, including charges of misdemeanor criminal offending. During the colonial period, these courts were the courts of last resort because there were no appeals (Surrency, 1967). Throughout the 1600s and early 1700s, the administration of justice in these courts was a "source of constant complaint" (Surrency, 1967, p. 254). With this backdrop (and many other complaints about injustices), the framers included guarantees of the right to jury trial, due process of law, and the right to counsel in the United States Constitution (U.S. Const., art. III, amend. V, VI). Despite the adoption of Article III and the Fifth and Sixth Amendments, defendants accused of minor crimes were not afforded the same constitutional protections as more serious offenders. Many of the minor crimes continued to be heard by nonlawyer judges.

By the 1800s, society and the law became more complex, and legal scholars became more critical of justices who had no legal training (Surrency, 1967). Many perceived these courts as having too much discretion and too little oversight (Newton, Welch, & Hamilton, 2012). In a stinging rebuke, Roscoe Pound, in 1920, referred to nonlawyer judges as "a humiliating anachronism" (Pound, 1920, p. 146). Despite these criticisms, the challenge to non-attorney judges was not forged until the 1960s—discussed later in the chapter—and the Supreme Court's early decisions legitimized these informal courts by narrowly interpreting "crimes" and "criminal prosecutions" to exclude "petty" offenses, and thereby depriving those cases of the right to jury trial (*Callan v. Wilson*, 1888). The *Callan* decision stimulated 100 years of debate and discussion on what amounted to a "petty" or trivial offense and which rights were guaranteed these lesser offenses.

An offense that was "grave [in] character affect[ed] the public at large," and these offenders were entitled to trials by jury (*Callan v. Wilson*, at 556). Individuals charged with "the class or grade of offense called 'petty offense,' which, under common law, may be proceeded against summarily in any tribunal legally constituted for that purpose ..." were not entitled to this constitutional right (*Callan v. Wilson*, at 556–7). In a series of cases between 1889 and 1917, the Supreme Court consistently held that "there may be many offenses called 'petty offenses' which do not rise to the degree of crimes within the meaning of Article 3, and in respect of which Congress may dispense with a jury trial, is settled" (*District of Columbia v. Colts*, 1930).[1] Petty offenses, which may be disposed of by summary proceedings before a magistrate, included ordinance violations with a penalty of $25 and imprisonment of not more than 30 days (*Natal v. Louisiana*, 1891). In 1894, the Supreme Court upheld a conviction for the destruction of fishing nets, valued at $15 apiece, without a jury because the value of property at stake was insubstantial (*Lawton v. Steele*, 1894).[2] The Court harkened to history, noting that

> from time immemorial the practice has been to try persons charged with petty offenses before a police magistrate, who not only passes upon the question of guilt, but metes out the proper punishment. This has never been treated as an infraction of the Constitution, though technically a person may in this way be deprived of his liberty without the intervention of a jury.
>
> (Lawton v. Steele, *1894, pp. 141–2*)

Whether defendants were entitled to jury trials turned on the definition of "crimes." A later Court in 1904 relied on *Blackstone*'s Commentaries—the influential eighteenth-century treatise on the common law of England—to define "crimes," because they reasoned that the framers of the Constitution would have been familiar with his definition:

> A crime, or misdemeanor, is an act committed, or omitted, in violation of a public law either forbidding or commanding it. This general definition comprehends both crimes and misdemeanors; which, properly speaking, are mere synonymous terms; though in common usage the word 'crimes' is made to denote such offenses as are of a deeper and more atrocious dye; while smaller faults and omissions of less consequence are comprised under the gentler name of 'misdemeanors' only.
>
> (Schick v. United States, *1904, p. 68*)

The Schick Court concluded that the framers intended to exclude petty criminal offenses from that class of crime afforded the right to jury trial (*Schick v. United States*, 1904, p. 70). It was this early history of justices of the peace and police magistrates and summary disposition without a jury, which included imposed punishments from commitments to jail, workhouses, and houses of correction that influenced later decisions by the Supreme Court to justify trials without juries for misdemeanor offenses (*District of Columbia v. Clawans*, 1937).

To determine whether a crime was petty, or not, the Court examined the nature of the offense and the severity of the punishment. It was the latter factor that posed the most difficulty for the Court. Was a 90-day jail sentence so serious that a jury trial was necessary? This was the question that the Supreme Court grappled with in the *Clawans* case. Again, the Court looked backward, noting that at the time the Constitution was adopted, "ninety days or more was not an unusual punishment for petty offenses, tried without a jury" (*District of Columbia v. Clawans*, 1937, p. 625). So, the Court held that a defendant subjected to a 90-day jail term for a misdemeanor offense was not entitled to a jury trial. A judge could preside over the case, convict the defendant, and pass a jail sentence of 90 days.

Thirty years later, the Court held that a contempt conviction (for failing to abide by a court order), which carried a term of imprisonment of six months did not warrant a jury trial (*Cheff v. Schnackenberg*, 1966; *Green v. United States*, 1958; *U.S. v. Barnett*, 1964). Six months imprisonment, the Court concluded, was a trivial penalty and therefore triable without a jury (*Cheff v. Schnackenberg*, p. 379). Two years after *Cheff*, the Supreme Court heard *Duncan v. Louisiana* (1968), where the accused was charged in state court with simple battery, a misdemeanor that carried up to two years in prison and a $300 fine. The trial judge denied Duncan's request for a jury trial; he was convicted and sentenced to 60 days in prison with a $150 fine (*Duncan v. Louisiana*, 1968, p. 146). The *Duncan* Court reaffirmed its prior decisions but drew the line at six months: "Crimes carrying possible penalties up to six months do not require a jury trial if they otherwise qualify as petty offenses" (*Duncan v. Louisiana*, 1968, p. 159). Even though Duncan was sentenced to only 60 days in jail, the Court held that it was the potential and authorized punishment of up to two years imprisonment that amounted to a serious crime, not a petty offense (*Duncan v. Louisiana*, 1968, p. 162). In arriving at this decision, the Court relied on history and practicality: "So-called petty offenses were tried without juries both in England and in the Colonies and have always been held to be exempt from the otherwise comprehensive language of the Sixth Amendment's jury trial provisions" (*Duncan v. Louisiana*, 1968, p. 162).

The consequences of petty offense convictions were insufficient to warrant the expense of the jury trial; a crime punishable by two years in prison was a serious, not a petty offense (*Duncan v. Louisiana*, 1968, p. 162). In 1970, the Supreme Court extended the Duncan holding to offenses with the potential for sentences over six months (*Baldwin v. New York*, 1970, p. 69). Six years later, the Supreme Court upheld the Massachusetts' two-tiered system, which authorized the prosecution of a non-petty offense—one punishable by more than six months in jail—to be tried by a judge as long as the defendant had the right to appeal that decision and obtain a jury trial *de novo* on appeal (*Ludwig v. Massachusetts*, 1976). The Court found that the additional financial cost associated with a second trial, the chance of a harsher sentence following the trial *de novo*, and the increased psychological and physical hardships of two trials did not amount to an unconstitutional burden on the exercise of the right to trial by jury (*Ludwig v. Massachusetts*, 1976). In arriving at this decision, the Supreme Court determined that it need not reconsider *Callan*, which distinguished petty crimes subject to summary proceedings and those that required trial by jury in the first moment, because (1) the Article III language, providing "[t]he Trial of all Crimes ... shall be by Jury," applied only in the federal courts, and (2) the two-tiered system in the District of Columbia, which required that defendants be "fully tried" in the first tier before taking an appeal, was different from Massachusetts' system, which permitted the accused to circumvent trial in the first tier (*Ludwig v. Massachusetts*, 1976). The Court concluded that Massachusetts guaranteed trial by jury for those accused of serious crimes, even if that review was on appeal, so the system was fair and not unduly burdensome (*Ludwig v. Massachusetts*, 1976, p. 630).

Misdemeanors and the Right to Counsel

The rights to jury trial and counsel have two different histories. Although the right to counsel was granted to defendants in felony prosecutions in 1963, in *Gideon v. Wainwright*, this right was not extended to misdemeanor prosecutions for nearly ten more years, and even then, it was not universally applied to all misdemeanor defendants. Similar to the right to jury trial, the curtailing of the constitutional right to counsel was justified on the ground that misdemeanor offenses were petty and unworthy of due process.

In 1965, President Johnson established the Commission on Law Enforcement and Administration of Justice. This group undertook a comprehensive assessment of the criminal justice system, making more than 200 specific recommendations for improvement (Katzenbach, 1967). This report found inequity, indignity, and ineffectiveness in the lower courts, concluding that these courts were in crisis (Katzenbach, 1967).

Following this report, the Supreme Court began holding that misdemeanor defendants were entitled to some fundamental protections and due process: the right to a speedy trial (*Klopfer v. North Carolina*, 1967, p. 226), a public trial and the right to be informed of the charges against them (*In re Oliver*, 1948, p. 257), the right to confront and cross examine witnesses (*Pointer v. Texas*, 1965, p. 400), and the right to call and compel witnesses in their defense (*Washington v. Texas*, 1967, p. 14). It wasn't until 1972, however, that the Court held that *some* misdemeanor defendants had the right to counsel (*Argersinger v. Hamlin*, 1972). In *Argersinger v. Hamlin,* the Court held that misdemeanor defendants who are prosecuted for crimes with the potential for serving jail as a punishment, no matter how short the jail term, are entitled to counsel.

Argersinger, charged with carrying a concealed weapon, was tried without a jury or counsel. He was convicted and sentenced to 90 days in jail. On petition to the Florida Supreme Court, he argued that he was deprived of his right to counsel—under *Duncan*, he was not entitled to a jury because the maximum punishment for his crime was six months in jail, a $1,000 fine, or both. The Florida Supreme Court followed the reasoning in *Duncan* to hold that the right to court-appointed counsel extended only to trials for offenses carrying more than six months imprisonment (*Argersinger v. Hamlin*, 1970).

The United States Supreme Court reversed, extending the right to counsel to misdemeanor crimes that resulted in any incarceration. The *Argersinger* Court distinguished the rights to counsel and jury trial (*Argersinger v. Hamlin*, 1972). The Court reasoned that the jury trial had a different history with many court proceedings presided over by a judge alone. The jury was intended to protect against overzealous prosecutors and government corruption. Only "serious criminal cases" were worthy of a jury trial. On the other hand, these limits to counsel were not found in history; the right to counsel was the foundation for fairness.

The importance of lawyers in defending those accused of criminal misconduct date to before the Constitution was adopted and ratified. In 1770, British soldiers fired into a crowd of protestors, killing five civilians (Finkel & Adams, 2011; Boston Massacre Historical Society). The incident became known as the Boston Massacre, and John Adams—who later became President and was a leader of the colonial resistance—came forward to defend the eight British soldiers. He did so because he believed in the rule of law. He argued the soldiers acted in self-defense against an unruly mob, and six of the eight soldiers were acquitted (Finkel & Adams, 2011).

Counsel is the foundation to ensuring fair trials, and even in "petty" cases, the law and constitutional issues can be complex (*Argersinger v. Hamlin*, 1972). The Argersinger Court was influenced by the President's Commission Report, which outlined the problems associated with misdemeanor and petty offenses, including the volume of cases and the lack of due process (*Argersinger v. Hamlin*, 1972). The Court held that counsel was a necessary ingredient to ensuring fairness in the lower courts:

> Beyond the problem of trials and appeals is that of the guilty plea, a problem which looms large in misdemeanor as well as in felony cases. Counsel is needed so that the accused may know precisely what he is doing, so that he is fully aware of the prospect of going to jail or prison, and so that he is treated fairly by the prosecution.
>
> (Argersinger v. Hamlin, *1972, p. 34*)

Despite the breadth of this language and the recognition of widespread issues, the Court limited its holding to only the case at hand, which is not unusual, so only defendants who were sentenced to *actual* incarceration were entitled to counsel under *Argersinger.*

The *Argersinger* decision that actually incarcerated defendants were entitled to counsel left open a number of legal questions, including whether the threat of jail was enough to trigger counsel. Over the next few years, this question was answered differently by a number of state courts. Many states held that appointed counsel was necessary when there was the potential for a jail term based on the maximum sentence, whereas others held that appointed counsel was necessary only when incarceration was a possibility, and still other states appointed counsel when the potential jail term reached a threshold minimum of three or six months (Ford, 1974). Some states only appointed counsel when defendants were actually jailed (*Scott v. Illinois*, 1979; Sixth Amendment Center).

In 1979, the conflict among the states was resolved. Taking a narrow approach to the Sixth Amendment, the Supreme Court, in *Scott v. Illinois* (1979), refused to extend the right to appointed counsel when defendants merely faced the threat of incarceration. The *Scott* Court called into doubt that the Sixth Amendment, as originally drafted, contemplated a guarantee to the right to counsel (*Scott v. Illinois*, 1979). The Scott Court decisively ruled that

> the Sixth and Fourteenth Amendment to the United States Constitution require only that no indigent criminal defendant be sentenced to a term of imprisonment unless the State has afforded him the right to assistance of appointed counsel in his defense.
>
> (Scott v. Illinois, *1979, pp. 373–4*)

Though the decision sounded like the final word on the right to counsel in misdemeanor prosecutions, it was not.

Two questions arose in the aftermath of *Scott*: (1) whether uncounseled misdemeanor convictions may be used to enhance subsequent charges and (2) whether suspended or conditional sentences invoked the Sixth Amendment. Just a year later, the Court answered the first question but 14 years later reversed that decision. Initially, the Court held that an uncounseled misdemeanor could not be used to later enhance a criminal offense from a misdemeanor to a felony, which carried a prison term (*Baldasar v. Illinois*, 1980). This decision was overruled, in *Nichols v. United States* (1994). The *Nichols* Court held that "an uncounseled misdemeanor conviction, valid under *Scott* because no prison term was imposed, is also valid when used to enhance punishments at a subsequent conviction" (*Nichols v. United States*, 1994, p. 748). Nichols, who entered a plea to federal felony, conspiracy to possess cocaine with the intent to distribute, argued that an uncounseled state misdemeanor conviction for driving under the influence conviction should not be used to increase his sentence. The Supreme Court held that since Nichols was not entitled to counsel for the driving under the influence offense because he was fined, not incarcerated, it was a lawful conviction and may be relied on to enhance a later criminal sentence. The Court held that appointed counsel was only required when a criminal proceeding resulted in incarceration, until 2002.

In 2002, the Supreme Court answered the second question, left open by *Scott v. Illinois*: whether suspended or conditional sentences invoked the right to counsel. Shelton represented himself and took his case to trial without a jury. The judge convicted him of third-degree assault, which carried a maximum sentence of one year in jail and a $2,000 fine. He appealed. In Alabama, Shelton was entitled to a new trial before a jury on appeal. Again, he represented himself, and he was convicted. Shelton was sentenced to 30 days in jail, but the trial judge suspended that sentence and placed him on two years of probation and imposed court costs, a fine, and restitution. Shelton appealed his case to the United States Supreme Court. The Court concluded that "[a] suspended sentence is a prison term imposed for the offense of conviction" (*Alabama v. Shelton*, 2002, p. 662). This was the case because upon violation of probation, Shelton would be imprisoned on the underlying offense, and therefore the Court held that defendants who were subjected to potential incarceration had the right to court-appointed counsel (*Alabama v. Shelton*, 2002).

The Right to Appeal

Due process does not require appellate review (*District of Columbia v. Clawans*, 1937; *McKane v. Durston*, 1894). In 1894, the Supreme Court, *in dicta*,[3] noted that the matter of an appeal was wholly in the discretion of the state courts (*McKane v. Durston*, 1894, p. 687). As Robertson (2013) has explained, an appeal is a "matter of grace and not a necessary ingredient of justice" (p. 1221). The right to appeal has been nearly universally adopted by federal law and in 48 of the states by either statute or constitution (Robertson, 2013). In the two states that do not have a statutory or constitutional provision allowing for the right of defendants to appeal—New Hampshire and West Virginia—the right to an appeal is guaranteed by court rule. Although the Supreme Court has not recognized the right to an appeal as a matter of due process, it has held, that when a state affords defendants that right (by statute, constitution, or court rule), equal protection is violated when appellate remedies are restricted for indigent defendants (*Griffin v. Illinois*, 1956).

In *Douglas v. California* (1963), the Supreme Court held that defendants who had the right to appeal by statute, constitution, or rule then had to be afforded the right to counsel on that appeal. The court reasoned that it would not be fair that someone had benefits on appeal if they were rich, but disadvantaged if they were poor:

> [T]he rich man, who appeals as of right, enjoys the benefit of counsel's examination into the record, research of the law, and marshalling of arguments on his behalf, while the indigent, already burdened by a preliminary determination that his case is without merit, is forced to shift for himself.
>
> (Douglas v. California, *1963, p. 358*)

The right to counsel only applies to defendants appealing as a matter-of-right, second-level appeal, or discretionary petition for review. However, the Supreme Court held that the Fourteenth Amendment and Due Process do not require the appointment of counsel for discretionary state appeals or applications for review to the Supreme Court of the United States. So, poor defendants who want to appeal beyond the first review are not entitled to counsel (*Ross v. Moffitt*, 1974).

An interesting quirk in the constitutional law of misdemeanor cases is that defendants may not have the right to counsel at trial, but when they appeal their uncounseled convictions, then they have the right to counsel. Justice Burger, in his concurring opinion in *Argersinger v. Hamlin* (1972), highlighted the anomaly and futility of providing counsel on appeal after denying counsel at trial:

> There is little ground, therefore, to assume that a defendant, unaided by counsel, will be any more able adequately to defend himself against the lesser charges that may involve confinement than more serious charges. Appeal from a conviction after an uncounseled trial is not likely to be of much help to a defendant since the die is usually cast when judgment is entered on an uncounseled trial record.
>
> *(p. 41)*

Right to an Attorney Judge

At the time the Constitution was adopted, many crimes were considered petty and "tried summarily without a jury, by justices of the peace ... and by police magistrates or corresponding judicial officers[,]" who were able to punish defendants to serve jail terms or to workhouses, and even houses of correction (*District of Columbia v. Clawans*, 1937). Many of these justices and police magistrates were not lawyers—a practice that was brought to the colonies from England (Ashman & Lee, 1977).

Although most of Europe replaced lay judges with professional judges by 1789, England retained and expanded their use (Ashman & Lee, 1977). With few educated lawyers in Colonial America, sparse populations, and poor transportation, lay justices served a vital role. These colonial courts with little guidance from England evolved in growth, operation, and administration (Surrency, 1967). Over time, these courts presided over many local matters, including criminal cases, and they were the courts of last resort because there was no right to an appeal (Surrency, 1967).

By the early 1700s, many complaints had been lodged against the administration of justice by these nonlawyer judges, ranging from a lack of due process, dilatory proceedings, and incompetence (Surrency, 1967). These complaints intensified into the 1800s when society became more complex and the legal system more sophisticated (Ashman & Lee, 1977). Claims of abuse of power were rooted in justices' wide discretion with little oversight (Newton et al., 2012).

With the growth of lawyers in the 1900s, many of them—including Roscoe Pound, a distinguished American legal scholar—criticized these courts as undermining the administration of justice, dated, and "humiliating" (Pound, 1920). Several organizations, including the American Bar Association, wrote harsh critiques of the use of nonlawyer judges and called for the abolishment of the justices of the peace in the 1920s and 1930s (Alfini, 1981; Newton et al., 2012). Despite this widespread and relentless criticism, it was not until the 1960s that 14 states moved to eliminate these courts and others restricted their authority, and the 1970s, when lawyers began to challenge the constitutionality of these courts (*Ditty v. Hampton*, 1972; *Gordon v. Justice Court for Yuba Judicial District of Sutter County*, 1974; Newton et al., 2012; *Shelmidine v. Jones*, 1976).

These early challenges to the constitutionality of nonlawyer justices followed the *Argersinger v. Hamlin* decision, in 1972. Lawyers argued that nonlawyer judges violated defendant's right to counsel when they were subjected to the possibility of incarceration. The Kentucky Court of Appeals rejected this argument, distinguishing the role of defense counsel and judge. Defense attorneys were advocates; judges provided nothing more than a fair and impartial proceeding

(*Ditty v. Hampton*, 1972). The Supreme Court of Utah did not address the right-to-counsel argument, but rather found that nonlawyer judges were a matter of necessity due to the scarcity of lawyers (*Shelmidine v. Jones*, 1976). The only court that agreed with the lawyers challenging the legitimacy of nonlawyer justices was the Supreme Court of California, which held that the increased complexity of criminal law and procedure made it likely that untrained lay judges would have a difficult time in understanding arguments, thereby diluting defendants' right to effective counsel (*Gordon v. Justice Court for Yuba Judicial District of Sutter County*, 1975).

The Supreme Court of California stood alone in its position. The courts in Texas, New Mexico, Minnesota, and New York found that the use of lay judges did not violate the constitution, particularly when defendants were given the right to trial *de novo*[4] on appeal (*Ex Parte Ross*, 1975; *In re Hewitt*, 1975; *State v. Lindgren*, 1956; *Tsiosdia v. Rainaldi*, 1976). These courts rejected a range of constitutional challenges that lay justices violated not only the right to counsel, but due process and equal protection of the law as well.

Due process requires fairness in the process of dispensing justice, even by nonlawyer judges. The Supreme Court, in 1927, held that due process is violated by a judge who presides over a criminal matter, who has a "direct, personal, substantial, pecuniary interest in reaching a conclusion against [a defendant]" (*Tumey v. Ohio*, 1927, p. 523). In Tumey, the Mayor of the Village of North College Hill, Ohio, was also the presiding judge in the town, and he was compensated for his judicial role from the costs he imposed against convicted defendants (*Tumey v. Ohio*, 1927). The Supreme Court concluded that

> a system by which an inferior judge is paid for his service only when he convicts the defendant has not become so embedded by custom in the general practice either at common law or in this country that it can be regarded as due process of law, unless the costs usually imposed are so small that they may be properly ignored as within the maxim *de minimis non curat lex.*[5]
>
> (Tumey v. Ohio, *1927, p. 531*)

Although the imposed cost to Tumey was only $12, the Court found the mayor received $696.35 from fees and costs levied by him to supplement his normal salary, and that amount of money (in 1927) was not insignificant (*Tumey v. Ohio*, 1927, pp. 523–33).

Almost 50 years later, the Supreme Court confronted another case involving a mayor, who was also the town judge in cases of ordinance violations and certain traffic offenses (*Ward v. Monroeville*, 1972). The Mayor of Monroeville had wide executive powers and he was the justice of the peace. A major part of the village income was collected through fines, forfeitures, costs, and fees imposed by him in his role on the mayor's court (*Ward v. Monroeville*, 1972). Ward argued that the mayor, acting as the judge, was not impartial as required by due process. The test for determining partiality was whether the situation was one

> which would offer a possible temptation to the average man as a judge to forget the burden of proof required to convict the defendant or which might lead him not to hold the balance nice, clear and true between the State and the accused....
>
> (Ward v. Monroeville, *1972, p. 60, quoting Tumey, 1927, p. 532*)

The Court found the mayor lacked impartiality because he benefited from filling his executive coffers with imposed costs from convicted defendants. The Supreme Court also rejected the argument that any unfairness at the trial level could be corrected on appeal with a trial *de novo*—a new trial before a different judge and in some instances a jury—because, the Court reasoned that the "petitioner is entitled to a neutral and detached judge in the first instance" (*Ward v. Monroeville*, 1972, p. 61).

The problem with the mayor courts was that those judges had an improper interest in committing defendants to generate fees. That the mayors were not lawyers was not at issue. It was not until 1976 that a challenge to the constitutionality of nonlawyer judges reached the Supreme Court. In that case, the Supreme Court upheld—against constitutional attack on due process and equal protection grounds—the use of nonlawyer judges even when an accused is subject to possible imprisonment when trial *de novo* on appeal is available (*North v. Russell*, 1976). Lonnie North was accused of driving while intoxicated; he asked for a jury trial. Police court magistrate Russell, who was not a lawyer, denied his request, and North was convicted and sentenced to 30 days in jail. Nonlawyer judges were permitted under Kentucky law to preside over cases in smaller towns. In larger cities, judges had to be lawyers. Kentucky also had a two-tiered misdemeanor court system, which meant that defendants, like North, had the right to appeal a decision by a police judge to a circuit court where all judges were lawyers and jury trials were available (*North v. Russell*, 1976).

North argued that he was denied equal protection under the law because defendants in larger cities were tried by judges who were legally trained lawyers. He also claimed that due process required a judge with a law degree when incarceration was possible (*North v. Russell*, 1976). North argued that his right to counsel, under *Argersinger*, was meaningless without a lawyer-judge, who could understand the arguments of counsel. North also asserted that substantive and procedural law had evolved and became so complex that all judges should be required to be lawyers "to be able to rule correctly on the intricate issues lurking even in some simple misdemeanor cases" (*North v. Russell*, 1976, p. 335).

The Supreme Court did not reach the question of whether defendants were entitled to lawyer judges when subject to incarceration because in Kentucky's two-tiered system, defendants were entitled to be tried *de novo* by a lawyer in an appeal that automatically vacated a conviction by the police court (*North v. Russell*, 1976). Although the Court recognized that many defendants may appear in police court without an attorney, and they may be unaware of their right to a *de novo* trial, the court made several assumptions that due process was ensured by nonlawyer judges. First, the Court "assume[d] that police court judges recognize their obligation under *Argersinger v. Hamlin*, to inform defendants of their right to a lawyer if a sentence of confinement is to be imposed" (*North v. Russell*, 1976, p. 335). Also,

> assume[d] [was] that police court judges … recognize their obligation to inform all convicted defendants, including those who waived counsel, or for whom imprisonment was not imposed, of their unconditional right to a trial *de novo* and of the necessity that an 'appeal' be filed within 30 days in order to implement that right.
>
> (North v. Russell, *1976, p. 335*)

Harkening to its 1972 decision, in *Colten v. Kentucky*, in which the Court upheld Kentucky's two-tiered system that was challenged on other grounds, the Court emphasized and reiterated that continuing with nonlawyer judges was important to reduce the "'increasing burdens on state judiciaries' and the 'interest of both the defendant and the State, to provide speedier and less costly adjudications' than those provided in courts 'where the full range of constitutional guarantees is available'" (*North v. Russell*, 1976, p. 336). This reasoning too is founded on the assumption that more due process by a lawyer judge would slow proceedings and raise costs. The Court noted the "convenience" of being tried in or near your town, rather than having to travel a long distance for a hearing by a lawyer-trained judge (*North v. Russell*, 1976, p. 336). And the Court assumed that—much like at the time of colonial America—there are insufficient lawyers to fill these judicial vacancies. Finally, the Court noted that it is important that judicial functions be carried out independently, neutrally, and with detached judgment; none of those functions required legal training. In rejecting the equal protection challenge, the Court found that people within a given city were treated equally, and citizens of similarly sized cities treated equally. These differences based on population and other factors justified different classifications within the court system, and therefore the differentiated system did not violate the Equal Protection Clause (*North v. Russell*, 1976).

Conclusion

Today, millions of defendants in the United States are charged with misdemeanor crimes. These are not "minor" crimes or civil traffic infractions. These are crimes that may subject defendants to incarceration, crimes that impact their right to live in public housing or receive a student loan. These are also crimes that may subject defendants to deportation. Yet the vast majority of these defendants are deprived of their fundamental rights to counsel and jury trial. Hundreds of thousands appear before nonlawyer judges, who are permitted to hold those positions in 22 states. Although the Supreme Court recognized the constitutional right to a jury trial for misdemeanor crimes that subject defendants to incarceration longer than six months in jail, and the right to counsel when defendants are actually incarcerated or subject to incarceration, this leaves the vast majority of defendants without either right.

The Supreme Court has relied on history—that is, what types of rights were conferred to defendants at the time the Constitution was adopted—and fundamental assumptions about how misdemeanor courts operate. In 1967, the President's Commission Report highlighted problems associated with the prosecution of misdemeanor crimes, including the lack of due process, and the essential unfairness of the proceedings (Katzenbach, 1967). Since 1967, empirical research has been conducted on the misdemeanor courts, emphasizing continued violations of due process and fairness as well as the long-term consequences of misdemeanor convictions. Much of this research is discussed in the remainder of this book. Perhaps, the Court will take a closer look at the misdemeanor courts, their lack of due process and the long-term impact of misdemeanor convictions to find that standards have evolved—much like the abandoning of the lashing and the stocks—and require misdemeanor defendants have the same fundamental rights afforded defendants charged with felonies.

Notes

1 Citing *Schick v. United States* (1904, p. 65); *Natal v. Louisiana* (1891, p. 624); *Lawton v. Steele* (1894); *State v. Rodgers*, 91 N.J. Law 212, 214, 6 *Gummere* 212, 102 A. 433 (1917).
2 The Court also upheld the conviction by a nonlawyer judge. This topic is discussed later in this chapter.
3 *Dicta* is the part of an opinion that does not concern the issue before the court, and it has no precedential value beyond the opinion of the particular justice.
4 *De novo* means anew, so in this context, defendants were entitled to trials before lawyer judges on appeal.
5 *De minimis non curat lex* translated from Latin mean that the law ignores insignificant details.

References

Alabama v. Shelton, 535 U.S. 654 (2002).
Alfini, J. (1981). Understanding misdemeanor courts: A review of the literature and recent case law. In J. Alfini, (Ed.), *Misdemeanor courts: Policy concerns and research perspectives* (pp. 1–28). Washington D.C.: U.S. Department of Justice.

Argersinger v. Hamlin, 236 So. 2d 442, 443 (Fla. 1970).
Argersinger v. Hamlin, 407 U.S. 25 (1972).
Ashman, A., & Lee, D.L. (1977). Non-lawyer judges: The long road north, *Chicago-Kent Law Review, 53*, 565–595.
Baldasar v. Illinois, 446 U.S. 222 (1980).
Baldwin v. New York, 399 U.S. 66 (1970).
Boston Massacre Historical Society. Retrieved from www.bostonmassacre.net/facts-and-numbers.htm
Callan v. Wilson, 127 U.S. 540 (1888).
Cheff v. Schnackenberg, 384 U.S. 373, 375 86 S.Ct. 1523, 16 L.Ed.2d 629 (1966).
Colten v. Kentucky, 407 U.S. 104 (1972).
District of Columbia v. Clawans, 300 U.S. 617, 57 S.Ct. 660, 81 L.Ed. 843 (1937).
District of Columbia v. Colts, 282 U.S. 63, 51 S.Ct. 52, 75 L.Ed. 177 (1930).
Ditty v. Hampton, 490 S.W.2d 772 (Ky. 1972), *appeal dismissed as moot*, 414 U.S. 885 (1973).
Douglas v. California, 372 U.S. 353 (1963).
Duncan v. Louisiana, 391 U.S. 145 (1968).
Ex Parte Ross, 522 S.W.2d 214 (Tex. Ct. Crim. App. 1975), *cert. denied*, 423 U.S. 1018 (1975).
Finkel, E., & Adams, J. (May 2011). Gets his day: The first lawyer-president set a standard for representing unpopular causes. *ABA Journal*. Retrieved from www.abajournal.com/magazine/article/john_adams_gets_his_day
Ford, B.B. (1974). *Argersinger v. Hamlin* and the collateral use of prior misdemeanor convictions of indigents unrepresented by counsel at trial. *Ohio State Law Journal, 35*, 168–189.
Gideon v Wainwright, 372 U.S. 335 (1963).
Gordon v. Justice Court for Yuba Judicial District of Sutter County, 12 Cal. 3d 323, 525 P.2d 72,115 Cal. Rptr. 632 (1974), *cert. denied*, 420 U.S. 938 (1975).
Green v. United States, 356 U.S. 165, 78 S.Ct. 632, 2 L.Ed.2d 672 (1958).
Griffin v. Illinois, 351 U.S. 12 (1956).
In re Hewitt, 81 Misc. 2d 202, 365 N.Y.2d 760 (Tompkins County Ct. 1975).
In re Oliver, 333 U.S. 257 (1948).
Katzenbach, N. (1967). *The challenge of crime in a free society: A report by the President's Commission on Law Enforcement and Administration of Justice*. U.S. Government Printing Office: Washington, DC. Retrieved from www.ncjrs.gov/pdffiles1/nij/42.pdf
Klopfer v. North Carolina, 386 U.S. 213 (1967).
Lawton v. Steele, 152 U.S 133, 14 S.Ct. 499, 38 L.Ed. 385 (1894).
Ludwig v. Massachusetts, 427 U.S. 618 (1976).
McKane v. Durston, 153 U.S. 684, 687 (1894).
Natal v. Louisiana, 139 U.S. 621, 624, 11 S.Ct. 636, 35 L.Ed. 288 (1891).
Newton, S.P., Welch, T.L., & Hamilton, N.G. (2012). No justice in Utah's justice courts: Constitutional issues, systemic problems, and the failure to protect defendants in Utah's infamous local courts. *Utah Law Review Online, 1*, 27–72.
Nichols v. United States, 511 U.S. 738 (1994).
North v. Russell, 427 U.S. 328 (1976).
Pointer v. Texas, 380 U.S. 400 (1965).
Pound, R. (1920). Anachronisms in law. *Journal of American Judicature Society, 3*, 142–148.
Robertson, C. B. (2013). The right to appeal. *North Carolina Law Review, 91*, 1219–1282.
Ross v. Moffit, 417 U.S. 600 (1974).
Schick v. United States, 195 U.S. 65 (1904).
Scott v. Illinois, 440 U.S. 367 (1979).
Shelmidine v. Jones, 550 P.2d 207 (Utah 1976).
State v. Lindgren, 235 N.W. 2d 379 (1956).
State v. Rodgers, 91 N.J. Law 212, 214, 6 Gummere 212, 102 A. 433 (1917).
Surrency, E.C. (1967). The courts in American colonies. *The American Journal of Legal History, 11*(3), 253–276.

The Sixth Amendment Center, *Drawing the line at actual imprisonment*. Retrieved from http://sixthamendment.org/the-right-to-counsel/history-of-the-right-to-counsel/drawing-the-line-at-actual-imprisonment/

Tsiosdia v. Rainaldi, 547 P.2d 553 (N.M. 1976).

Tumey v. Ohio, 273 U.S. 510 (1927).

United States v. Barnett, 376 U.S. 681, 692, 84 S.Ct. 984, 12 L.Ed.2d 23 (1964).

Washington v. Texas, 388 U.S. 14 (1967).

Ward v. Monroeville, 409 U.S. 57 (1972).

3

THE PROCESS IS THE PUNISHMENT REVISITED

Forty-Year Anniversary Review

Jennifer Earl

The Process is the Punishment (hereafter *TPP*) was originally published to wide acclaim in 1979 (Feeley, 1992). Feeley was one of the first major authors to shine a light on the substantial role of lower courts in the criminal justice system, inspiring a wave of subsequent research on the lower courts. He observed New Haven, Connecticut's lower courts during a period of broadly expanded due process rights in which the adversarial U.S. legal system should have been at its peak, ensuring that false negatives, not false positives, dominated the errors made within the system. What Feeley famously observed was far different from what casual observers would have anticipated. Instead of adversarial court processes, including trials, leveraging due process rights to ensure that individuals were not falsely convicted, he found a world where those accused of small crimes paid a price through a punishing process—a process that became ever more punishing as one extended their engagement with it. Far from maximizing the use of due process rights, this punishing process led many defendants to opt-out of the system as soon as possible, often by failing to appear or by taking pleas. Formal sentences were the least of defendants' punishments. These observations, and the open systems model[1] that *TPP* helped to popularize, have had a major impact on our understanding of the criminal courts broadly, especially lower criminal courts.

In celebration of these major contributions, I published a 30-year anniversary long-form review of *TPP* in *Law and Social Inquiry* (Earl, 2008). That review explored the range of accolades and criticisms that *TPP* received in the era of its initial publication and also conducted a painstaking empirical review of how *TPP* had been cited, in terms of the literatures and debates that *TPP* was being used in and how it was being used, which ranged from being one member of a longer string citation (e.g., research on sentencing disparities) to serious and substantive engagement with key arguments (e.g., research on pretrial punishments and on understudied actors such as bail bondsmen). Since only ten years have passed since that review, making it unlikely that there have been seismic shifts in *TPP*'s areas of impact, this 40-year anniversary review takes a fundamentally different tact.

This review imagines how *TPP* may help us to understand a dramatically different criminal justice system than when Feeley originally wrote, sometimes in ways that *TPP* might not have originally anticipated and even in ways that may be at odds with some of Feeley's views at the time. Indeed, while Feeley wrote at a time best marked by the expansion of due process rights, his book is now being read and used in an era indelibly associated with mass incarceration and the intense racialization of incarceration and criminal supervision. While my prior review was a celebration of Feeley's book on its own terms and written around its own intellectual wake, I celebrate *TPP* now by focusing on how its core arguments may be recast to speak to key issues in the contemporary criminal justice system. At times this means taking issue with some of Feeley's arguments in *TPP* even while extending others to their theoretical conclusions.

Specifically, two arguments from *TPP* are persistently and powerfully useful to understanding today's criminal justice system, including lower courts. First, the "title track argument" (Earl, 2008)—that pretrial processes can be more punishing than lower court sentences, leading defendants to fail to appear or plead guilty—is even more useful than Feeley imagined in understanding how inequality operates in the criminal justice system, and this has become even more true in the age of mass incarceration. Second, Feeley's arguments about the open system in which actors who are not formally supposed to influence adjudication and sentencing nonetheless substantially influence pretrial costs (e.g., bail bondsmen) also remain important today. When one considers additional actors, not considered by Feeley, this argument has even more purchase. I begin by reviewing the arguments as originally presented by Feeley and then move to understanding how these arguments deepen our understanding of criminal justice, and the lower courts specifically, today.

Reviewing the "Title Track": The Process is the Punishment Today

TPP's core contribution was its weighing of the severity of sentences against the informal costs that took place pre-adjudication. Feely set up a simple calculation: If pretrial costs are greater than sentence severities, then defendants are incentivized to plead guilty or fail to appear entirely because it is too costly to contest the charges. Some of the costs that Feeley noted were financial: Most must pay a bail bondsman a fee to post bail and be released; those poorer individuals who could not afford bail would have to remain in jail until their case was disposed of; attorneys may need to be hired; work must be missed while in jail and for subsequent court appearances; childcare may be needed for both situations as well; etc. Many other costs are emotional, relational, and/or reputational: Feeley's

> description of these costs is often rich—as when he describes the confusion and difficulty involved in trying to find an attorney while in jail, especially when one does not know any attorneys personally—and strongly conveys the nonpecuniary costs of pretrial experiences, expenses paid in the currencies of stress, conflict, and confusion.
>
> *(Earl, 2008, p. 744)*

Importantly, these costs escalate with involvement in the system. The more one persists in the system, the more court appearances, missed work, child care, lawyers' fees, stress, and conflict one experiences. But, the formal punishments that the courts would eventually mete out tend to be relatively minor (e.g., small fines or a night in jail when Feeley was observing New Haven).

Although I discuss each of these more later, the punishing nature of the process has two important implications: (1) Poor defendants have greater incentives to plead guilty or fail to appear than wealthier defendants because they may not be able to afford to do otherwise, and (2) Both innocent and guilty defendants suffer process-related punishments prior to any determination of guilt, meaning that arrest is really the gatekeeper for punishment, not conviction. Feeley (1992) does not stress these points, although they are clear implications of his claims, because he is also committed to other claims in *TPP*: that this system may still render substantive justice, but in accordance with the efficiency dictates of the court, and that defendants were likely guilty of something, even if they are not guilty of what they were arrested for, which is similar to the way police often view defendants.

In my 30-year anniversary essay, I criticized *TPP* on both points. After all, Feeley is studying lower courts, which means that police are often arresting individuals without having engaged in significant investigations or vetted the arrest and charges with a prosecutor. Thus, unless we believe that police are virtually infallible in their initial assessments of situations, it must be true "that some (if not many) defendants are innocent" (Earl, 2008, p. 754). If this is the case, then it is hard to imagine that substantive justice is being done by a system that so heavily incentivizes guilty pleas; it is likely that many innocent defendants do not even enjoy the privilege of protesting their innocence and must instead consign themselves to participate in their own judicial undoing as the mathematics of pretrial punishments make a guilty plea, or a failure to appear, the only options (Albonetti, 1986; Alschuler, 1981; 1983; Bibas, 2004; Earl, 2005; Figueira-McDonough, 1985). As was noted shortly after the publication of TPP, while false confessions and false convictions are important and consequential travesties of justice, "what accounts for probably the largest number of false-convictions are guilty pleas entered to avoid some of the burdens and risks of dealing with the criminal justice system" (as also quoted in Earl, 2008; Weinstein, 1981, p. 449).[2] Letting go of the related ideas that substantive justice is being done on presumptively guilty defendants are important steps to unlocking the power of *TPP* for understanding justice in the lower courts today because it allows us to see guilty pleas as a result of an incentive system instead of a justice system. Building on this insight, in the next several sub-sections, I evaluate some of the implications of this incentive system to understanding lower courts in the age of mass incarceration.

Assessing Pretrial Costs in the Era of Mass Incarceration and Quality-of-Life Policing

The history of mass incarceration, including rising jail populations—from both pretrial detention and convictions with sentences of less than a year (which would come from lower courts)—is well known. Other cogs in the wheels of mass incarceration are also well known: The United States went through a prison build boom, hired many new police officers, prosecutors, and correctional officers, and created specialized courts to handle high caseloads around drug crimes. While we often think about what the government was doing that enabled mass incarceration, many fail to think about the ways in which mass incarceration was also built on the back of a heavy load of guilty pleas. As Devers (2011) noted near the peak of mass incarceration: "While there are no exact estimates of the proportion of cases that are resolved through plea bargaining, scholars estimate that about 90%–95% of both federal and state court cases are resolved through this process" (p. 1).

One of my central arguments is that *TPP*'s basic equation—something we could express mathematically as "pretrial costs > sentences"—likely became ever truer during the rise of mass incarceration. The importance of pretrial costs over sentencing outcomes was a necessary aid for mass incarceration as the courts would face a crushing inability to process defendants, especially if a fraction of pleas were instead decided by bench or jury trials. As one bail reform advocate, Steinberg, is quoted as saying: "The current bail system is designed to extract guilty pleas from the most vulnerable people in our society. If people were empowered to demand their right to a fair trial, the system would grind to a halt" (as quoted in May, 2018). In other words, I am arguing that mass incarceration and the press of pretrial costs enabled the intensification of each other.

The basic building blocks of this argument have to do with what happens to pretrial costs as the load of cases becomes dramatically heavier, even if sentences are also becoming stiffer for some crimes. One of the most basic costs that Feeley discusses is bail, especially since one's inability to pay bail ensures a jail stay until trial. Despite increases in average bail levels (although data on lower court bails is hard to track nationally), there is a lack of profit motivation for bail bondsmen to cover small bails (i.e., bails of a few thousand dollars or less; Pinto, 2015), and shifts in the inability of about half of Americans household to absorb unexpected costs of even a few hundred dollars (Federal Reserve, 2018) have all led to a rise in the number and proportion of people who are in jails on pretrial detention (Pinto, 2015). The Prison Policy Institute claims that between 11 and 13 million Americans enter a jail in the United States each year and that "99% of the growth in jails over the last 15 years has been a result of increases in the pretrial population" (Wagner, 2015). Popular estimates of the number of individuals in jails on any given day in the United States due to an inability to pay their bail is close to a half million people (Pinto, 2015). This means that an incredibly large number of people are experiencing one of the biggest costs in the pretrial model.

Mass incarceration and the crush of over ten million people cycling through jails per year has also arguably changed the jail experience. While Feeley remarked on shabby courtrooms and court personnel who had chips on their shoulders about working in lower criminal courts, he did not talk about extreme neglect or predation in jails or excessive pretrial jail stays. Poor conditions are now a fixture of many jails, with some jails like New York's Rikers Island being so poor that they are being slowly closed. These deplorable conditions can range from poor nutrition to risks of physical and sexual abuse by both guards and other inmates (Beck, Berzofsky, Caspar, & Krebs, 2014). While data on prison violence are becoming more available, systematic data on jail violence are hard to come by; anecdotal evidence about jail conditions is very alarming (e.g., Kalief Browder's three-year pretrial detention at Rikers Island on theft of a backpack charge, see, e.g., *The New Yorker*).

The time to disposition has also increased, although systematic national data on lower courts are again difficult to find. This is obviously salient for those who could not make bail, but as Feeley originally noted, it is tough on defendants who are out on bail. Some state-level reports exist but they vary in whether they report on overall times to disposition or pretrial detention periods, making even what data are available difficult to compare. For example, research on New Mexico courts found that "many misdemeanants are detained for some time in detention facilities throughout the state, with an overall median of 80 days ranging up to a median of 106 days at one facility" (Denman, 2016, p. 1), while reporting on New York shows time to disposition of misdemeanor cases routinely taking longer than a year and sometimes into multiple years (Glaberson, 2013). Given that even model standards for state court misdemeanors would only require 98% of cases to be resolved after 180 days (National Center for State Courts, 2011), it is likely that lower court cases are taking longer to resolve today than they did when *TPP* was published. If Feeley's defendants were facing uncertainty on the orders of months and through a half dozen or so court appearances, defendants now may be facing, depending on jurisdiction and other factors, years of uncertainty and the possibility of over a dozen court appearances.

Other costs, such as attorneys' costs or the ability to secure actual time and attention from a public defender, have also worsened over time, as attorneys' caseloads climb. One can imagine that the nonpecuniary costs that Feeley identified have also risen alongside worsening jail conditions, increased costs, and increased time to disposition. If these were decisive costs when the physical condition of jails was better and less dangerous and when pretrial processes only stretched for months, then these stressors should be expected to be ever more decisive now. Some have also argued that even the stigma of being caught up in the criminal justice system has been exacerbated by mass incarceration (Alexander, 2012).

Of course, mass incarceration is not the only factor influencing the worsening fate of those charged with lower crimes. Sentences for some minor crimes have increased, particularly where drugs are involved. "Wobblers"—cases that could be charged as misdemeanors or felonies—have long been used to push defendants to plea bargain into a misdemeanor in order to avoid a wobbler felony. But, overcharging may be more common now even though court rulings have made it difficult to collect data on the exercise of such prosecutorial discretion (Alexander, 2012). Quality-of-life policing, discussed at greater length in another chapter of this volume, has also uniquely contributed to the number of people facing minor violations and crimes. Where once these minor violations and crimes might have gone entirely unnoticed, and certainly unpoliced, broken-windows-inspired policing initiatives have meant that aside from what is happening in prisons, the number of those facing very minor violations and crimes has risen dramatically. When the subjects of quality-of-life policing are arrested, the small sentences are quickly outweighed by pretrial costs. In sum, I am claiming that mass incarceration and the sanctioning process have fed one another, and their relationship has been intensified further by quality-of-life policing, making *TPP* even more important as a core socio-legal text.

Police and the Open Systems Model of Pretrial Costs

While not heavily discussed in *TPP*, two things are necessarily true when the process becomes the punishment: (1) The police become central actors in determining who will be punished and how much, particularly in the lower courts where initial arrests are unlikely to be the result of indictments, and (2) As long as punishment is happening pretrial, both innocent and guilty defendants are receiving these punishments.

On the first point, Feeley investigated a variety of actors who contributed to the punishing nature of the process, but he oddly did not include much discussion of police, even though for lower courts, police often make the decision to arrest and, in instances when citations or desk appearance tickets could be given, are making the decision about whether to make custodial arrests. This major source of discretion is lawful, so long as there is probable cause. Given how the punishing nature of the process has grown, this means that there is a significant amount of punishment for which police effectively become judge and jury. Exacerbated by rulings such as *Atwater vs. Lago Vista* (2001), in which the United States Supreme Court authorized the use of police discretion in making custodial arrests for fine-only offenses without even requiring the police deem the arrest necessary for some reason, the ability of police to use the process as a strategic tool for punishment is now the law of the land. Furthermore, the already punishing nature of arrests can be coupled with other intentional informal penalty enhancements by police such as so-called "rough rides," in which police drive dangerously with subjects in their cars or vans, through overly tight handcuffs, stress positions, etc. Moreover, these custodial arrests for fine-only offenses can result in lawful searches of both the arrestee and their proximate property (including a vehicle) even without the legal need for the suspicion that would otherwise have to exist to justify such a search.

The rise of quality-of-life policing, which, earlier, was framed as enhancing the mutually reinforcing relationship between mass incarceration and increasing pretrial punishments, also expands the role of the police as effective judge and jury for innocent and guilty defendants who may now lawfully be subjected to substantial pretrial punishment for suspicion of such minor crimes as jaywalking. In other words, when police agencies decide to implement quality-of-life policing and empower officers to make custodial arrests for fine-only offenses, the process gets much more punitive, much more quickly. This threat is not unknown or unleveraged by police.

Alexander (2012) argues that the fear of custodial arrests in otherwise petty or fine-only offenses provides police with significant leverage in encounters in which they were interested in searching property but lacked probable cause, allowing them to implicitly trade on the threat of a custodial arrest to extract a "consensual" search of property for which officers would otherwise not have the necessary suspicion to search. In other words, I am arguing that *TPP* becomes ever more relevant if we account for the role of police in playing the gatekeeper for pretrial punishment, effectively playing the role of the judge of some aspects of pretrial punishment severity, and in trading on their ability to do both to force search (through searches incident of custodial arrests) or leverage searches (through "consensual" searches undertaken in the shadow of the threats of custodial arrests) that otherwise lack sufficient suspicion.

Buying Your Way Out of Sentencing, but Not Punishment

Also relevant to police interests in instigating a punishing process for defendants, even when alleged crimes are fine-only crimes, is the increasing role of fines and fees in creating an incentive system for police agencies, cities, and counties to heavily police minor crimes, including heavily policing traffic offenses and quality-of-life crimes. The heavy reliance of some municipalities and police departments on fines and fees came to public attention in the wake of investigations of Ferguson, Missouri. Subsequent research drawing on data from over 9,000 cities shows that the use of fines and fees is both common and much more likely if the city has more black residents (Sances & You, 2017). These fines and fees themselves can be quite punishing, particularly when defendants do not have the funds to pay the fines and fees, leading defendants to be placed on payment plans that also cost money. This creates a situation in which some people face skyrocketing fine debt and/or a custodial arrest for an inability to pay fines.

It is also important to note that not only are fees and fines more likely in cities with larger African American populations, but research shows that major fine generating infractions such as traffic violations are concentrated in poorer areas of cities (United States Commission on Civil Rights, 2017). This means that fines and fees both generate a profit motive to police small infractions, and when these infractions are disproportionately policed in poorer areas, this further concentrates the punishing nature of pretrial process in these areas.

Alongside the rise of fines and fees has been a dramatic rise in civil asset forfeiture, which was not even on Feeley's radar in the 1970s. With burglaries down and civil asset forfeiture on the rise, in 2014 the federal government alone took in more money from civil asset forfeiture seizures than burglars took in burglaries that year (Ingraham, 2015). While early drug war seizures might have made significant amounts on a smaller number of large seizures, many seizures today are of relatively small sums of money taken during encounters as routine traffic stops (Sallah, O'Harrow, Rich, & Silverman, 2014). While certainly asset forfeitures happen in relation to suspected felonious activity, very minor encounters often trigger seizing assets today. When small amounts of money are in play, and when assets are seized from those who do not have the resources to contest their seizure, it is not surprising that a very substantial proportion of assets are seized without a legal contest. Alexander (2012) argues that asset seizures expand the role of police in punishment directly and by allowing police to implicitly suggest a willingness to take assets in exchange for foregoing a custodial arrest.

In considering both the role of the police as pretrial punishers and their increasing power and profit motives, it is important to recall the second key implication of Feeley's argument mentioned at the beginning of this section: Summary punishment is happening to defendants who are innocent and guilty, and all of whom have not yet been found guilty. In other words, one of the important, even critical, implications of *TPP*'s argument is that this is happening to innocent individuals without recourse, reinforcing the extent to which we have developed an incentive system and effective taxation system, but not necessarily a justice system. Put differently, by considering the police as themselves actors that heavily influence pretrial punishment, we can understand how police have been able to become judge and jury for minor offenses, especially fine-only offenses, how the threat of lawful custodial arrest for fine-only and other minor offenses has expanded both the power of police to summarily punish through the process, but also to leverage the discretion to punish to gain consent for searches that would otherwise be impermissible, and how police have even been incentivized to do so through fines, fees, and asset seizures, which themselves are tied to both income and racial inequality.

Conclusion

This chapter pays tribute to *TPP*, not by uncritically rehearsing its arguments or by tracing its academic usage as has been done already, but instead by showing that *TPP* offers an incredibly powerful tool for understanding punishment and plea bargaining in the United States, particularly for lower courts, today. While written before the rise of mass incarceration, quality-of-life policing, massive increases in fines, fees, and civil asset forfeiture, this amazing book nonetheless can help us to understand better the potential role and consequences of each of these. Understanding plea bargaining as organized around an incentive system for guilty pleas is critical to evaluating the role of the lower courts in American society and in the realization of justice. Pretrial punishments and their strong incentives for guilty pleas also have enabled mass incarceration, even while the worsening pretrial conditions that follow from mass incarceration have intensified costs, creating a reciprocal relationship between pretrial punishments and mass incarceration.

TPP's open systems approach also allows us to re-evaluate the role of police in the criminal justice system. When read alongside the pretrial process model, *TPP* implies that modern American policing may be shifting more heavily into role of judge and jury, making the police critical, but informal, sanctioners who control the gateway to punishment and have wide discretion in intensifying punishment. Discretion in applying pretrial punishment can be heavily leveraged; police can entirely prevent pretrial punishment for specific subjects if they fail to pursue charges, but this also can serve as leverage encouraging subjects to submit to searches or allowing their assets to be seized. Profit-motivated policing, implementing police funding through fines, fees, and seized assets, also promotes the expansion of police engagement around minor offenses, contributing to the volume of pretrial punishment experienced by defendants accused of very minor offenses.

Finally, this chapter intends to spark a broader consideration of the use of pretrial processes and punishments. For instance, is the potential for reduced pretrial punishment being leveraged in immigration settings, since immigration detention likely shares many of the same features as criminal detention? One way to remember great works is to celebrate them on their own terms; another route is to see them as living theoretical lenses that may be adaptable to settings and circumstances they did not imagine.

Notes

1 An open systems approach to courts tends to view courts as organizations with various internal workgroups (e.g., courthouse workgroup) that include actors who may lack a formal role in the courtroom but nonetheless impact its operations and the processes and outcomes experienced by defendants (e.g., bail bondsman). An open systems' approach also sees the courthouse workgroup as being impacted by environmental forces (Eisenstein & Jacob, 1977).

2 For an example exercise for teaching on this point, see the extended Endnote 12 in Earl (2008).

References

Albonetti, C. A. (1986). Criminality, prosecutorial screening, and uncertainty - toward a theory of discretionary decision-making in felony case processings. *Criminology, 24*(4), 623–644.

Alexander, M. (2012). *The new Jim Crow.* New York: New Press.

Alschuler, A. W. (1981). The changing plea bargaining debate. *California Law Review, 69*(3), 652–730.

Alschuler, A. W. (1983). Implementing the criminal defendants right to trial: Alternatives to the plea bargaining system. *University of Chicago Law Review, 50*(3), 931–1050.

Atwater v. Lago Vista, 532 U.S. 318 (2001).

Beck, A. J., Berzofsky, M., Caspar, R., & Krebs, C. (2014). *Sexual victimization in prisons and jails reported by inmates, 2011–12-Update.* Bureau of Justice Statistics, U.S. Department of Justice.

Bibas, S. (2004). Plea bargaining outside the shadow of trial. *Harvard Law Review, 117*(8), 2463–2547.

Denman, K. (2016). *Pretrial detention and case processing measures: A study of nine New Mexico counties.* New Mexico Statistical Analysis Center: Institute for Social Research. Retrieved from www.jrsa.org/pubs/sac-digest/vol-26/nm-pretrial-detention-and-case-processing.pdf

Devers, L. (2011). *Plea and charge bargaining: Research summary.* Washington, DC: Bureau of Justice Assistance, Department of Justice.

Earl, J. (2005). You can beat the rap, but you can't beat the ride. *Research in Social Movements, Conflict, and Change, 26*, 101–139.

Earl, J. (2008). The Process is the punishment: 30 years later. *Law and Social Inquiry, 33*(3), 737–778.

Eisenstein, J., & Jacob, H. (1977). *Felony justice: An organizational analysis of criminal courts.* Boston: Little & Brown.

Federal Reserve (2018). *Report on the economic well-being of U.S. households in 2017.* Washington, DC: Federal Reserve.

Feeley, M. (1992). *The Process is the punishment: Handling cases in a lower criminal court.* New York: Russell Sage Foundation.

Figueira-McDonough, J. (1985). Gender differences in informal processing: A look at charge bargaining and sentence reduction in Washington, DC. *Journal of Research in Crime and Delinquency, 22*(2), 101–133.

Glaberson, W. (2013, April). In misdemeanor cases, long waits for elusive trials. *The New York Times.* Retrieved from https://archive.nytimes.com/www.nytimes.com/2013/05/01/nyregion/justice-denied-for-misdemeanor-cases-trials-are-elusive.html

Ingraham, C. (2015, November 23). Law enforcement took more stuff from people than burglars did last year. *Washington Post.* Retrieved from www.washingtonpost.com/news/wonk/wp/2015/11/23/cops-took-more-stuff-from-people-than-burglars-did-last-year/?utm_term=.893c09736586

May, K. T. (2018, August 31). How the bail system in the US became such a mess — and how it can be fixed. *We Humans.* Retrieved from https://ideas.ted.com/how-the-bail-system-in-the-us-became-such-a-mess-and-how-it-can-be-fixed/

National Center for State Courts (2011). *Model time standards for state trial court.* Retrieved from www.ncsc.org/Services-and-Experts/Technology-tools/~/media/Files/PDF/CourtMD/Model-Time-Standards-for-State-Trial-Courts.ashx

Pinto, N. (2015, August 15). The bail trap. *New York Times.* Retrieved from www.nytimes.com/2015/08/16/magazine/the-bail-trap.html

Sallah, M., O'Harrow Jr., R., Rich, S., & Silverman, G. (2014, September 6). Stop and seize: Aggressive police take hundreds of millions of dollars from motorists not charged with crimes. *Washington Post.* Retrieved from www.washingtonpost.com/sf/investigative/2014/09/06/stop-and-seize/?utm_term=.14de78b57ad9

Sances, M.W., & You, H.Y. (2017). Who pays for government? Descriptive representation and exploitative revenue sources. *The Journal of Politics, 79*(3), 1090–1094.

The New Yorker (n.d.), *Kalief Browder.* Retrieved from www.newyorker.com/topics/kalief-browder-in-the-new-yorker.

United States Commission on Civil Rights. (2017, September). Targeted fines and fees against low-income communities of color: Civil rights and constitutional implications. Washington, DC. Retrieved from www.usccr.gov/pubs/2017/Statutory_Enforcement_Report2017.pdf

Wagner, P. (2015, August 14). *Jails matter. But who is listening?* Prison Policy Institute. Retrieved from www.prisonpolicy.org/blog/2015/08/14/jailsmatter/

Weinstein, J. B. (1981). Eyewitness testimony by Elizabeth F. Loftus. *Columbia Law Review, 81*(2), 441–457.

SECTION 2

Research and Scholarly Work on Misdemeanors Today

4

THE IMPACT OF BROKEN-WINDOWS POLICING ON LOWER CRIMINAL COURTS

Jacinta M. Gau and Nicholas Paul

In the 1980s, police agencies started adopting a commitment to reducing disorderly conditions and behaviors. Disorder remains a high priority in policing today. This approach is grounded in broken-windows theory (Wilson & Kelling, 1982), which holds that police can reduce crime by stringently enforcing laws regulating behaviors such as public drinking, panhandling, vandalism, and so forth. Broken-windows theory does not prescribe specific tactics for disorder reduction, so police agencies vary in how they implement this style of policing. Some attempt to prevent or alleviate disorder through problem-solving and community-based efforts, while others go about it through aggressive enforcement of laws against low-level crimes and disorderly behavior (Braga, Welsh, & Schnell, 2015). Arrests for these low-grade offenses and street stops of people who police believe appear to have criminal intent have become the two signature tactics of aggressive order maintenance. Police proactively seek out people who jaywalk, panhandle illegally, or appear suspicious, and they arrest, cite, or briefly detain and question them (potentially resulting in arrest).

Police departments that employ the aggressive-enforcement version of broken-windows policing generate large volumes of misdemeanor arrests that the courts must then handle. The cases flowing into courts are of low relative severity, carrying small or trivial potential criminal penalties. Courtroom workgroups adapt to this high-volume, low-stakes operation by prioritizing efficient dispositions over the manner in which defendants are treated or the sentences they receive (Feeley, 1992). The goal of speedy case disposition eclipses most considerations about due process (Heumann, 1978). This raises questions about fundamental fairness of the criminal process. Additionally, it undermines deterrence. Deterrence works when people fear the stigma of criminal conviction and the penalty it carries (Gau, 2019). Producing large quantities of people with convictions strips the conviction of its power to stigmatize and shame. Furthermore, the penalties associated with these convictions are minimal. Offenders are sentenced to punishments such as time served, a suspended sentence, or a small fine.

This chapter examines the implications of broken-windows policing for the lower courts that must deal with the incoming flow of misdemeanor arrests. In particular, the focus is on how this style of policing degrades due process and undermines deterrence. It is argued that strict enforcement of laws against minor misbehavior ultimately does a disservice to the courts and the law by delegitimizing the criminal process and watering down the deterrent properties of criminal sanctions.

Broken-Windows Theory and Aggressive Order Maintenance

The past few decades have seen the emergence of multiple policing strategies, including community-oriented policing, problem-oriented policing, and intelligence-led policing (Goldstein, 1990; Ratcliffe, 2008). One of the most widely adopted police practices is the aggressive enforcement of low-level disorder. This tactic emerged from Wilson and Kelling's (1982) broken-windows theory. The theory proposes that leaving social and physical disorder unattended triggers a downward slide. Individuals who live in these communities start to alter their routines out of fear of encountering frightening or dangerous people. They avoid certain businesses or walkways and spend more time indoors, which weakens a neighborhood's ability to informally manage crime (Reisig, 2010). The atmosphere of decay and the absence of people using public spaces for work and recreation is a milieu in which offenders perceive an area to lack effective social controls and to therefore be a safe haven for criminal activity. This process leads to an environment pervaded by crime, deviance, delinquency, and urban decay (Wilson & Kelling, 1982).

Many police agencies saw broken windows as the holy grail of policing in the 1990s (Harcourt, 1998). Broken windows is a theoretical model of how crime takes root in a community; it is not a blueprint for *how* police should stave off disorder and its negative effects. When police departments started taking notice of the broken-windows idea, they were free to fashion their own methods for disorder-based policing. In the end, aggressive enforcement of laws prohibiting disorder and minor crimes became the model approach. "Aggressive" in this context means officers seek opportunities to intervene when someone is behaving incorrectly. Today, police departments routinely construe the premise of the theory as requiring staunch, widespread emphasis on traditional enforcement activities aimed at the proactive pursuit of low-level disorderly behaviors (Fagan & Davies, 2000).

Not all departments go about aggressive order maintenance in the same way. The various strategies range from "zero-tolerance policing," "quality-of-life policing," and "order-maintenance policing" (Cordner, 1998). Nonetheless, the core themes are consistent. Police seek out people engaging in behavior that is criminal and deemed socially problematic, such as public intoxication, unauthorized vending, or the commission of vandalism or graffiti. When an officer encounters a disorderly person, department policy requires or encourages the officer to make an arrest or issue a citation (an order to appear in court). Another hallmark of this type of order maintenance is the street stop. Street stops are brief field detentions. Police are legally entitled to detain people when there is reasonable cause to believe that those people are engaged in criminal activity. If officers have reasonable suspicion that a person they have stopped is armed or otherwise a threat to officer safety, they can pat down (frisk) the outer layer of the person's clothing (*Terry v. Ohio*, 1968). Street stops can lead to arrest if officers confirm that a person is indeed committing a crime, if a frisk recovers drugs or an illegal weapon, or if an encounter becomes acrimonious and the person is arrested for an offense such as assaulting a police officer. When a police department implements a policy of aggressive enforcement, the volume of arrests and summons for misdemeanor offenses increases dramatically (Kohler-Hausmann, 2018).

Impacts on Misdemeanor Arrests

Departments that implement broken windows based policing strategies encourage more self-initiated stops, searches, and arrests of citizens with the belief that these tactics will prevent or reduce serious crime (Kelling & Sousa, 2001). During the 1990s, the New York City Police

Department (NYPD) was the most notable example of a committed adoption of aggressive order maintenance. The NYPD's experience served as a model for several other police agencies wanting to adopt order-maintenance approaches.

The NYPD initiative also fueled numerous scholarly inquiries into the outcomes of the aggressive enforcement of low-level, public-order crimes. Howell (2009) analyzed non-felony arrests in New York City between 1989 and 1998, a time period that spanned before and after the implementation of broken windows. Results revealed a drastic increase in the number of arrests annually. Before the start of broken-windows policing, there were approximately 86,000 arrests for misdemeanors per year. By 1998, once aggressive order maintenance was firmly established, the annual number of non-felony arrests rose to approximately 176,000. In other words, non-felony arrests increased by almost 90,000 *per year* due to the impact of broken-windows policing. Additionally, the demographics of arrestees changed. There was increase in arrests of citizens with no prior criminal records, especially youths between 16 and 20 years of age. The proportion of whites arrested for misdemeanors decreased, while the proportion of minorities sharply increased. Finally, the seriousness of the charges changed. Howell (2009) separated misdemeanors into three categories: harm to people, harm to property, and public-order offenses. Consistent with the aims of broken-windows theory, the number of arrests for public-order misdemeanor offenses rose sharply. Howell (2009) also compared slow days and busy days in the NYPD to find out what officers did when they had time to engage in order maintenance. Results showed that the overwhelming majority (approximately 80%) of the differences in the numbers of low-level arrests between slow days and busy days were offenses to public order. Thus, broken-windows policing created hundreds of extra arrests per day that were exclusively focused on petty offenses related to public disorder.

Arrests for low-level drug possession also contributed to the spike in misdemeanor arrests during the heyday of NYPD's disorder crackdown. Howell (2009) found that most of the public-order arrests were for minor drug offenses like possession of cannabis or drug paraphernalia, suggesting that on slow days, police proactively identify people who they would otherwise not pay attention to if they were busy with more serious offenses and offenders. Overall, from 1994 to 2000 the number of arrests for marijuana possession increased from 1,851 arrests in 1994 to over 51,000 in 2000, an increase of 2,670% annually (Harcourt & Ludwig, 2007).

In a recent analysis of NYPD's order-maintenance practices, Chauhan, Tomascak, Cuevas, Hood, and Lu (2018) examined misdemeanor arrests from 1993 to 2016. They divided offenses into two categories: those more likely to be complaint driven (persons and property crimes), and those less likely to be complaint driven (minor drug offenses and so on). The analysis indicated that the number of misdemeanor charges for crimes unlikely to be complaint driven saw the most dramatic increase. For example, the number of arrests for theft of service (such as for jumping subway turnstiles) and misdemeanor drug possession more than doubled from 54,813 in 1993 to 118,514 in 2000. Moreover, the authors found similar results as Howell (2009) in that arrests of minorities and young people outpaced those of whites and older citizens. Other studies of racial patterns in street stops in New York City likewise found that blacks and Hispanics were stopped at higher rates than whites (Fagan & Davies, 2000). Furthermore, hit rates (the proportion of stops that result in arrest) were lower among blacks and Hispanics relative to whites (Gelman, Fagan, & Kiss, 2007), suggesting that some street stops of people of color are grounded on shaky evidence, while stops of whites perhaps tend to rest on more reliable indicators of guilt. Perhaps not surprisingly given these findings, a federal appeals court recently declared NYPD's use of widespread stops (which are often accompanied by frisks) unconstitutional due to the pervasive racial skew in stops and frisks (*Floyd v. City of New York*, 2013).

Impacts on Lower Courts

The growth in arrest rates under zero-tolerance forms of broken-windows policing significantly burdens lower criminal courts. These courts already face limited resources and high caseloads. The influx of misdemeanor arrests when a police department adopts a zero-tolerance approach to reducing disorder creates a court system that undercuts due process and fails to produce meaningful experiences or punishments.

Kohler-Hausmann (2018) used a mixed-methods approach to analyze how the broken-windows policing initiative in New York City impacted both the lower courts and the hundreds of thousands of people arrested for misdemeanor offenses. Findings revealed that lower courts in New York City employ a managerial approach that utilizes the rules of criminal procedure as a tool to manage and control offenders; in other words, court actors strategically use the process as a way to make determinations about how individual cases should be handled. Moreover, Kohler-Hausmann (2018) discovered that case-dismissal rates increased and conviction rates fell after the advent of order-maintenance policing. Conviction rates for misdemeanors were approximately 45% in 1985, but decreased steadily since the early 1990s and have been less than 20% since prior to 2010 (Kohler-Hausmann, 2018). In other words, in spite of (or, more likely, because of) the significant increase in arrests being funneled into the courts, 80% of offenders are never convicted. The next section discusses the reasons for this low conviction rate.

Court Processing of High-Volume, Low-Stakes Cases

There are two primary features of the misdemeanor arrests generated by aggressive order maintenance that significantly impact how lower courts adapt to the influx. The first feature is the sheer volume of these types of arrests. Hundreds or thousands of extra cases enter a local court system each year when a police department engages in this type of policing. The second impactful feature is that the cases are low-level, frequently non-serious crimes with no victims of personal harm or property destruction. The combination of these two factors (a high volume of low-stakes cases) pushes courtroom workgroups to find easy, fast ways to dispose of cases (Feeley, 1992; Heumann, 1978), in an assembly-line fashion (Packer, 1968).

To enhance efficiency, attorneys and judges turn away from formalized adherence to due-process requirements and toward informal processes like plea bargaining. The reliance on informality transforms the court system into an arrangement of negotiations and deals. Perhaps ironically, in this system prosecutors and defendants are often aligned in terms of their ultimate goals and what they are willing to do to reach them. Prosecutors want guilty pleas, and defendants want to get out of jail and to be done with the court process as soon as possible. As such, prosecutors will typically offer to reduce charges or recommend sentence reductions in exchange for defendants' guilty pleas, and defendants are generally happy to comply. The plea-bargaining-based system circumvents the original goal (enshrined in the nation's constitution) of seeking justice through an adversarial process. Court actors instead develop going rates for crimes, offer defendants breaks in exchange for guilty pleas, and in so doing push cases through quickly (Feeley, 1992; Packer, 1968; Walker, 1993). This is a form of bureaucratic justice. It is a managerial model of workload processing that prioritizes efficient dispositions over the manner in which defendants are treated and the fairness of the sentences they receive (Kohler-Hausmann, 2018; Nardulli, Flemming, & Eisenstein, 1985). In adopting this managerial model, the criminal courts join agencies of other branches of the criminal justice system (policing and corrections) in which immediate bureaucratic and administrative needs (staffing, budgets, and so forth) take precedence over long-term goals such as crime reduction or offender rehabilitation (Gordon, 1991).

Although assembly-line processing benefits defendants in some ways (such as being able to get out of jail right away and not miss days of work for court appearances), some of these supposed benefits are misleading. There are consequences to going rates. Defendants facing similar charges are issued routine and equivalent bonds and plea offers with little or no regard for personal circumstances like income, or for case-specific factors like the constitutionality of police searches (Walker, 1993). Defendants who might have been victims of illegal police behavior or who might earn sympathy from a jury or judge if they went to trial are never vindicated and, indeed, might not even be made aware that challenging the charges against them is a viable option.

Part of the reason for the push toward a crime-control oriented model (Packer, 1968) is that exercising due-process rights is costly. The court system operates on a congested schedule that is not always compatible with defendants' work and family routines, transportation situation, and so on. Defendants are forced to miss work and other obligations to make several mandatory court appearances that often result in continuations even after the accused has been significantly inconvenienced by waiting all day (Howell, 2016). These procedural hurdles are often more of a punishment than the actual sentence an accused offender will receive (Feeley, 1992).

Overwhelmed courts have also moved toward a managerial model wherein convictions and punishments are only one of multiple end goals (Kohler-Hausmann, 2018; see also Gordon, 1991). Managing the workload becomes the goal in and of itself. Prosecutors will sometimes decline to file charges at all. Reasons can vary from questions about the constitutionality of the method of acquiring evidence to a prosecution not serving the interests of justice (e.g., a cancer patient caught with a small amount of marijuana). When prosecutors do file charges, defendants are often offered the opportunity to participate in diversion programs, and they avoid conviction if they complete the terms of the program. It is only when defendants repeatedly fail to comply with the terms of the programs that prosecutors pursue convictions and formal punishments (Kohler-Hausmann, 2018). Instead of focusing on the actual offense and punishing it, actors of the lower courts use hassles created by the process (such as showing up to court repeatedly) as a way to determine an offender's ability to abide by rules and to be governable or controlled (Kohler-Hausmann, 2018). It is the assessment of the offender's performance during these obstacles that usually determines how the case is resolved.

Although the present inquiry focuses on the lower courts handling of misdemeanors, it is noteworthy that the problem of low conviction rates is not isolated to these crimes. Journalists investigating the Washington, D.C. Police Department's use of aggressive stop and frisks to confiscate illegal firearms found that 40% of cases in which offenders were charged with gun-related crimes were dismissed. It is impossible to pinpoint with certainty why so many cases are dropped, but the most likely culprit is concern about the legality of the stops and frisks (Madden, 2018). If either a stop or a frisk violates the Fourth Amendment, the weapon is inadmissible in court and the defendant must be released. A significant proportion of stops rest on questionable evidence or are clearly unconstitutional (Gould & Mastrofski, 2004), and analyses of NYPD stop data showed that only 64% of stops clearly met the reasonable-suspicion standard. Of the remaining stops, 14% were unconstitutional and 22% lacked sufficient information for a determination of legality (see Fagan & Davies, 2001).

Undermining Due Process

Due-process protections are spelled out in the Bill of Rights and the Fourteenth Amendment to the U.S. Constitution, which engrains them in the foundational fabric of the country's laws and sense of justice. Defendants have access to court-appointed counsel if they are unable to afford private representation, jury trials (in most cases), cross-examination, compulsory process, and other rights fundamental to the fairness of the criminal process. One overarching purpose of these rights is to guard against wrongful convictions. Another is to ensure the integrity of the criminal process such that police and prosecutors do not violate the law themselves as they pursue arrests and convictions of guilty people.

The operations of criminal courts have been described as appearing either due-process oriented or crime-control oriented (Packer, 1968). As noted previously, there is also a managerial model that describes case processing as more administrative than either crime-control or due-process oriented (Kohler-Hausmann, 2018). The due-process model describes court operations as adhering closely to an adversarial concept of justice and constitutional protections for the accused. The presumption of innocence features prominently in the due-process model.

The crime-control model represents a more efficiency-oriented system of processing wherein defendants are presumed guilty and the end result (conviction and punishment) is considered more important than textbook adherence to procedural rules. The managerial model holds that prosecutors, judges, and defense attorneys come to see their jobs as revolving around supervision and social control. In this model, defendants must prove themselves worthy of leniency by adhering to court-imposed rules.

Both the crime-control and the managerial model function on a presumption of guilt. While defendants are legally innocent until proven guilty, in reality most are assumed to be guilty. The only questions typically asked concern whether circumstances that mitigate culpability (e.g., the defendant being very young) exist and appropriateness of the sentence imposed upon conviction (see Feeley, 1992). In and of itself, this may not be inherently problematic if most defendants are guilty, and they prefer to handle their cases in the relative privacy of the plea-bargaining process. Guilty defendants benefit from disposing of their cases quickly and avoid lengthy, embarrassing public trials.

Where trouble arises is if a court operating under a crime-control or managerial model experiences such unwieldy caseloads that courtroom workgroups cannot devote sufficient time on each case. Excessive caseloads can cause court actors' priorities to shift from the integrity of the process toward fast dispositions. Whether disposition is by guilty plea, dismissal, or diversion, the goal is to make decisions quickly. Defendants are often dissuaded from exercising their procedural rights. If they indicate that they want jury trials, they are warned of the serious penalties they face upon conviction. Defendants may have difficulty presenting defenses or proclaiming their innocence. Case-by-case consideration suffers.

It might also be difficult to address violations of defendants' constitutional rights by police. Public defenders frequently read defendants' case files for the first time, moments before preliminary hearings (Howell, 2016), leaving almost no time for them to examine police procedures or develop strategies for appealing to judges for leniency. As discussed earlier, a sizeable portion of police stops (and frisks) are questionable or clearly unconstitutional (Fagan & Davies, 2000; Gould & Mastrofski, 2004). There may be countless unlawful detentions, frisks, searches, or arrests that occur as a result of broken-windows style policing that lower courts do not have the ability to detect and address (Kohler-Hausmann, 2018). Rushed processing makes it difficult for defense attorneys to provide adequate oversight to potential illegal or questionable police procedure. This undercuts the core values of defense attorneys as an institution, which are to deter police and prosecutorial misconduct (Heumann, 1978). As Howell (2009) points out, without accountability from lower courts, the police can arrest people on minor charges whether or not probable cause exists, they can stop and frisk citizens without reasonable suspicion, and the legality of these actions will almost never be tested or questioned.

Workload is compounded by the petty nature of the types of offenses people are charged with under an order-maintenance scheme. Prosecutors, defense attorneys, and judges commonly view non-serious crimes disparagingly. They call them names like "junk," "garbage," and "nickel–dime" (Heumann, 1978, p. 38). Since these offenses carry only minor penalties and convictions do not significantly impact someone's criminal record (compared to the effect of having a felony conviction), there may a tendency to think it is no big deal for someone to be convicted of such an offense. This mentality facilitates the fast processing of cases, as it likely increases court actors' tolerance of error.

Undermining Deterrence

Broken-windows policing is often implemented with the premise that adopting zero-tolerance policies toward low-level infractions will deter individuals from committing more serious offenses (Harcourt, 1998). However, heavy-handed enforcement of misdemeanor laws may be more likely to erode deterrence. This might initially seem contrary to expectations since more arrests should increase the certainty of punishment, but the deterrence literature supports this notion.

Sanctions can be formal or informal. Formal punishments include consequences such as being arrested, convicted, or imprisoned. Informal penalties involve feelings of guilt or shame, unemployment, victim retaliation, and loss of respect (Braithwaite, 1989; Grasmick & Bursick, 1990). These two mechanisms work together, such as when a formal procedure like an arrest leads to informal penalties like loss of a job or the stigma attached to having a criminal history (Pate & Hamilton, 1992).

Effective deterrence depends on people's perceptions of the certainty and severity of punishment. People do not accurately assess arrest probabilities or punishment severity (Kleck, Sever, Li, & Gertz, 2005). This alone is not the end of deterrence, however, because what matters more than objective certainty and severity is that people *believe* the chances of arrest and punishment are high (Waldo & Chiricos, 1972). People tend to overestimate both certainty and severity (Paternoster, 1987). Certainty is more important than severity at causing people to shy away from crime (Bridges & Stone, 1986; Nagin, 2013; Paternoster, 1987, 2010).

Individuals' perceptions about legal sanctions are fluid (Loughran, Paternoster, Chalfin, & Wilson, 2016). When people have experience with either punishment or punishment avoidance, they "update" their risk perception upward or downward (Apel, 2013; Paternoster, 2010). Offenders who are arrested and suffer no or minor consequences are likely to lower their future perceived risk assessment for that behavior, downgrading their fears about future arrest and punishment. Indeed, people who committed delinquency or crime in the past and were punished appear more likely to reoffend than those whose misdeeds were never detected and penalized (Paternoster & Piquero, 1995).

Because of experiential effects, the justice system is a more effective deterrent when it *limits* people's exposure to arrest and court processing. Aggressive order-maintenance policing does the opposite by expanding such contact and demonstrating how low the objective certainty of punishment is. Even with strict enforcement that increases the total volume of arrests, the average panhandler, drug addict, or prostitute still gets caught for a very small percentage of his or her total transgressions (Ratcliffe, 2008). Moreover, individuals who are arrested for misdemeanor offenses frequently do not suffer significant consequences or receive the necessary correctional resources to fix underlying problems (Goldstein, 1979). Likewise, prosecutors and judges are mindful of local jail capacity and will actively seek to avoid issuing jail sentences

(Heumann, 1978). Thus, offenders are not held accountable in a meaningful way and are not provided services to help treat issues (e.g., drug addiction) that contribute to their misbehavior. In all, the frustrating and arbitrary assembly-line process that defendants experience usually serves as the only real consequence for criminal behavior (Feeley, 1992).

Informal sanctions are as (or more) powerful than formal ones at deterring crime. When people contemplate hypothetically committing a crime and the consequences they might face, they include shame, guilt, embarrassment, social degradation, and loss of respect from the community as potential unpleasant outcomes (Braithwaite, 1989; Cochran, Chamlin, Wood, & Sellers, 1999; Grasmick & Bursick, 1990). Hyper-aggressive enforcement of minor crimes drastically increases the number of people within a given community who have the stigma of an arrest or label of "criminal." This diminishes the emotional and social impact of the label.

Aggressive enforcement of laws against minor offenses also risks creating a widespread impression of unfairness and anger. Sherman (1993) theorized that individuals react to feelings of shame in two distinct ways. If they perceive the process by which they were arrested and punished to be fair, they are likely to acknowledge and internalize the feelings of shame. However, if offenders believe the sanction was unjust, they will reject shame and develop a level of defiance that could increase the chances of future criminal behavior. Order-maintenance policing is perilous to public perceptions of fairness because not everyone agrees on the definition of "disorder" (Vera Sanchez & Gau, 2015). Large portions of the public also disapprove of police frequently stopping, searching, and arresting people for petty crimes (Weitzer, 1999) and those who have experienced such treatment feel poorly about the police as a result (Gau & Brunson, 2010). Therefore, by bringing rigid enforcement to bear upon minor infractions, officers may be eroding the deterrent effect of shame and creating a hostile, defiant reaction that leads to less respect for the law overall (Sherman, 1993).

Conclusion

This chapter discussed the consequences of aggressive order-maintenance policing for due process in the lower courts and for deterrence more broadly. Broken-windows theory holds that disorderly conditions generate fear and weaken social fabric within a community, which then makes the community vulnerable to criminals. Many police departments have interpreted broken-windows theory as a mandate to aggressively enforce laws pertaining to public order. This generates large quantities of misdemeanor arrests. Local courts must find ways to adapt to the high volume of low-level cases, and they typically do so by emphasizing speed of processing. Efficiency is not inherently flawed, but there is a danger that efficiency will be prioritized to the detriment of ensuring defendants are treated fairly, that innocent defendants are not pressured to plead guilty, and that constitutional rights are duly respected. Furthermore, the supposed deterrent effect of strict enforcement of laws regulating public order runs counter to what scholarly research has revealed about the factors that deter people from criminal behavior. Contact with police and courts can actually increase the chances of future offending. Departments that adopt an aggressive style of order maintenance do a disservice to the criminal law by weakening its capacity to shape people's decision-making about crime. Nothing in broken-windows theory requires police departments to rely on rigid enforcement or street stops. Some departments employ problem-solving methods that attempt to stop disorder using creative means that avoid or minimize arrests. Police should take disorder seriously, but disorder reduction should be done thoughtfully and in a manner that does not negatively impact courts and the law itself.

References

Apel, R. (2013). Sanctions, perceptions, and crime: Implications for criminal deterrence. *Journal of Quantitative Criminology, 29*(1), 67–101.

Braga, A. A., Welsh, B. C., & Schnell, C. (2015). Can policing disorder reduce crime? A systematic review and meta-analysis. *The Journal of Research in Crime and Delinquency, 52*(4), 567–588.

Braithwaite, J. (1989). *Crime, shame, and reintegration*. Cambridge: University Press.

Bridges, G. S., & Stone, J. A. (1986). Effects of criminal punishment on perceived threat of punishment: Toward an understanding of specific deterrence. *The Journal of Research in Crime and Delinquency, 23*(3), 207–239.

Chauhan, P., Tomascak, S., Cuevas, C., Hood, Q. O., & Lu, O. (2018). *Trends in arrests for misdemeanor charges in New York City, 1993–2016*. New York: New York.

Cochran, J. K., Chamlin, M. B., Wood, P. B., & Sellers, C. S. (1999). Shame, embarrassment, and formal sanction threats: Extending the deterrence/rational choice model to academic dishonesty. *Sociological Inquiry, 69*(1), 91–105.

Cordner, G. (1998). Problem-oriented policing vs. zero tolerance. In T. O. Shelley & A.C. Grant (Eds.) *Problem-oriented policing: Crime-specific patterns, critical issues, and making POP work* (pp. 24–34). Washington D.C.: Police Executive Research Forum.

Fagan, J., & Davies, G. (2000). Street stops and broken windows: Terry, race and disorder in New York City. *Fordham Urban Law Journal*, 28(2), 457–503.

Feeley, M. M. (1992). *The process is the punishment: Handling cases in a lower criminal court*. New York: Russell Sage Foundation.

Floyd v. City of New York, 959 F.Supp 2d 540 (2013).

Gau, J. M. (2019). *Criminal justice policy: Origins and effectiveness*. New York, NY: Oxford University Press.

Gau, J. M., & Brunson, R. K. (2010). Procedural justice and order maintenance policing: A study of inner-city young men's perceptions of police legitimacy. *Justice Quarterly, 27*(2), 255–279.

Gelman, A., Fagan, J., & Kiss, A. (2007). An analysis of the New York City police department's "stop-and-frisk" policy in the context of claims of racial bias. *Journal of the American Statistical Association, 102*(479), 813–823.

Goldstein, H. (1979). Improving policing: A problem-oriented approach. *NPPA Journal, 25*(2), 236–258.

Goldstein, H. (1990). *Problem-oriented policing*. New York, NY: McGraw-Hill, Inc.

Gordon, D. (1991). *The justice juggernaut: Fighting street crime, controlling citizens*. New Brunswick, NJ: Rutgers University Press.

Gould, J. B., & Mastrofski, S. D. (2004). Suspect searches: Assessing police behavior under the US Constitution. *Criminology & Public Policy*, 3(3), 315–362.

Grasmick, H., & Bursik, R. (1990). Conscience, significant others, and rational choice: Extending the deterrence model. *Law and Society Review, 24*(3), 837–862.

Harcourt, B. (1998). Reflecting on the subject: A critique of the social influence conception of deterrence, the broken window theory, and order-maintenance policing New York style. *Michigan Law Review, 97*(2), 291–389.

Harcourt, B. E., & Ludwig, J. (2007). Reefer madness: Broken windows policing and misdemeanor marijuana arrests in New York City, 1989–2000. *Criminology & Public Policy, 6*(1), 165–182.

Heumann, M. (1978). *Plea bargaining: The experience of prosecutors, judges, and defense attorneys*. Chicago, IL: The University of Chicago Press.

Howell, K. B. (2009). Broken lives from broken windows: The hidden costs of aggressive order-maintenance policing. *NYU Review of Law and Social Change, 33*, 271–327.

Howell, K. B. (2016). The costs of broken windows policing: Twenty years and counting. *Cardozo Law Review, 37*, 1059–1073.

Kelling, G. L., & Sousa, W. H. (2001). *Do police matter? An analysis of the impact of New York City's police reforms*. Center for Civic Innovation at the Manhattan Institute.

Kleck, G., Sever, B., Li, S., & Gertz, M. (2005). The missing link in general deterrence research. *Criminology, 43*(3), 623–660.

Kohler-Hausmann, I. (2018). *Misdemeanorland: Criminal courts and social control in an age of broken windows policing*. Princeton, NJ: Princeton University Press.

Loughran, T., Paternoster, R., Chalfin, A., & Wilson, T. (2016). Can rational choice be considered a general theory of crime? Evidence from individual level panel data. *Criminology, 54*(1), 86–112.

Madden, P. (2018, October 24). D.C.'s aggressive confiscation of illegal guns leaves residents feeling targeted. Retrieved from www.npr.org/2018/10/24/659980871/d-c-s-aggressive-confiscation-of-illegal-guns-leaves-residents-feeling-targeted.

Nagin, D. S. (2013). Deterrence in the twenty-first century. *Crime and Justice, 42*(1), 199–263.

Nardulli, P. F., Flemming, R. B., & Eisenstein, J. (1985). Criminal courts and bureaucratic justice: Concessions and consensus in the guilty plea process. *Journal of Criminal Law and Criminology, 76*(4), 1103–1130.

Packer, H. (1968). *The limits of the criminal sanction*. Stanford, CA: Stanford University Press.

Pate, A., & Hamilton, E. (1992). Formal and informal deterrents to domestic violence: The Dade County spouse assault experiment. *American Sociological Review, 57*(5), 691–697.

Paternoster, R. (1987). The deterrent effect of the perceived certainty and severity of punishment: A review of the evidence and issues. *Justice Quarterly, 4*(2), 173–217.

Paternoster, R. (2010). How much do we really know about criminal deterrence? *The Journal of Criminal Law and Criminology, 100*, 765–824.

Paternoster, R., & Piquero, A. (1995). Reconceptualizing deterrence: An empirical test of personal and vicarious experiences. *Journal of Research in Crime and Delinquency, 32*(3), 251–286.

Ratcliffe, J. (2008). *Intelligence-led policing*. Collumpton, Devon: Willan Publishing.

Reisig, M. (2010). Community and problem-oriented policing. *Crime and Justice, 39*(1), 1–53.

Sherman, L. W. (1993). Defiance, deterrence, and irrelevance: A theory of the criminal sanction. *The Journal of Research in Crime and Delinquency, 30*(4), 445–473.

Terry v. Ohio, 392 U.S. 1 (1968).

Vera Sanchez, C., & Gau, J. M. (2015). Racially neutral policing?: Puerto Rican and Mexican young adults' experiences with order maintenance strategies. *Journal of Qualitative Criminology and Criminal Justice, 3*, 166–194.

Waldo, G. P., & Chiricos, T. G. (1972). Perceived penal sanction and self-reported criminality: A neglected approach to deterrence research. *Social Problems, 19*(4), 522–540.

Walker, S. (1993). *Taming the system: The control of discretion in criminal justice, 1950–1990*. New York: Oxford University Press.

Weitzer, R. (1999). Citizens' perceptions of police misconduct: Race and neighborhood context. *Justice Quarterly, 16* (4), 819–846.

Wilson, J. Q., & Kelling, G. L. (March 1982). Broken windows: The police and neighborhood safety. *Atlantic Monthly, 249*, 29–38.

5

PROVIDING COUNSEL FOR DEFENDANTS

Access, Quality, and Impact

Andrew Davies and Kirstin A. Morgan

America's lower criminal courts are the real face of the justice system. They are the place that most defendants are brought to be prosecuted. They are also the places that will hear, process, and ultimately dispose of their cases. In these courts, decisions are made about whether a person will be released during pretrial, and how much bail he or she must pay to obtain their liberty. They can require defendants to pay fines, perform community service, or serve time under the supervision of departments of probation or (in some places) in jail and prison.[1] They also have the responsibility of assuring that accused defendants are represented by counsel for their defense.

Yet supplying counsel to defendants often proves a real challenge for lower criminal courts (Boruchowitz, Brink, & Dimino, 2009; Harvey, Rosenfeld, & Tomascak, 2018). In what follows, we first assess how often access to counsel is provided in these venues. Second, we look behind the numbers to describe barriers to access to counsel in four categories—systemic, logistical, procedural, and individual. Third, we examine the impact of defendants not having counsel. How do courts treat uncounseled defendants differently, and what does that mean for defendants' experiences of adjudication and the quality of justice those courts deliver? We close with concluding thoughts on ways to improve access to counsel in the future.

Defining Access to Counsel

While the Sixth Amendment to the Constitution guarantees that "[i]n all criminal prosecutions, the accused shall enjoy the right...to have the Assistance of Counsel for his defense," it wasn't until 1932 in the 'Scottsboro Boys' case, *Powell v. Alabama*, that the United States Supreme Court first held that a person facing capital charges should be provided an attorney at government expense if they suffered from "ignorance, feeble mindedness, illiteracy, or the like" (p.72). Thirty-one years later in *Gideon v. Wainwright* (1963), the Court decided that such a right extended to all persons accused of any felony offense; nine years after that, it expanded it further to all persons sentenced to incarceration (*Argersinger v. Hamlin*, 1972). No longer conditioned on the defendant's mental capacity, the right also now extended to all that could not afford to hire an attorney privately.

While the Court expanded the right to counsel on paper, however, it left certain questions around how defendants might access counsel unaddressed. Did *Argersinger* mean that defendants should have counsel if jail was possible, but unlikely? Did the right to counsel attach at defendants' first appearances in court, or some other time? Should the state retain the services of full-time lawyers institutionalized into public defender offices to represent defendants, or could it contract with private lawyers and pay them by the hour, or by the case? And how might states assess whether representation was of adequate quality?

The Court allowed state and local governments to make their own decisions about how to supply access to counsel, resulting in significant variety. Twenty states go beyond *Argersinger* and provide counsel to any misdemeanor defendant facing even the possibility of incarceration (Simpson, 2000). Fourteen states guarantee counsel at defendants' first appearance in court, while the rest do not (The Constitution Project, 2015). Twenty-two states supply defense services through statewide agencies, while the rest do something else (Strong, 2016). Actual funding for defense services themselves, meanwhile, vary widely by state—around ten-fold in per-capita terms (Davies & Worden, 2009).

The result is wide variation in the extent to which defendants in lower courts access counsel (Boruchowitz et al., 2009). National data suggest around a quarter of jail inmates convicted of misdemeanors were not represented by counsel, but this figure masks wide regional variation (Harlow, 2000). In New York, for example, courts reported finding between 70% and 100% of defendants eligible for assignment of counsel (New York State Office of Indigent Legal Services, 2016). Meanwhile, in Texas, the range in the rate at which misdemeanor defendants obtained government-funded counsel in 2017 ran the gamut. In some counties, 100% of misdemeanor defendants were represented, in others the figure was 0%; on average, the rate was 46% (Indigent Defense Data for Texas, n.d.).[2] Access to counsel varies, therefore, both in terms of their eligibility for court appointed counsel and whether defendants obtain access to attorneys at all.

The roles that defense attorneys play in lower criminal courts don't always match the popular image of vigorous advocates challenging prosecution evidence and standing up for the poor (Feeley, 1979). Rather, lower courts tend to operate according to pre-established routines that defense lawyers have little power to challenge (Flemming, Nardulli, & Eisenstein, 1993). Indeed, strong defense advocacy may disadvantage lawyers and defendants alike should they irritate a judge (Nardulli, 1978). In urban places, lower criminal courts can operate so fast that it is not clear they really consider each case on their merits at all, instead treating cases in an 'assembly-line' fashion (Boruchowitz et al., 2009; Harvey et al., 2018). In rural areas, courts can be so small that they lack basic facilities, are hard to find, and are frequently overseen by judges who are not themselves lawyers (Davies & Clark, 2018; Smith, Maddan, Price, & Tvedt, 2016). If the promise of the Sixth Amendment is that a defendant will 'have his day in court,' what does it mean if that day is, in reality, just three minutes long (Smith & Maddan, 2011)?

The consequences of misdemeanor convictions can be quite serious. Many jurisdictions have increased the fines and fees assessed in misdemeanor cases which can quickly create unmanageable debt for defendants (Atkinson, 2016; Hampson, 2016). Defendants in misdemeanor cases are still routinely at risk of pretrial detention stays, and those who are in jail for even a few days risk the loss of employment and housing, and the exacerbation of medical and psychological conditions (Clark, 2016; Levin, 2008; Western, 2002). Defendants' families may experience significant disruption when defendants are the main financial providers in the household. Collateral consequences of conviction may include losing the right to vote; denial of access to government-funded housing, food assistance, education grants, and other types of public assistance; ineligibility for certain jobs or programs; and referral to immigration authorities for deportation (Chin & Holmes, 2002; Katzmann, 2014).

Counsel could, in principle, act as a defendant's guide through the baffling process of prosecution. Criminal defense lawyers, according to national standards, should act as the defendant's advocate, their loyal confidante, and their expert advisor (American Bar Association, 2016). And yet defendants must often navigate the lower court experience with counsel that lacks those essential qualities or with no counsel at all.

Explaining Access to Counsel

What accounts for the variations in access to counsel across the country? We offer four factors that may be at play. Systemic factors have to do with the governmental decisions about how to fund and organize defense. Procedural factors have to do with the steps that defendants must take to actually obtain access to counsel, including establishing their financial eligibility and, in some places, payment of an application fee. Logistical factors have to do with practical flaws of defense systems. Individual characteristics have to do with the characteristics of defendants themselves.

Systemically, poor funding for defense systems tends to limit defendant access to counsel (American Bar Association, 2004). Several studies, for example, have shown that attorneys who were paid flat fees for representing juveniles (and who would not therefore be compensated more if they put more effort into the case) tended to request fewer expert witnesses, file fewer motions, request release of defendants less often, and move for fewer dismissals than salaried lawyers (Houlden & Balkin, 1985; Schwall, 2017; Yamashiro, Azzam, & Himmelfarb, 2013). Leaders of public defense organizations in better funded jurisdictions tend to show greater commitment to the quality of the services they provide, and demonstrate more creative leadership of their agencies (Davies & Worden, 2017). With increased funding, defenders are better able to connect clients to needed services and obtain better outcomes for them in court (Labriola, Farley, Rempel, Raine, & Martin, 2015; Luchansky, 2010). Spending on defense, moreover, is significantly related to the political, economic, and demographic realities of states and localities (Davies & Worden, 2009, 2017; Lefstein, 2011; Worden & Worden, 1989).

Procedurally, the application processes that defendants must go through to obtain defense counsel can be burdensome. Almost all defense programs employ some type of 'eligibility screening' process to determine whether defendants are truly unable to afford to hire attorneys.[3] These serve to draw the line between defendants with adequate means and those without, and provide limits for program caseloads, which could lead to the possibility of unfair denials (Spangenberg, Wilson, Smith, & Lee, 1986). Referring to an income threshold in wide use across the country, Gross noted that

> [a] defendant making just above 125% of the Federal Poverty Guidelines receives federal assistance to pay for food, heat, and medical care for his children but is somehow not regarded by some states as too poor to hire a lawyer.
>
> *(2013, p. 1208)*

Fraud detection measures may themselves discourage applications for counsel. Authorities in McLennan County, Texas, for example, sought to control the costs of defense by appointing a detective from the Sheriff's Office to investigate whether persons applying for counsel were concealing assets or income (Butts, 2014). The detective made two arrests for fraud, and another 20 arrests by finding and identifying individuals with outstanding warrants during the applicant investigations.[4]

Forty-three states also charge application fees for defendants seeking assignment of counsel (Shapiro, 2014). Not only might such fees discourage accessing counsel, they can also usher defendants toward taking an unfavorable plea deal. Smith and Maddan (2011) reported on a procedure in Broward County, Florida, for example, whereby defendants would be charged a \$50 application fee for a defender if choosing to plead at arraignment, but \$350 if choosing to plead thereafter, effectively conditioning access to counsel on willingness to plead guilty.

Other court procedures surrounding the assignment process might also cause defendants not to accept the assistance of counsel. In a now-repealed Colorado statute, for example, defendants' applications were required to be "deferred until after the prosecuting attorney ha[d] spoken with the defendant" (Colo. Rev. Stat. § 16–7–301(4)). The deferral provided prosecutors an opportunity to offer defendants the chance to plead guilty before ever meeting with an attorney (Carroll, 2010).

Logistically, access to counsel may be lost when systems are simply not well designed to transmit information between courts, attorneys, and defendants. Sometimes, such errors are fleeting instances of 'teething problems,' as occurred during a Chicago project to provide early access to counsel where defenders receiving calls for service did not receive enough information to locate their clients (Chicago Appleseed Fund for Justice, 2017). But other times, they are ingrained within the defender systems. Gilboy's study of 'horizontal representation'—the practice of switching attorneys mid-case—noted that "information may be entirely lost" by attorneys when passing cases one to another (1981, p. 1044).

Sometimes, simple geography reduces access to counsel. Rural areas often suffer from severe shortages of lawyers (Pruitt et al., 2018). In New York, counsel is provided by defender systems organized at the county level, while courts are organized at the city, town, and village levels, with the result that single defender offices may be responsible for providing representation in as many as 60 courts (Davies & Clark, 2018). The task of getting counsel to all of those courts is so complex that in many places it simply has not historically been done (Worden, Davies, Shteynberg, & Morgan, 2017).

Last, limited access to counsel is sometimes due to individual characteristics. Non-English-speaking defendants, for example, may face obstacles in communicating with attorneys. In a 1999 survey of defense services in large counties in the United States, only 70.2% expended any funds for interpreters (DeFrances & Litras, 2000). Persons of color may also face disadvantages in how their lawyers see them. Work by Eisenberg and Johnson (2004) and later by Richardson and Goff (2013) suggests lawyers are likely to be susceptible to implicit bias in how they assess defendants. Edkins (2011) found that when defendants are persons of color, attorneys expect, and will recommend defendants accept less favorable plea offers. When considering the reality of access to counsel, therefore, individual defendants may face specific obstacles—some of which may be inflicted upon them by the very persons assigned to represent them.

The Difference Access to Counsel Makes

Lacking access to high-quality counsel can have serious effects for all defendants, and for the court system at large. First, uncounseled defendants may receive worse outcomes than comparable defendants with counsel. Second, uncounseled defendants may perceive the justice system as less fair, leading to lower levels of trust in that system, and even increasing their likelihood of reoffending. Third, looking beyond individual defendants, barriers to access to counsel may reduce the quality of justice as a whole by diminishing adversarial testing and efficacy, which is necessary to avoid wrongful convictions.

Equity demands that all defendants have an equal chance at liberty. Yet carefully controlled studies of the impact of attorneys on pretrial processes have shown that even for perfectly matched samples of defendants the presence of an attorney can substantially alter the courses of their cases. Where counsel is provided earlier in the judicial process, for example, studies have shown it can prevent defendants from making incriminating statements, help them advocate for release on recognizance or a more manageable bail, and help connect defendants with needed pretrial services (Colbert, Paternoster, & Bushway, 2002; Fazio et al., 1984; Ho, 2013; Worden, Morgan, Shteynberg, & Davies, 2018).

The presence of counsel early in a case can change the bail-setting practices of judges, sometimes dramatically, as they either set lower bail, set larger numbers of defendants at liberty without any bail at all, or hold defendants for shorter periods.[5] Pretrial liberty can have far-reaching consequences. Fazio et al. (1984) showed defendants assisted by attorneys earlier concluded their cases more rapidly, had them dismissed more often, and obtained shorter sentences on average. Recent research has reaffirmed the association between the inability to secure release or make bail and higher rates of guilty pleas (Didwania, 2018; Heaton, Mayson, & Stevenson, 2017) and receiving a jail or prison sentence (Sacks & Ackerman, 2014).

The quality of counsel can also change case outcomes. Abrams and Yoon (2007), for example, found that where attorneys were more experienced, the same defendant tended to get more lenient case outcomes than if the attorney had been less experienced.

In a jurisdiction with random lawyer assignments, Anderson and Heaton (2012) compared public defender and court-appointed lawyer outcomes. Anderson and Heaton found statistically significant differences in the outcomes of murder cases depending on whether the attorney was a public defender or a court-appointed, private lawyer. Although the public defenders achieved better outcomes, they theorized that the results may have been influenced by the support of their institutions (Anderson & Heaton, 2012). Other research has shown that private attorneys and public defenders obtain similar adjudication and sentencing outcomes for clients, but assigned counsel gets less favorable results (Cohen, 2014). Potential explanations for these findings are rooted in the possible appointment of attorneys with less skill, experience, or qualifications (Iyengar, 2007; Roach, 2014). Meanwhile, Agan, Freedman and Owens (2018) showed that attorneys tended to get better outcomes for defendants who retained them privately than for those whom they were appointed by the state, suggesting attorneys may be doing better work for paying clients. Each of these findings raises questions about the ability of appointed lawyers to provide effective representation of equal standard to all defendants.

Lack of access to counsel can also limit defendants' comprehension and participation in the justice system, with negative impacts on their perceptions of attorney quality and system legitimacy (Boccaccini, Boothby, & Brodsky, 2004; De Mesmaecker, 2014). Many defense providers, especially public defender offices, have such high caseloads that time spent per case is very limited (Farole & Langton, 2010). Defendant comprehension of the process and outcomes of their case suffer when attorneys can spend little more than hours or minutes on each case (Boruchowitz et al., 2009; Smith & Maddan, 2011). Some defendants complain they lack access to basic information about their cases such as court dates, next steps in the process, and the consequences of certain charges or plea bargains (Boccaccini et al., 2004; De Mesmaecker, 2014). Defendant participation in legal decision-making, and thus their perceptions of attorney quality and procedural justice, also suffers when access to counsel is limited (Boccaccini et al., 2004).

Counseled defendants may be more likely to perceive the justice system as fair. The interdisciplinary literature on defendant perceptions demonstrates that beliefs about the fairness of both court processes and outcomes are related to overall beliefs about the legitimacy of the criminal justice system (De Mesmaecker, 2014; Lind & Tyler, 1988; Raaijmakers, Keijser, Nieuwbeerta, & Dirkzwager, 2015) and even to reoffending (Tyler & Huo, 2002). Some of that research has suggested defendants' judgments are intimately impacted by quality of counsel (Casper, 1978; Boccaccini et al., 2004). Colbert et al. (2002), for example, found that defendants represented by counsel regarded the bail determination as fairer and better informed. The implication is that the provision of counsel to defendants may not only improve their subjective experience, but may lead to higher levels of acceptance for justice system verdicts and thus lower levels of future offending (Sandys & Pruss, 2017).

A similar claim for reduced future offending is made by practitioners of 'holistic defense' (Steinberg, 2005). Holistic defenders seek to assist defendants by going above and beyond criminal defense services to offer "comprehensive and effective solutions to the social service, psychological, and human needs they have, [in order to] help clients chart their own paths toward futures free from criminal justice involvement and incarceration" (p. 630). There is indeed evidence that lawyers can be more effective as advocates by improving their knowledge of and relationships with defendants. Brewer (2005), for example, showed that jurors were substantially more willing to consider evidence in mitigation of a defendant's guilt in a capital murder case if they perceived the relationship between the lawyer and his or her client to be a warm one.

There are few extant evaluations of holistic defense, however, and those which exist show mixed results. McCarter (2016), for example, showed a range of benefits including reductions in aggressive behavior among juvenile holistic defender clients compared to controls. Anderson, Buenaventura and Heaton (2019), meanwhile, were able to show that holistic defense clients received substantially lower periods of incarceration at sentencing but detected no difference in long-term recidivism. DeHart, Lize, Priester and Bell (2017), meanwhile, showed few differences between holistic and non-holistic clients in North Carolina. With more research, greater clarity might emerge on what works in the field of holistic defense practice, and what does not (Lee, Ostrom, & Kleiman, 2015).

Effective defense may also offer benefits to the justice system. Some assessments have revealed that investing in defense may save money. Cost-benefit assessments of social worker collaborations with defenders have shown substantial savings in incarceration costs through sentencing advocacy (Buchanan & Nooe, 2017; Geurin, Otis, & Royse, 2013), while one analysis projected the city of Chicago could save over $12 million by implementing early representation by counsel (Sykes, Solowiej, & Patterson, 2015).

More profoundly, defenders have at times played instrumental roles in preserving the integrity of the justice system against executive overreach and wrongful convictions. Colgan (2017), for example, charted the role of the defense function in "spotting and making public the pattern of abuses in Ferguson [Missouri]'s municipal court" in the story of reform in that city (p. 1219). Defender litigation effectively increased the political costs of the operation of the municipal court in Ferguson, argues Colgan, changing the calculus of prosecutors and political leaders about its viability. Similarly, a small number of studies have pointed to the instrumental role played by adequate and experienced counsel in reducing wrongful convictions (Gould, Carrano, Leo, & Hail-Jares, 2014; Harmon & Lofquist, 2005; Worden, Davies, & Brown, 2014).

Conclusions

Notwithstanding the mandates of Supreme Court jurisprudence, access to counsel is not always guaranteed in lower criminal courts. The consequences for defendants can be serious, leaving them vulnerable to conviction and incarceration, financial penalties, and other collateral consequences. Defense services are, from one perspective, a mandate on taxpayers to help defend people of questionable character. But they can also offer value to society by acting as a check on injustice for both individual defendants and systems at large.

Recent work on defense has shown the possibilities for positive change in the services defense providers deliver. Evaluations of innovations to improve early access to counsel (Worden et al., 2017), overhaul poorly regulated defense providers (Fabelo, Reynolds, & Tyler, 2013), and inject new funds into resource-starved defense systems (Labriola et al., 2015) have each shown the value that defense services can offer. Defenders may be only one of the parties in the court room, but there is real evidence that with adequate resources and an expanded role they can help systems become more equitable, better informed, and more just.

Notes

1 Lower-level courts vary on whether they have jurisdiction over cases that can result in incarceration. The Sixth Amendment Center reports that of the 31 states that allow nonlawyers to act as judges, 22 also allow those judges to take a person's liberty (Carroll, 2016).

2 Texas' numbers actually compare the number of cases where defense attorneys were paid with the number of new cases opened in the year in the county's courts. Because newly opened cases are counted at case inception, and cases paid are counted at point of closing, it is possible the metric is slightly misleading in these extreme cases. We take note, however, that several counties had such extreme results, as they have done for many of the prior years for which data are available.

3 We say 'almost' all because there are some occasions where, in the interests of efficiency, defendants may not be screened where court proceedings are imminent and brief, as they may be immediately after arrest. We do not know of any context anywhere in the country where defendants could receive extended representation without an eligibility screening, however.

4 Though the contemporary reporting suggested the program saved money, in part by deterring people from applying for counsel, a subsequent investigation by the Texas Indigent Defense Commission could find no evidence of changes in application rates, and consequently no evidence of budgetary savings (Texas Indigent Defense Commission, 2014).

5 Early access to counsel means something slightly different in each study. Fazio et al. (1984) provided counsel to randomly selected felony defendants within 24 hours, rather than the more typical wait time of approximately two weeks. Colbert and colleagues (2002) provided representation to randomly selected defendants at initial bail hearings in Baltimore. Worden et al. (2018) evaluated the impact of introduction of a program to provide representation at both scheduled and unscheduled first appearances before judges in a variety of upstate New York courts.

References

Abrams, D., & Yoon, A. (2007). The luck of the draw: Using random case assignment to investigate attorney ability. *University of Chicago Law Review, 74*(4), 1145–1177. Retrieved from https://chicagounbound.uchicago.edu/uclrev/vol74/iss4/1

Agan, A., Freedman, M., & Owens, E. (2018). *Is your lawyer a lemon? Incentives and selection in the public provision of criminal defense* (Working Paper No. 24579). Cambridge, MA: National Bureau of Economic Research.

American Bar Association. (2004). *Gideon's broken promise: America's continuing quest for equal justice*. Chicago, IL: ABA. Retrieved from www.americanbar.org/content/dam/aba/administrative/legal_aid_indigent_defendants/ls_sclaid_def_bp_right_to_counsel_in_criminal_proceedings.authcheckdam.pdf

American Bar Association. (2016). *Criminal justice standards for the defense function*. Chicago, IL, ABA. Retrieved from www.americanbar.org/groups/criminal_justice/standards/DefenseFunctionFourthEdition-TableofContents/

Anderson, J., Buenaventura, M., & Heaton, P. (2019, forthcoming). The effects of holistic defense on criminal justice outcomes. *Harvard Law Review*. Retrieved from www.law.upenn.edu/live/files/8282-holisticdefensev201

Anderson, J., & Heaton, P. (2012). How much difference does the lawyer make? The effect of defense counsel on murder case outcomes. *Yale Law Journal, 122*(1), 154–217.

Argersinger v. Hamlin, 407 US 25 (1972).

Atkinson, T. (2016). A fine scheme: How municipal fines become crushing debt in the shadow of the new debtors' prisons. *Harvard Civil Rights-Civil Liberties Law Review, 51*(1), 189–238.

Boccaccini, M. T., Boothby, J. L., & Brodsky, S. L. (2004). Development and effects of client trust in criminal defense attorneys: Preliminary examination of the congruence model of trust development. *Behavioral Sciences & the Law, 22*(2), 197–214.

Boruchowitz, R., Brink, M., & Dimino, M. (2009). *Minor crimes, massive waste: The terrible toll of America's broken misdemeanor courts*. Washington, DC: National Association of Criminal Defense Lawyers.

Brewer, T. W. (2005). The attorney–client relationship in capital cases and its impact on juror receptivity to mitigation evidence. *Justice Quarterly, 22*(3), 340–363.

Buchanan, S., & Nooe, R. M. (2017). Defining social work within holistic public defense: Challenges and implications for practice. *Social Work, 62*(4), 333–339.

Butts, S. (2014, May 30). Investigator making dent in county's indigent defense costs. *Waco Tribune*. Retrieved from www.wacotrib.com/news/courts_and_trials/investigator-making-dent-in-county-s-indigent-defense-costs/article_1a2dd7ad-4b83-5680-ab5d-808f4b31f0b4.html

Carroll, D. (2010, December 12). Gideon Alert: Lawsuit challenges Colorado law refusing appointment of counsel until after clients meet with DA. Washington, DC: National Legal Aid & Defender Association. Retrieved from www.nlada.net/jseri/gideon-blog/co_complaintfiledinmisdrsuit 12-12-2010_gideonalert

Carroll, D. (2016, December 12). Should non-lawyer judges be sending people to jail? SCOTUS asked to review. Retrieved from http://sixthamendment.org/should-non-lawyer-judges-be-sending-people-to-jail-scotus-asked-to-review/

Casper, J. D. (1978). *Criminal courts, the defendant's perspective*. Washington, DC: Law Enforcement Assistance Administration.

Chicago Appleseed Fund for Justice. (2017). *Station-house representation in Chicago at six months: Outcomes, obstacles, and recommendations*. Chicago, IL. (Unpublished report, available upon request from the chapter author).

Chin, G., & Holmes, R. (2002). Effective assistance of counsel and the consequences of guilty pleas. *Cornell Law Review, 87*(3), 697–742.

Clark, J. (2016). Finishing the job: Modernizing Maryland's bail system. *The Abell Report, 29*(2), 1–19.

Cohen, T. H. (2014). Who is better at defending criminals? Does type of defense attorney matter in terms of producing favorable case outcomes. *Criminal Justice Policy Review, 25*(1), 29–58.

Colbert, D., Paternoster, R., & Bushway, S. D. (2002). Do attorneys really matter? The empirical and legal case for the right of counsel at bail. *Cardozo Law Review, 23*, 101–165.

Colgan, B. (2017). Lessons from Ferguson on individual defense representation as a tool of systemic reform. *William and Mary Law Review, 58*, 1171–1252.

Colo. Rev. Stat. § 16–7–301, Pub. L. No. 16–7–301, § 16–7–301, 16–7–301 16–7–301 (2013).

Davies, A. L. B., & Clark, A. M. (2018). Access to counsel in local courts in New York state. *New York State Bar Association Government Law and Policy Journal, 17*(1), 15–21.

Davies, A. L. B., & Worden, A. P. (2009). State politics and the right to counsel: A comparative analysis. *Law & Society Review, 43*(1), 187–220.

Davies, A. L. B., & Worden, A. P. (2017). Local governance and redistributive policy: Explaining local funding for Public defense. *Law & Society Review, 51*(2), 313–345.

De Mesmaecker, V. (2014). *Perceptions of criminal justice*, 1st Edition. New York, NY: Routledge.

DeFrances, C. J., & Litras, M. F. X. (2000). *Indigent defense services in large counties, 1999* (Bulletin No. NCJ 184932). Washington, DC: Bureau of Justice Statistics.

DeHart, D., Lize, S., Priester, M. A., & Bell, B. A. (2017). Improving the efficacy of administrative data for evaluation of holistic defense. *Journal of Social Service Research, 43*(2), 169–180.

Didwania, S. H. (2018). *The immediate consequences of pretrial detention: Evidence from federal criminal cases* (SSRN Scholarly Paper No. ID 2809818). Rochester, NY: Social Science Research Network. Retrieved from https://papers.ssrn.com/abstract=2809818

Edkins, V. A. (2011). Defense attorney plea recommendations and client race: Does zealous representation apply equally to all? *Law and Human Behavior, 35*(5), 413–425.

Eisenberg, T., & Johnson, S. (2004). Implicit racial attitudes of death penalty lawyers. *DePaul Law Review, 53*(4), 1539–1556.

Fabelo, T., Reynolds, C., & Tyler, J. (2013). *Improving indigent defense: Evaluation of the Harris County public defender.* Austin, TX: Center for State Governments. Retrieved from http://harriscountypublic defender.org/wp-content/uploads/2013/10/JCHCPDFinalReport.pdf

Farole, D., & Langton, L. (2010). *County-based and local public defender offices, 2007* (Special Report No. 231175). Washington, DC: Bureau of Justice Statistics.

Fazio, E. J., Wexler, S., Foster, T., Lowy, M. J., Sheppard, D., & Musso, J. A. (1984). *Early representation by defense counsel field test*. San Francisco, CA: Ursa Institute.

Feeley, M. (1979). *The process is the punishment: Handling cases in a lower criminal court*. New York, NY: Russell Sage.

Flemming, R., Nardulli, P., & Eisenstein, J. (1993). *The craft of justice: Politics and work in criminal court communities*. Philadelphia, PA: University of Pennsylvania Press.

Geurin, L., Otis, M. D., & Royse, D. (2013). Increasing alternative sentencing in the juvenile justice system through a partnership between public defenders and social workers. *Journal of Forensic Social Work, 3*(3), 261–277.

Gideon v. Wainwright, 372 US 335 (1963).

Gilboy, J. A. (1981). The social organization of legal services to indigent defendants. *Law & Social Inquiry, 6*(4), 1023–1048.

Gould, J. B., Carrano, J., Leo, R. A., & Hail-Jares, K. (2014). Predicting erroneous convictions. *Iowa Law Review, 99*, 471–522.

Gross, J. P. (2013). Too poor to hire a lawyer but not indigent: How states use the federal poverty guidelines to deprive defendants of their Sixth Amendment right to counsel. *Washington and Lee Law Review, 70*(2), 1173.

Hampson, C. D. (2016). The new American debtors' prisons. *American Journal of Criminal Law, 44*(1), 1–48.

Harlow, C. W. (2000). *Defense counsel in criminal cases* (Special Report No. NCJ 179023). Washington, DC: Bureau of Justice Statistics.

Harmon, T. R., & Lofquist, W. S. (2005). Too late for luck: A comparison of post-Furman exonerations and executions of the innocent. *Crime & Delinquency, 51*(4), 498–520.

Harvey, T. B., Rosenfeld, J. H., & Tomascak, S. (2018). Right to counsel in misdemeanor prosecutions after *Alabama v. Shelton*: No-lawyer-courts and their consequences on the poor and communities of color in St. Louis. *Criminal Justice Policy Review, 29*(6–7), 688–709.

Heaton, P., Mayson, S., & Stevenson, M. (2017). The downstream consequences of misdemeanor pretrial detention. *Stanford Law Review, 69*(3), 711–794.

Ho, H. L. (2013). The privilege against self-incrimination and right of access to a lawyer: A comparative assessment. *Singapore Academy of Law Journal, 25*, 826–846.

Houlden, P., & Balkin, S. (1985). Quality and cost comparisons of private bar indigent defense systems: Contract vs. ordered assigned counsel. *Journal of Criminal Law and Criminology, 76*(1), 176–200.

Indigent Defense Data for Texas. (n.d.). Retrieved from http://tidc.tamu.edu/Public.Net/

Iyengar, R. (2007). *An analysis of the performance of federal indigent defense counsel* (Working Paper No. 13187). Cambridge, MA: National Bureau of Economic Research.

Katzmann, R. A. (2014). When legal representation is deficient: The challenge of immigration cases for the courts. *Daedalus, 143*(3), 37–50.

Labriola, M., Farley, E., Rempel, M., Raine, V., & Martin, M. (2015). *Indigent defense reforms in Brooklyn, New York*. New York, NY: Center for Court Innovation.

Lee, C., Ostrom, B., & Kleiman, M. (2015). The measure of good lawyering: Evaluating holistic defense in practice. *Albany Law Review, 78*(3), 1215–1238.

Lefstein, N. (2011). *Securing reasonable caseloads: Ethics and law in public defense*. Chicago, IL: American Bar Association.

Levin, D. (2008). *Reading the tea leaves: Utilizing jail inmate surveys for examining the relationships between income, legal representation, and pretrial release*. Rockville, MD: Pretrial Justice Institute.

Lind, E. A., & Tyler, T. R. (1988). *The social psychology of procedural justice*. New York: Plenum Press.

Luchansky, B. (2010). *The public defense pilot projects Washington state office of public defense*. Olympia, WA: Looking Glass Analytics.

McCarter, S. A. (2016). Holistic representation: A randomized pilot study of wraparound services for first-time juvenile offenders to improve functioning, decrease motions for review, and lower recidivism. *Family Court Review, 54*(2), 250–260.

Nardulli, P. (1978). *Courtroom elite: An organizational perspective on criminal justice*. Cambridge, MA: Ballinger. Retrieved from www.ncjrs.gov/App/Publications/abstract.aspx?ID=53645

New York State Office of Indigent Legal Services. (2016). *Determining eligibility for assignment of counsel in New York: A study of current criteria and procedures and recommendations for improvement*. Retrieved from www.ils.ny.gov/files/Hurrell-Harring/Eligibility/Final%20Background%20Study/Background%20Study%20Full%20FINAL%20021216.pdf

Powell v. Alabama, 287 U.S. 45 (1932).

Pruitt, L., Kool, A., Lucas, L. S., Statz, M., Conway, D., & Haksgaard, H. (2018, forthcoming). Legal deserts: A multi-state perspective on rural access to justice. *Harvard Law and Policy Review, 12*. Retrieved from https://works.bepress.com/lisa_pruitt/48/

Raaijmakers, E., Keijser, J. W. de, Nieuwbeerta, P., & Dirkzwager, A. J. E. (2015). Criminal defendants' satisfaction with lawyers: Perceptions of procedural fairness and effort of the lawyer. *Psychology, Crime & Law, 21*(2), 186–201.

Richardson, L.S., & Goff, P. A. (2013). Implicit racial bias in public defender triage. *Yale Law Journal, 122*(8), 2626–2649.

Roach, M. A. (2014). Indigent defense counsel, attorney quality, and defendant outcomes. *American Law and Economics Review, 16*(2), 577–619.

Sacks, M., & Ackerman, A. R. (2014). Bail and sentencing: Does pretrial detention lead to harsher punishment? *Criminal Justice Policy Review, 25*(1), 59–77.

Sandys, M., & Pruss, H. (2017). Correlates of satisfaction among clients of a public defender agency. *Ohio State Journal of Criminal Law, 14*(2), 431–461.

Schwall, B. (2017). More bang for your buck: How to improve the incentive structure for indigent defense counsel. *Ohio State Journal of Criminal Law, 14*(2), 553–578.

Shapiro, J. (2014, May 19). As court fees rise, the poor are paying the price. Retrieved from www.npr.org/2014/05/19/312158516/increasing-court-fees-punish-the-poor

Simpson, B. M. (2000). A fair trial: Are indigents charged with misdemeanors entitled to court appointed Counsel? *Roger Williams University Law Review, 5*(2), 417–439.

Smith, A., & Maddan, S. (2011). *Three-minute justice: Haste and waste in Florida's misdemeanor courts.* Washington, DC: National Association of Criminal Defense Lawyers. Retrieved from www.nacdl.org/reports/threeminutejustice/

Smith, A., Maddan, S., Price, D. D., & Tvedt, C. (2016). *Rush to judgment: How South Carolina's summary courts fail to protect constitutional rights.* Washington, DC: National Association of Criminal Defense Lawyers.

Spangenberg, R., Wilson, R., Smith, P., & Lee, B. (1986). *Containing the costs of indigent defense: Eligibility screening and cost recovery procedures.* Washington, DC: National Institute of Justice. Retrieved from www.ncjrs.gov/pdffiles1/Digitization/103682NCJRS.pdf

Steinberg, R. G. (2005). Beyond lawyering: How holistic representation makes for good policy, better lawyers, and more satisfied clients. *New York University Review of Law & Social Change, 30,* 625–635.

Strong, S. (2016). *State-administered indigent defense systems, 2013* (Special Report No. NCJ 250249). Washington, DC: Bureau of Justice Statistics. Retrieved from www.bjs.gov/index.cfm?ty=pbdetail&iid=5826

Sykes, B., Solowiej, E., & Patterson, E. (2015). The fiscal savings of accessing the right to legal counsel within twenty-four hours of arrest: Chicago and Cook County, 2013. *University of California- Irvine Law Review, 5*(4), 813–842.

Texas Indigent Defense Commission. (2014). *Procedures for appointing counsel in McLennan County* (Internal memo, available from author).

The Constitution Project. (2015, March). *Don't I need a lawyer? Pretrial justice and the right to counsel at first judicial bail hearing.* Washington, DC: National Right to Counsel Committee. Retrieved from https://constitutionproject.org/wp-content/uploads/2015/03/RTC-DINAL_3.18.15.pdf

Tyler, T. R., & Huo, Y. J. (2002). *Trust in the law: Encouraging public cooperation with the police and courts.* New York, NY: Russell Sage Foundation.

Western, B. (2002). The impact of incarceration on wage mobility and inequality. *American Sociological Review, 67*(4), 526–546.

Worden, A. P., Davies, A. L. B., & Brown, E. K. (2014). Public defense in an age of innocence: The innocence paradigm and the challenges of representing the accused. In M. Zalman & J. Carrano (Eds.), *Wrongful Conviction and Criminal Justice Reform* (pp. 209–226). New York, NY: Routledge.

Worden, A. P., Davies, A. L. B., Shteynberg, R. V., & Morgan, K. A. (2017). Court reform: Why simple solutions might not fail? A case study of implementation of counsel at first appearance. *Ohio State Journal of Criminal Law, 14*(2), 521–551.

Worden, A. P., Morgan, K. A., Shteynberg, R. V., & Davies, A. L. B. (2018). What difference does a lawyer make? Impacts of early counsel on misdemeanor bail decisions and outcomes in rural and small town courts. *Criminal Justice Policy Review, 29*(6–7), 710–735.

Worden, A. P., & Worden, R. E. (1989). Local politics and the provision of indigent defense counsel. *Law & Policy, 11*(4), 401–424.

Yamashiro, C., Azzam, T., & Himmelfarb, I. (2013). Kids, counsel and costs: An empirical study of indigent defense services in the Los Angeles juvenile delinquency courts. *Criminal Law Bulletin, 49*(6), 1351–1378.

6

MISDEMEANOR JUSTICE IN RURAL COURTS

Alissa Pollitz Worden and Alyssa M. Clark

In both the popular imagination and social science research, our understanding of the criminal courts is governed by what we have learned about urban and metropolitan jurisdictions. Since Abraham Blumberg's (1967) landmark expose, *Criminal Justice*, researchers have portrayed the adjudication process in cities such as Chicago, Detroit, New York, Miami, and Pittsburgh as an anonymous, bureaucratized, crowded assembly line of rapid-fire hearings, bewildered defendants, and jaded lawyers and judges. It is not surprising, therefore, that the problems of high-volume urban courts have dominated the past 50 years of analyses, critiques, and reform initiatives, even as some observers argued that these efforts overlooked the diverse practices and needs of lower courts (President's Commission on Law Enforcement and Administration of Justice, 1967; Alfini & Doan, 1977; Bartol, 1996; King, 2013).

This chapter's focus is primarily on the lower courts in rural areas. While there is no agreed-upon taxonomy of courts, we locate rural courts at the intersection of three characteristics. First, these courts have *limited jurisdiction*, both substantively and geographically. They handle misdemeanor cases (and in some states lesser infractions and violations), and often the early stages of felony charges, usually along with an array of minor civil claims. It has been estimated that, across the states, there are 14,000–16,000 courts that meet this definition; and these courts process 66% of all court cases (Cornell, 2012). According to the National Center for State Courts, only seven states have no limited jurisdiction courts for criminal matters: California, Connecticut, Illinois, Iowa, Maine, Minnesota, Missouri, and Vermont (Court Statistics Project, 2018).

Second, these courts are located in *rural counties or communities*. Of course, there is no uniform definition for "rural" communities. They might be defined as geographic jurisdictions with populations under a specified number, by population per square mile; or definitions might involve small incorporated cities under a certain size (Bell, 1986; Nugent-Borakove & Mahoney, 2011). In an ongoing project on pretrial incarceration, the Vera Institute defines rural counties as those with small cities of 10,000–50,000 (micropolitan) as well as those areas with no defined micro- or metropolitan areas. By this definition, in the 44 states with local jails, 1,936 of the nation's 3,074 counties, comprising 15% of the nation's population, are rural (Kang-Brown & Subramanian, 2017).

Third, these courts are at least partially *independent* of other courts in the state's legal system; they are not parts of larger circuit, district, or county courts, and most of them are funded fully or partially through local revenues. While their decisions are subject to appellate review, few appeals are filed from them, and most of their judges are locally elected, so there are few real constraints on their discretion. This definition is imperfect, but it should suffice to begin an analysis of the challenges of administering justice in these seldom-studied venues. These courts go by many names: For example, municipal courts (Alabama, Oklahoma), justice courts (Texas, Utah), town or village courts (New York, Indiana), and magisterial or magistrate courts (Pennsylvania, Georgia).

Why study these rural courts? Over thirty years ago, Silbey observed that these courts are "invisible, neglected by the bar, scholars and the citizenry, and at the same time are the only judicial experience for most who enter the court system" (Silbey, 1981, p. 13). In New York, a state that makes extensive use of over 1,200 town and village courts (also called justice courts), the Office of Court Administration recently estimated that almost all New Yorkers outside of New York City will have their "first and only" interaction with the criminal justice system through one of these justice courts (New York State Unified Court System, 2018). But in these courts, as we shall see, there is reason to believe that community characteristics, as well as court structure and courthouse culture, produce different expectations for justice, and different patterns of case outcomes, than might be found in urban or even suburban courts operating under the same statutory and procedural law. If that is true, then small town courts may offer both benefits and costs to citizens who find themselves before the bench; but they may also face obstacles to innovations and reforms designed with urban jurisdictions in mind. Hence, in the following sections, we consider (1) the historical origins of small town courts, (2) the role of community characteristics in shaping expectations for justice in small towns and rural areas, (3) the commonalities and diversities of practices that observers have recorded in these courts, as well as the implications of community and court culture on case processing, and, finally, (4) what critics and reformers have to say about the future of rural courts.

Historical Origins of Limited Jurisdiction Courts

Like many features of contemporary American criminal justice, today's small town courts, where they exist, are living vestiges of practical efforts by early colonists to create workable institutions to settle many kinds of disputes. While much of the detail of these creations is lost to history, what we know about their establishment suggests that they were very localized adaptations of English models intended to efficiently resolve conflicts and reduce friction among community members.

In the colonies, in the absence of a clearly established legal system, courts were established in settlements and villages, where community leaders appointed "justices of the peace" whose substantive jurisdiction was broad and not clearly bounded (Smith, 1927). In some colonies, there was little legislative authority for the founding of these local courts, other "than the fact that the office was established in each county" (Surrency, 1967, p. 258), and the traditional English custom of delegating the power to establish local courts to governors and local officials. These courts were convened as needed, probably seldom in a courthouse but more likely in other convenient public buildings such as churches.

Much later, after the Revolution, some state legislatures legitimized the existence of these informal local courts through constitutions and statutes, though eventually those same legislatures created more formally structured court systems with more clearly identified jurisdictional boundaries, avenues of appeal, and eventually specialization between civil and criminal matters (Friedman, 2005). The strong tradition of federalism in the new nation reinforced the legitimacy of these sorts of justice courts, however: Centered on communities, they persevered even after structured systems of district or county courts, circuit courts, and courts of appeal were institutionalized. In many states they remain a critical piece of the justice infrastructure, even as they function somewhat independently of the state court system.

received by felony offenders; in contrast, extralegal factors were of greater importance when accounting for sentences in rural and suburban courts (Austin, 1981). However, little research has focused on misdemeanor sentences – again, perhaps because data on those sentences is difficult to access. Both Bartol (1996) and Edmundson (1996) speculated that judges in small town courts took time to tailor sentences to individual defendants, taking into account his or her capacity to give back to the community harmed. This might be due to the judges' familiarity with defendants, or because the judge, as a community leader, believes he or she knows what is best for the community.

Defendants are not the only parties who are affected by court decisions. Many limited jurisdiction courts are authorized to grant *ex parte* orders of protection, issued most commonly in cases of alleged domestic violence. A study in three rural counties in Kentucky found that those seeking orders of protection encountered more barriers in rural areas (Logan, Shannon, & Walker, 2005). Victims have less access to advocates in rural communities than in urban areas, and once granted, protective orders are more difficult to serve in rural jurisdictions. Unsurprisingly, rural women believed that access to the criminal justice system "largely depended on one's social and political connections and socioeconomic status" (Logan et al., 2005, p. 893).

Many limited jurisdiction courts, both rural and urban, are not courts of record: No court clerk or reporter records the proceedings in real time and preserves that record for the possibility of an appeal. For example, the overwhelming majority of justice courts in New York State had no ability to record proceedings until 2006, when the State Office of Court Administration mandated funds for the purchase and distribution of recorders (Kaye & Lippman, 2006). If an official record needed to be produced, judges were instructed to conduct a reconstruction hearing, based on his or her handwritten notes from the court proceeding (Kaye & Lippman, 2006). In Texas, Mississippi, Indiana, and Ohio, some or all lower courts are not courts of record. That said, since so many cases resolve by guilty pleas in these courts, very few are appealed (Smith & Maddan, 2011).

Finally, rural courts' accountability to the larger judicial systems and their standards is compromised by their ambiguous standing in those systems. Alfini wrote that even though lower courts operate within statewide administrative systems, paradoxically court unification efforts have left them with a "large degree of local autonomy" (1981, p. 7). Fetter and Stott suggested that isolation causes judges, attorneys, and other court personnel to feel disconnected from colleagues, leading to court actors "losing their sense of participating in a statewide court system" (1977, p. 2). And, conversely, because of this isolation, state judicial systems and other political leaders "may become less sensitive to rural court problems and needs" because they do not have "regular contact with rural court personnel" (Fetter & Stott, 1977, p. 2).

The Future of Rural Courts

> While the justice of the peace system has a long history and has been firmly imbedded in the fundamental laws of the states, yet it is an anachronism in our jurisprudence the perpetuation of which cannot be justified... The administration of justice by these lay magistrates is uncertain, unequal and unstable, and in truth, the system as such, is a denial of justice according to our highest conception of that term.
>
> *(Smith, 1927)*

This passage was written nearly a century ago, by a Tulane University law professor. His disdain for small local courts, and that of colleagues and peers who then, and now, might concur, reduces rural courts to vestigial and corrupted vestiges of a primitive legal apparatus. Much more recently, in an interview with North Country Radio, attorney Rosemary Phillips responded to criticisms of New York town justices: "It's not just a job. This is them trying to take care of their community and trying to make it better and trying to help people be better" (Rosenthal, 2018).

This more optimistic perspective argues for acknowledgement that in sparsely populated districts, these courts may provide more immediate access and personalized justice than bureaucratized and centralized alternatives. The future of rural courts may reside, therefore, in initiatives to modernize them, albeit through efforts that openly acknowledge their differences from the urban courts that are often models and testing grounds for court reform. We conclude this chapter with some thoughts on how to improve our understanding of these courts, and consideration of directions such reforms might take.

The first challenge in improving rural courts is learning more about how they work, and what they need. Case studies tell us that their practices are not uniformly determined by their size and location, so, building on existing case studies, researchers should prioritize investigation of unanswered, but important questions: Do the discretionary decisions of these courts differ from decisions in similarly charged cases in larger courts? Do lay judges make decisions that differ substantively from those of law-trained judges? How, and how consistently, does early representation of clients by attorneys impact short- and long-term outcomes? And they should also invest in understanding more about these rural courts' siblings in suburban communities: Do structurally similar courts have easier access to resources, social services, and treatment programs, and if so, how have they capitalized on those assets? Do their higher tax bases allow them to operate more effectively?

Policy makers should pay particular attention to the deficits that have been identified, with a practical eye toward remedies. Foremost among concerns in these courts is the deficit of legal counsel for defendants, at all stages of adjudication but particularly at the first appearance and bail hearing. In areas where lawyers are scarce, some states, such as Maine, South Dakota, and Arkansas, have experimented with incentives for young lawyers to relocate to rural communities, including loan repayment plans, fellowships for legal aid work, and stipends for establishing practices (Pruitt et al., 2015; Donvan & Goetzinger, 2018; University of Maine Law School, 2018). Others have proposed to institute multi-county indigent defense systems so counties can share the cost of a full-time indigent defense provider (Vetter & Clark, 2012), sharing the costs to conduct legal seminars or training (Mahoney, Carlson, & Baehler, 2006), and utilizing multi-county entities to reduce pretrial incarcerated populations (Levin & Haugen, 2018).

To ensure competent, educated judges, researchers have recommended that judges, especially lay judges, complete a certain number of credits each year for judicial training. In New York, judges are required to earn twelve credits of continuing judicial education. Six credits must be earned by participating in ethics courses, while the other six credits can be in elective credits that have been pre-approved. However, there have been few, if any, systematic evaluations of the effectiveness of these dosages of training. This is particularly troubling insofar as, once elected or appointed, most rural judges work in isolation from other judicial authorities. Many prosecutors and public defenders have established mentoring and shadowing programs; similar models might orient new judges into their roles.

Some experts have also recommended that rural courts utilize technology to compensate for problems of geographic distance and communication deficits. Rural courts could adopt payment services that spare defendants the time and effort to travel to court to pay fines (and save the time of clerks accepting those fines) (Nugent-Borakove & Mahoney, 2011). Judges and court clerks could also utilize technology to complete legal training and conduct legal research to save costs of attending in-person trainings. To reduce transportation costs for detained defendants, attorneys, and judges, rural court personnel could institute videoconferencing. For example, Utah uses videoconferencing that permits participants to see all parties participating in the hearing through split screens.

Yet others argue in favor of consolidation of these small courts (Fetter & Stott, 1977; Nugent-Borakove & Mahoney, 2011). While on the surface this recommendation is appealing, in sparsely populated places such plans might only multiply the challenges of geographic dispersion. In these small constituencies, strong attachment to longstanding local courts may doom any political attempt to alter their identities; the voters of New York, for example, have persistently resisted efforts to abolish or replace their local courts through constitutional amendment (Glaberson, 2006).

So perhaps the most promising future for rural courts will entail more ambitious reforms of criminal justice and criminal law. Those reforms might start with funding. In those states and counties where local governments must fund their local courts, judges are faced with at least tacit responsibility for generating revenue. For example, in upstate New York, town and village governments get a portion of fines paid to their courts. In 2010, the Office of the State Comptroller reported that the justice courts in New York collected over $246.3 million in fines. Of this, $115.7 million was distributed to the State government, $10.7 million went to the counties, and $119.9 million remained in towns' and villages' budgets (Division of Local Government and School Accountability, 2010). In Nevada, when police officers shifted their focus towards more serious crimes instead of lower level offenses and traffic violations, the chief justice of the Nevada Supreme Court warned that the judicial system was running out of money (Ford, 2015). The conflict of interest inherent in this financing system could be alleviated by state funding of these local courts (as is provided for courts of general jurisdictions); such a change would clarify judges' objective role in meting out justice.

Finally, and most ambitiously, some of those who have investigated rural courts most carefully have concluded that many of the challenges they face might be alleviated by legal and practical reforms that would also address universal problems in criminal adjudication. Some of these reforms would require new resources for many local courts. In urban areas, treatment programs, drug courts, community service opportunities, and the like can be delivered, if not wholesale, at least at levels that create some economies of scale. Rural areas may require more retail investment styles, which of course will come with greater costs. However, other policy proposals might not only offset those costs, but also reduce high levels of pretrial and post-conviction incarceration, and along with those reductions, mitigate the collateral consequences that defendants often face. Decriminalization of misdemeanor offenses that do not impact public safety, use of summonses and appearance tickets by law enforcement, in lieu of bail at arraignment to ensure court appearances, and diversion of low-risk cases into community supervision and treatment might not only reduce caseloads, but also allow judges to concentrate on the most problematic cases (Boruchowitz, Brink, & Dimino, 2009; Levin & Haugen, 2018).

References

Alfini, J. J. (1981). Introductory essay: The misdemeanor courts. *The Justice System Journal, 6*(1), 5–12.

Alfini, J. J., & Doan, R. N. (1977). A new perspective on misdemeanor justice. *Judicature, 60*(9), 425–434.

Alfini, J. J., & Passuth, P. M. (1981). Case processing in state misdemeanor courts: The effect of defense attorney presence. *The Justice System Journal, 6*(1), 100–116.

Argersinger v. Hamlin, 407 U.S. 25 (1972).

Austin, T. L. (1981). The influence of court location on type of criminal sentence: The rural-urban factor. *Journal of Criminal Justice, 9*(4), 305–316.

Bartol, A. M. (1996). Structures and roles of rural courts. In T. D. McDonald, R. A. Wood, & M. A. Pflug (Eds.), *Rural criminal justice: Conditions, constraints, and challenges* (pp. 79–92). Salem, WI: Sheffield Publishing Company.

Bell, D. J. (1986). Domestic violence in small cities and towns: A pilot study. *Journal of Crime and Justice, 9*(1), 163–181.

Blumberg, A. (1967). *Criminal justice.* Chicago, IL: Quadrangle Books.

Boruchowitz, R. C., Brink, M. N., & Dimino, M. (2009). *Minor crimes, massive waste: The terrible toll of America's broken misdemeanor courts.* Washington, DC: National Association of Criminal Defense Lawyers.

Carroll, D. (2016, December 12). Should non-lawyer judges be sending people to jail? SCOTUS asked to review. Retrieved from http://sixthamendment.org/should-non-lawyer-judges-be-sending-people-to-jail-scotus-asked-to-review/

Center for Access to Justice. (2018). *Mississippi's no-counsel courts.* Atlanta, GA: Georgia State University.

Court Statistics Project. (2018). *State court structure charts.* National Center for State Courts. Retrieved from www.courtstatistics.org/OtherPages/State_Court_Structure_Charts.aspx

Church, T. W. (1985). Examining local legal culture. *Law and Social Inquiry, 10*(3), 449–510.

Cornell, J. G. (2012). *Limited-jurisdiction courts – Challenges, opportunities, and strategies for action.* Williamsburg, VA: National Center for State Courts.

Curtis, K., & Davies, A. L. B. (2014). *Summary report of the 2014 survey of town and village magistrates: Counsel at first appearance.* Albany, NY: New York State Office of Indigent Legal Services.

Davies, A. L. B., & Worden, A. P. (2017). Local governance and redistributive policy: Explaining local funding for public defense. *Law & Society Review, 51*(2), 313–345.

Division of Local Government and School Accountability. (2010). *Report on the justice court fund.* Albany, NY: Office of the State Comptroller.

Donvan, J. (Interviewer), & Goetzinger, P. (Interviewee). (2018). *Luring doctors and lawyers to rural America* [Interview Transcript]. Retrieved from www.nhpr.org/post/luring-doctors-and-lawyers-rural-america#stream/0

Edmundson, C. (1996). Rural courts, the rural community and the challenge of change. In T. D. McDonald, R. A. Wood, & M. A. Pflug (Eds.), *Rural criminal justice: Conditions, constraints, and challenges* (pp. 93–109). Salem, WI: Sheffield Publishing Company.

Eisenstein, J., & Jacob, H. (1977). *Felony justice: An organizational analysis of criminal courts.* Lanham, MD: University Press of America.

Eisenstein, J., Nardulli, P. F., & Flemming, R. B. (1988). *The contours of justice: Communities and their courts.* Philadelphia, PA: University of Pennsylvania Press.

Feld, B. C. (1991). Justice by geography: Urban, suburban, and rural variations in juvenile justice administration. *Journal of Criminal Law and Criminology, 82*, 156–210.

Fetter, T. J., & Stott, E. K. (1977). *Rural courts: Trends and implications.* Williamsburg, VA: National Center for State Courts.

Flanagan, T. J., & Longmire, D. R. (Eds.). (1996). *Americans view crime and justice: A national public opinion survey.* Thousand Oaks, CA: SAGE Publications, Inc.

Flemming, R. B., Nardulli, P. F., & Eisenstein, J. (1992). *The craft of justice: Politics and work in criminal court communities.* Philadelphia, PA: University of Pennsylvania Press.

Ford, M. (2015, April 2). The problem of funding government through fines. *The Atlantic.*

Friedman, L. (2005). *A history of American law, 3rd edition.* New York, NY: Simon & Schuster.

Glaberson, W. (2006, September 27). How a reviled court system has outlasted critics. *The New York Times.* Retrieved from: www.nytimes.com/2006/09/27/nyregion/27courts.html

Kang-Brown, J., & Subramanian, R. (2017). *Out of sight: The growth of jails in rural America.* New York, NY: Vera Institute of Justice.

Kaye, J. S., & Lippman, J. (2006). *Action plan for the justice courts.* Albany: State of New York Unified Court System.

King, J. D. (2013). Beyond "life and liberty": The evolving right to counsel. *Harvard Civil Rights – Civil Liberties Law Review, 48*, 1–49.

Levin, M.A. (1977). *Urban politics and the criminal courts.* Chicago, IL: The University of Chicago Press.

Levin, M., & Haugen, M. (2018). *Open roads and overflowing jails: Addressing high rates of rural pretrial incarceration.* Austin: Texas Public Policy Foundation.

Logan, T. K., Shannon, L., & Walker, R. (2005). Protective orders in rural and urban areas: A multiple perspective study. *Violence Against Women, 11*(7), 876–911.

Mahoney, B., Carlson, A., & Baehler, A. (2006). Strengthening rural courts. What should be done to improve court operations and enhance the quality of justice in rural America? *The Court Manager, 20*(4), 11–16.

McCarthy, J. (2016, October 14). Americans divided on priorities for criminal justice system. *Gallup.* Retrieved from https://news.gallup.com/poll/196394/americans-divided-priorities-criminal-justice-system.aspx

McKeon, J. C., & Rice, D. G. (2009). Administering justice in Montana's rural courts. *Montana Law Review, 70*(2), 201–220.

New York State Unified Court System. (2018). *City, town, and village courts.* Retrieved from: www.nycourts.gov/courts/townandvillage/

Nugent-Borakove, E., & Mahoney, B. (2011). The context of rural justice: Rural court networks. *Court Manager, 26*(2), 26–30.

Nugent-Borakove, E., Mahoney, B., & Whitcomb, D. (2011). *Strengthening rural courts: Challenges and progress.* Williamsburg, VA: National Center for State Courts. Retrieved from www.ncsc.org/~/media/Microsites/Files/Future%20Trends/Author%20PDFs/Borakove%20Mahone%20and%20Whitcomb.ashx

Patton, E. (2013). *The black-white and urban-rural divides in perceptions of racial fairness.* Washington, DC: Pew Research Center.

Phillips, M. T. (2012). *A decade of bail research in New York City: Final report.* New York: New York City Criminal Justice Agency, Inc.

President's Commission on Law Enforcement and Administration of Justice. (1967). *The challenge of crime in a free society.* Washington, DC: U.S. Government Printing Office.

Provine, D. M. (1986). *Judging credentials: Nonlawyer judges and the politics of professionalism.* Chicago, IL: University of Chicago Press.

Pruitt, L. R., McKinney, J. C., & Calhoun, B. (2015). Justice in the hinterlands: Arkansas as a case study for the rural lawyer shortage and evidence-based solutions to alleviate it. *University of Arkansas Little Rock Law Journal, 37*, 573–719.

Rosenthal, L. (2018, April 13). *After a 90-year fight to reform NY's court...What's changed?* Canton, NY: North Country Public Radio. Retrieved from www.northcountrypublicradio.org/news/story/36007/20180413/after-a-90-year-fight-to-reform-ny-s-courts-what-s-changed

Silbey, S. S. (1981). Making sense of the lower courts. *The Justice System Journal, 6*(1), 13–27.

Sixth Amendment Center. (2015). *The right to counsel in Utah: An assessment of trial-level indigent defense services.* Boston, MA: Sixth Amendment Center.

Smith, A., & Maddan, S. (2011). *Three-minute justice: Haste and waste in Florida's misdemeanor courts.* Washington, DC: National Association of Criminal Defense Lawyers.

Smith, A., Maddan, S., Price, D. D., & Tvedt, C. (2017). *Rush to judgment: How South Carolina's summary courts fail to protect constitutional rights.* Washington, DC: National Association of Criminal Defense Lawyers.

Smith, C. H. (1927). The justice of the peace system in the United States. *California Law Review, 15*(2), 118–141.

Spangenberg, R. L., & Beeman, M. L. (1995). Indigent defense systems in the United States. *Law and Contemporary Problems, 58*(1), 31–49.

Surrency, E. C. (1967). The courts in the American colonies. *The American Journal of Legal History, 11*(4): 347–376.

University of Maine Law School. (2018, September 18). *UMF partners with Maine law to give students more affordable path to law degree.* Retrieved from: https://mainelaw.maine.edu/news/umf-partners-with-maine-law-to-give-students-more-affordable-path-to-law-degree/

Vetter, S. J., & Clark, J. (2012). *The delivery of pretrial justice in rural areas: A guide for rural county officials.* Washington, DC: National Association of Counties.

Worden, A. P., Morgan, K. A., Shteynberg, R. V., & Davies, A. L. B. (2018). What difference does a lawyer make? Impacts of early counsel on misdemeanor bail decisions and outcomes in rural and small town courts. *Criminal Justice Policy Review, 29*, 710–735.

7

THE VALIDITY OF MISDEMEANOR PLEAS

Samantha Luna, Amy Dezember, and Allison D. Redlich

When most Americans think of a guilty plea, they assume it is as simple as a guilty person admitting their crime and accepting the punishment for their actions. However, it is not always that straightforward. For example, John Casey, a defendant who described himself as homeless, was charged with three misdemeanor offenses: trespassing, loitering, and having an open container in public (Bach, 2009). Judge Henry Bauer did not assign Casey an attorney and set Casey's bail inexplicably at $25,000. Without Casey even in the courtroom, Judge Bauer called the case and proceeded with a guilty plea, declaring: "The matter of People against John Casey was a plea and time served" (Bach, 2009, p. 100). After seven days, Casey was discharged from jail without ever having to come to court, with the judge effectively pleading guilty for him. Judge Bauer was later charged with, among other things, failing to inform defendants of their right to an attorney, coercing guilty pleas, and convicting defendants without a plea or trial and was eventually removed from the bench (Bach, 2009). While it is unclear whether the circumstances surrounding Casey's plea are common or an anomaly, it raises various questions and concerns about how the validity of misdemeanor pleas are handled by the courts.

In the United States, over 15 million criminal cases are filed in state courts every year, most of which are misdemeanors (Schauffler, LaFountain, Strickland, Holt, & Genthon, 2017). These criminal cases include felonies, misdemeanors, criminal appeals from limited jurisdiction trial courts, and other criminal cases. Due to this high volume of criminal cases flooding the system each year, the vast majority do not make it to trial. For example, of the 48,939 felony arrests in the 75 largest urban counties, 25% are dismissed, 2% go to trial, and 64% are convictions through guilty pleas (Bureau of Justice Statistics, 2013). Plea bargaining alleviates the overburdened criminal justice system by offering an alternative to time consuming and costly trials; many argue that the system simply could not function without it (Bibas, 2003). Although the high prevalence of pleas makes for a more efficient system, it may not make for a more just system if defendants are feeling coerced into making plea decisions in the hopes of being rewarded for saving the court time. Yet, because our system is often overburdened and over-capacity, plea decisions are often made in haste without adequate knowledge or information (Bibas, 2011; Lynch, 2003).

Though most literature has focused on felony cases, misdemeanors alone have accounted for over 75% of the criminal cases filed in state courts, and in some states the percentage of misdemeanor cases that actually make it to trial (either bench or jury) can be lower than 1% (Schauffler et al., 2017). Since the research shows that defendants charged with felonies often enter their pleas in haste, it can be assumed that these same pressures are felt by defendants charged with misdemeanors, raising questions about the validity of these pleas. For a plea to be considered valid, the defendant should have the necessary information (i.e., the decision should be made knowingly and intelligently), the defendant should enter the plea voluntarily, and the defendant should be factually guilty of the charges (Redlich, 2016). It is unclear, however, if these three elements are actually present in reality. In fact, some argue that misdemeanor defendants are not afforded the same due process rights as felony defendants (Natapoff, 2012a). The lack of research on misdemeanor pleas highlights a large gap in the literature surrounding plea bargains and the validity of pleading guilty in misdemeanor cases.

This chapter examines the validity of pleading guilty with a focus on misdemeanor cases. We begin with a review of the literature on plea decision-making and evaluating the validity of guilty pleas while also highlighting gaps in the literature. In this section, we highlight what we know, and do not know, about ensuring that pleas are made knowingly, intelligently, and voluntarily and how these issues may specifically impact misdemeanor guilty pleas. Finally, we conclude with potential ways to move the knowledge base forward by identifying consequences that potentially arise if the validity of guilty pleas is not properly evaluated and ideas for future research directions to address these concerns.

Understanding Guilty Pleas

To understand how to evaluate the validity of a guilty plea, it is important to understand the overall plea process. Defendants typically plead guilty as part of an arrangement with the district attorney, wherein the state ensures a conviction and the defendant receives some sort of deal or bargain (Bibas, 2004). These deals commonly include the state dropping charges, amending the charges to less severe ones, recommending a discounted sentence, or a combination of all three (Redlich, Bibas, Edkins, & Madon, 2017). Additionally, there are several different types of guilty pleas that defendants can enter, including a traditional guilty plea, a nolo contendere (no contest) plea, and the *Alford* plea. No contest pleas allow the defendant to enter a guilty plea without acknowledging guilt or innocence (Redlich, 2016). In contrast, the *Alford* plea allows the defendant who claims innocence but perceives their chances of acquittal at trial to be too much of a risk to plead guilty (*North Carolina v. Alford*, 1970). Regardless of the type of plea the defendant enters, the court is tasked with ensuring that the plea is valid and that a factual basis of guilt has been established before accepting the plea.

When considering why defendants might choose to plead guilty, some research has focused on the institutional or organizational influences on pleas, such as the role of judges, prosecutors, and defense attorneys working together toward the shared goal of disposing cases efficiently and minimizing uncertainty (Eisenstein & Jacobs, 1977). In other research, legal scholars and criminologists have considered that the various legal actors involved in the plea process make plea decisions "in the shadow of trial" (Bibas, 2004; Nagel & Neef, 1979). The "shadow of the trial" model argues that decisions to offer, accept, or reject pleas derive from the perceived probable outcome of a trial and that a rational, risk-neutral defendant would only accept a plea deal that is less than the expected value of the trial outcome (Bushway & Redlich, 2012). However, critics of the shadow model raise questions about its face validity—the degree to which a model subjectively covers the concept that it is measuring (Bibas, 2004). There is evidence indicating that defendants are not always rational actors, especially when innocent, and that myriad other factors can influence the decisions of defendants, attorneys, and judges (Bjerk, 2005; Tor, Gazal-Ayal, &

Garcia, 2010). Additionally, researchers have found that factors, such as prosecutorial discretion, defendant characteristics, and offense type, impact the plea bargain a defendant receives (King, Soule, Steen, & Weidner, 2005; Rhodes, 1979; Ulmer & Bradley, 2006). Regardless of why people plead guilty, it is important to determine if guilty plea decisions are valid.

Determining the Validity of Guilty Pleas

The United States Supreme Court has consistently ruled that guilty pleas must only be accepted if a plea has been entered knowingly, intelligently, and voluntarily (see *Boykin v. Alabama*, 1969; *Brady v. United States*, 1963). The primary mechanisms used to determine if a plea meets these standards (i.e., knowing, intelligent, voluntary) are the oral judicial plea colloquy (*Boykin v. Alabama*, 1969) and written tender-of-plea forms (Redlich, 2016). The colloquy consists of the judge asking the defendant a series of questions or statements aimed at determining the validity of the plea and must be preserved in court record (*Boykin v. Alabama*, 1969). These questions aim to address whether there were any pressures, threats, or promises made (i.e., voluntary), if the defendant understands the consequences of pleading guilty (i.e., knowing and intelligent), and if the defendant is incapacitated in any way and therefore unable to intelligently enter the guilty plea. Similarly, the tender-of-plea forms are intended to supplement the oral colloquy by informing defendants about information relevant to their plea, such as the charges being pled to, punishment ranges and maximums, and rights being waived (Redlich & Bonventre, 2015).

Federal Rule of Criminal Procedure 11 governs the entry of a guilty plea and outlines how the validity of guilty pleas should be examined to ensure the decision is made knowingly and intelligently, voluntarily, and that there is a sufficient basis of guilt. Despite this federal rule and two separate mechanisms (though the written version is optional) for determining the validity of pleas, each court, and even in some cases each judge, is able to implement their own version of an oral colloquy and tender-of-plea forms, leading to large variances in the information included (or excluded) from court to court. This is especially true in misdemeanor cases given that research indicates that misdemeanor cases are often rushed through the court process with mere minutes devoted to each plea hearing (Boruchowitz, Brink, & Dimino, 2009; Natapoff, 2015). Due to the potential for variation from court to court, it is not always clear how, or even whether, courts evaluate the validity of guilty pleas in misdemeanor cases to ensure that the pleas are entered knowingly, intelligently, and voluntarily as set out in state and federal rules for criminal procedure.

Knowing and Intelligent Plea Decisions

Federal Rule 11 Part 1, "*Advising and Questioning the Defendant*," lists measures that the court must address with the defendant in open court (e.g., rights being waived as a result of the plea, the charges against the defendant, and certain sentencing requirements). This list of 15 items is often what makes up elements of the judicial oral colloquy and is intended to ensure that the defendant is making a knowing and intelligent plea decision. Three important components are part of knowing and intelligent plea decisions: whether defendants (1) have the *capacity* to understand the information involved (i.e., adjudicative competence), (2) *actually* understand the information involved, and (3) are given enough information to make a knowing and intelligent decision (Redlich, 2016). Having the *ability* to enter a valid plea (i.e., adjudicative competence) and *actually making* a knowing, intelligent, and voluntary decision are not necessarily equivalent (*Godinez v. Moran*, 1993; Redlich & Summers, 2012). This chapter will focus on the validity of pleas entered by those presumed to have the capacity to make knowing, intelligent, and voluntary decisions. There is significant research that has addressed the issue of knowingness and intelligence in a variety of ways, including looking at defendants' competence to make plea/trial decisions (e.g., see Pirelli, Gottdiener, & Zapf, 2011 for a review of 40 years of competence research).

One area of research on understanding of the plea process looks at defendant comprehensibility of the language used by legal actors. Generally, research has found disparities between defendants' average reading and listening comprehensibility abilities and the levels required to fully understand the oral colloquy and written tender-of-plea forms (see Blackwood, 2009; Haigler, Harlow, O'Connor & Campbell, 1994; Redlich, 2016; Redlich & Bonventre, 2015). Limited defendant comprehension has also been found for the words used in written tender-of-plea forms (Kaban & Quinlan, 2004; Redlich & Shteynberg, 2016). For example, in a laboratory study, Redlich and Shteynberg (2016) asked participants to define the word "concession" as used in the legal context, and found that more than 90% of adults could not do so accurately. They also found that more than 50% of adults and juveniles in the study could not define "unlawful influence," which has implications not only for knowing and intelligent, but also voluntary decision-making. In addition, Redlich and Summers (2012) assessed comprehension of legal understanding among defendants who had just entered supposedly legally valid pleas, finding that two-thirds of their sample answered 60% or more of the questions incorrectly. Overall these studies indicate that even if defendants meet the threshold for adjudicative competence and enter legally valid pleas (either misdemeanor or felony) they may not fully understand the information necessary to actually make a knowing and intelligent plea decision. And while such studies have tended to focus on felony cases, it is reasonable to assume that felony defendants' understanding of the information involved in the guilty plea process is either on par with, or perhaps even higher, than misdemeanor defendants' understanding.

Another aspect of a knowing and intelligent plea decision is whether defendants are given sufficient information to make these decisions. Although the Supreme Court does not require that defendants be informed of collateral consequences, many legal scholars argue that defendants should be informed of the numerous collateral consequences associated with their pleas, such as consequences around employment, education, and welfare benefits, as this knowledge could lead to different plea decisions (Redlich, 2016). Another area of concern surrounding the information available to defendants during plea negotiations is exculpatory evidence (i.e., evidence that supports the idea that the defendant is not guilty). While the Supreme Court has been clear about the requirement to turn over exculpatory information for trials (*Brady v. Maryland*, 1963), the Supreme Court has held that a defendant who pleads guilty forgoes a fair trial, a plea may be voluntary without release of impeachment evidence, and exculpatory impeachment evidence (i.e., evidence that challenges the credibility of witnesses) need not be turned over to the defense (*United States v. Ruiz*, 2002). Legal scholars, however, argue that without knowing the full weight of the evidence against them, defendants are ill-equipped to negotiate deals with the prosecution that accurately represent the cases against them (Alkon, 2014). Additionally, innocent defendants may plead guilty without this knowledge for fear of losing at trial and risking harsher sentences (Bibas, 2004). To ensure that defendants are able to make a fully informed decision, proper safeguards should be in place that provide defendants with the sufficient information necessary to make a plea decision.

The sufficiency of information given to misdemeanor defendants may be even more limited, considering the "assembly-line process" used to resolve misdemeanor cases. As previously mentioned, misdemeanor cases are often rushed through the court process with only minutes devoted to each plea as a result of the court attempting to efficiently processes such high numbers of these types of cases (Boruchowitz et al., 2009; Natapoff, 2015). Boruchowitz et al., (2009) report that even for misdemeanor trials "defenders do not have enough time to see their clients or to prepare their cases adequately, there are no witness interviews or investigations, they cannot do the legal research required…" (p. 30). Without having adequate access to evidence and other elements related to a case, it is clear that defendants charged with misdemeanors may be missing vital information necessary to make an intelligent and informed plea decision.

Voluntary Plea Decisions

Federal Rule 11 Part 2, *"Ensuring That a Plea is Voluntary,"* requires that judges "address the defendant personally in open court and determine that the plea is voluntary and did not result from force, threats, or promises." Despite voluntariness being an integral part of making a valid plea decision, the legal requirement for voluntariness is not always clear.

There are many who view plea bargaining as inherently coercive because they offer defendants a "forced choice," that is the choice between a certain lesser punishment and an unknown risk of a far greater punishment (Kipnis, 1976; Langbein 1992; Lynch, 2003). Without clear standards for the voluntariness of pleas, the issue then becomes how much coercion is too much coercion? And at what point does coercion become "wrongful" or "undue"? While the answers to these questions are highly subjective, past research has addressed the issue of perceived plea voluntariness in a variety of ways.

In a study of recent plea-takers, Redlich and Summers (2012) found that most of the felony defendants interviewed reported being asked if it was their choice to plead guilty (96%) and most also claimed that it was in fact their voluntary choice (93%). However, an alarming 44% of defendants in the study incorrectly believed that guilty pleas do not have to be voluntary. Voluntariness has also been examined by looking at the external pressures experienced during the plea process and the potential for coercion. Bordens and Basset (1985) found that external pressure from prosecutors was a predominant reason for defendants pleading guilty. Additionally, Malloy, Shulman, and Cauffman (2014) found that 10%–14% of youthful offenders in their study reported pleading guilty for reasons related to duress. These findings are not surprising given the various social influence factors that can limit the perceived voluntariness of plea decision-making, such as time-limited offers, obedience to authority, and the value of the plea bargain itself (Redlich et al., 2017).

For misdemeanors specifically, external pressure to plead guilty may be especially worrisome. Misdemeanor caseloads are extremely high across the United States and can go far beyond the national standard of 400 cases per year (Boruchowitz et al., 2009). For example, defenders in Chicago reported having more than 2,000 misdemeanor cases per year. These large caseloads contribute to a "meet and plead" system for misdemeanors, where defendants often meet their attorney (if they are provided one),[1] become informed of their plea deal, and enter a plea, all within their first appearance (Boruchowitz et al., 2009). Unsurprisingly, this rushed process can result in intense pressure for defendants to plead guilty. Overworked defenders may pressure defendants to take plea deals as a way to save time and resources and prosecutors are able to pressure defendants by offering time-limited deals (Boruchowitz et al., 2009). Additionally, the misdemeanor process can be especially coercive for those incarcerated prior to trial. Those who are incarcerated prior to trial often cannot afford bail and end up pleading guilty as a way to avoid time in custody (Boruchowitz et al., 2009; Fellner, 2010; Natapoff, 2015). For example, Heaton, Mayson, and Stevenson (2017) found that detained misdemeanor defendants were 25% more likely to plead guilty than defendants in similar situations who were not detained. With high misdemeanor caseloads and minimal time with defense attorneys to discuss options, this could lead to defendants who may not even know that the plea is their choice to make and raises many concerns about the true voluntariness of guilty pleas in misdemeanor cases.

Factual Basis of Guilt

Federal Rule 11 Part 3, "*Determining the Factual Basis for a Plea*," requires that before judgment is entered on a guilty plea, the court must determine that a factual basis exists for a plea. This aspect, however, is often de-emphasized and conflated with a defendant's willingness to plead guilty (Bibas, 2014; Redlich, 2016). Research suggests that, in practice, judges either do not inquire about factual guilt or simply accept the plea itself as proof of factual guilt (Rakoff, 2014; Redlich et al., 2017). The de-emphasis of factual guilt is especially alarming given the lack of safeguards available when a defendant pleads guilty, such as the presumption of innocence and the ability to present evidence in your own defense (Redlich, 2016). It is unsurprising then that innocent persons have pled guilty to crimes they did not commit. While the exact number of false guilty pleas is largely unknown, the National Registry of Exonerations, to date, has documented 328 felony and 89 misdemeanor cases of false guilty pleas since 1989 (as of September 2018). However, it is important to note that the National Registry of Exonerations acknowledges that their database only includes information about known cases with publicly available information. Additionally, while most known wrongful convictions are the "wrong person" type (65% of National Registry cases), meaning a crime actually occurred and the wrong person was convicted, wrongful convictions can also occur when no crime is committed (Norris, Bonventre, & Acker, 2018). Misdemeanor cases may be especially likely to be the "no crime" type of wrongful convictions.[2] For example, Natapoff (2012b) notes that thousands of loitering arrests are made annually in Baltimore (as well as New York). However, failure to "move along," as described by Moskos (2008), does not fit the legal definition of loitering, and thus it is an open question whether these thousands of arrestees actually were loitering. Thus, it is possible that the likelihood of false guilty pleas among misdemeanor cases is much higher than those catalogued in the National Registry.

Future Research on the Validity of Misdemeanor Pleas

First and foremost, there is an overall lack of information on misdemeanor cases, indicating that there is a need for additional research to provide a foundation about the rates and frequency of misdemeanor pleas as well the characteristics of misdemeanor defendants themselves. Misdemeanor convictions are typically dismissed as low-level events that do not seemingly deserve the same attention awarded to felonies; yet ten million petty cases are filed every year and the vast majority of U.S. convictions are misdemeanors (Natapoff, 2012a). As noted throughout this chapter, the vast majority of research is on felonies, both in terms of the validity of guilty pleas and about guilty pleas in generally. This leaves a gap in the literature and knowledge surrounding guilty pleas in misdemeanor cases that researchers should address.

With regard to our knowledge about the validity of guilty pleas, there is also the need for additional research. When a defendant chooses to go to trial, he is guaranteed certain safeguards, such as the right not to be compelled to be a witness against himself, to confront persons against him, to present evidence in his defense, and the responsibility of the state to prove the charges against him beyond a reasonable doubt (Boruchowitz et al., 2009). However, as previously mentioned, our system is one in which the vast majority of cases never make it to trial, and when a defendant chooses to enter a plea those trial safeguards no longer apply. Therefore, ensuring that pleas are entered knowingly, intelligently, voluntarily, and with a factual basis of guilt is all the more imperative. And with a lack of research surrounding misdemeanor pleas, ensuring the validity for these pleas is an area that needs further attention.

While some may hold a common misconception that misdemeanor convictions are trivial and do not affect individuals in meaningful ways (Boruchowitz et al., 2009), this type of a conviction can have lasting and detrimental effects. Pleading guilty in misdemeanor cases, just like in felony cases, can have numerous collateral consequences impacting a variety of areas in a defendant's life (e.g., education, employment, access to public assistance programs, etc.). Though the punishment for misdemeanor convictions may pale in comparison to that of felonies, the collateral consequences of these convictions can expand far beyond the punishment associated with a misdemeanor (e.g., "time served" or one year in jail) (Natapoff, 2015). These collateral consequences can include disqualification from public housing, food assistance, educational opportunities, future employment, and the denial of professional licenses (Boruchowitz et al., 2009; Natapoff, 2015). Additionally, it has been argued that the "process is the punishment" when it comes to misdemeanor cases, meaning the real costs are not the fines and prison sentences, but the costs incurred before the case even comes before the judge, such as lost wages from missed work, commissions to bail bondsmen, attorney's fees, and wasted time (Feeley, 1992).

Given the lasting effect these convictions can have, it is vital that future research focus on ensuring that guilty pleas are made knowingly and intelligently. To ensure this, the language used during the oral colloquy and in the written-tender-of-plea forms needs to be made more accessible to defendants. Research has shown that disparities exist between the levels required to understand these legal processes and average defendant comprehension levels (Blackwood, 2009; Haigler et al., 1994; Redlich, 2016; Redlich & Bonventre, 2015). Future research should address this by examining how to make the plea process and inquiry more understandable for both felony and misdemeanor defendants. Additionally, since pleading guilty can have a variety of effects on an individual's life, defendants need to be provided with sufficient information about both direct and collateral consequences to make truly knowing and intelligent plea decisions. More research is needed on what information should be provided before a plea is entered, as well as on the impact of this information on plea decisions (e.g., does informing defendants of collateral consequences influence plea decisions?). Furthering the knowledge base around knowing and intelligent pleas can help ensure defendants have a full understanding of the decision-making process and the consequences they will experience as a result of their plea.

Additionally, numerous questions still exist about the true voluntariness of these choices. While it has been well established that defendants who plead guilty receive comparatively shorter sentences than individuals who are convicted of similar crimes at trial, the threat or risk of a lengthier sentence at trial, referred to as the "trial penalty" or "trial tax" may compel defendants to plead guilty (Ulmer & Bradley, 2006). Research looking at defendant's plea decision-making has found that defendants who plead guilty reported doing so because they felt that if they were to reject a plea deal, they would receive a stiffer penalty (Daftary-Kapur & Zottoli, 2014). While defendants charged with misdemeanors may not typically be faced with lengthy incarceration sentences, these findings raise concerns about prosecutors using the threat of longer sentences, including jail time over probation only, as a means of coercing pleas out of defendants. Future research should focus on examining perceptions of voluntariness of the plea decision among defendants to better understand the differing pressures defendants feel. Additionally, it is possible that defendants confuse satisfaction with the outcome of their case as a result of a plea with the actual voluntariness of the plea decision. For example, even if a defendant is pressured into pleading guilty, the defendant may still see the plea as a "good" deal simply because they received probation (rather than jail time) for a misdemeanor offense. Researchers have suggested that this issue could be addressed by comparing the perceptions of voluntariness between true and false guilty plea-takers as a way to disentangle the issues of "good deals" versus voluntary pleas (Redlich, 2016). Since the vast majority of misdemeanor charges result in guilty pleas, future research should focus on ensuring that these decisions are truly made voluntarily.

Finally, issues with voluntariness also raise concerns of innocent defendants feeling coerced into pleading guilty. These are not abstract fears, but rather a stark reality of our criminal justice system. As previously mentioned, the National Registry of Exonerations has to date identified 417 individuals who have entered false guilty pleas in felony and misdemeanor cases in the last 29 years, which is only a mere glimpse into how often this occurs. A very real possibility is that there are far more false guilty pleas that have gone and will continue to go unrecorded (see Redlich, 2016). As noted, safeguards are lacking in the plea process and even with the checks that do exist (i.e., oral colloquy and written tender-of-plea forms), a factual basis of guilt is often de-emphasized and potentially even ignored (Bibas, 2014; Redlich, 2016). For low-level crimes specifically, the possibility of false guilty pleas may be even greater (Bowers, 2008). For example, consider an innocent misdemeanor defendant who cannot afford bail. This defendant has the option of remaining in custody until his trial or pleading guilty to time served and being able to go home. It is not difficult to understand why this defendant would choose to enter a false guilty plea, especially if he was not provided information about the collateral consequences associated with a misdemeanor conviction. This scenario, while simplified, highlights the need to ensure that defendants are entering pleas voluntarily, knowingly, and factually to protect against false guilty pleas.

Conclusion

As it becomes clearer that our criminal justice system is a system of pleas, it is all the more imperative to ensure that guilty pleas, both at the misdemeanor and felony levels, are made knowingly, intelligently, voluntarily, and with a factual basis of guilt as the Supreme Court intended (*Boykin v. Alabama*, 1969). Misdemeanor pleas account for an overwhelming amount of the pleas processed in our courts systems (Schauffler et al., 2017), which means that it is even more important to make sure that these defendants have the information needed to make valid decisions and to ensure that situations like John Casey's (whose story started this chapter) do not occur. Casey should have been brought in front of the judge to confirm that he understood the nature of the charges against him, as well as the consequences of pleading guilty, rather than his case being processed without his presence. Further, a lack of knowledge or complete information coupled with pressures and incentives to plead guilty is likely leading to a number of people entering false guilty pleas at a rate much higher than is known or appreciated. This illustrates the importance of studying the validity of guilty pleas, especially in misdemeanor cases, in order to make sure that the safeguards in place provide defendants with the information and protections necessary to ensure that plea decisions are valid.

Notes

1 A significant percentage of misdemeanor defendants do not receive counsel (Boruchowitz et al., 2009). *Scott v. Illinois* (1979) held that petty offenders have no right to a lawyer if they have not been "actually incarcerated."

2 Indeed, of the 89 misdemeanor false guilty pleas in the National Registry of Exonerations, all but three were "no crime" wrongful convictions. However, many of these cases took place in Harris County, Texas which experienced a mass exoneration of drug cases.

References

Alkon, C. (2014). The right to defense discovery in plea bargaining fifty years after Brady v. Maryland. *New York University Review of Law & Social Change, 38*, 407–422.

Bach, A. (2009). *Ordinary justice: How America holds court.* New York, NY: Metropolitan Books.

Bibas, S. (2003). Harmonizing substantive criminal law values and criminal procedure; The case of Alford and Nolo Contendere pleas. *Cornell Law Review, 88*, 1361–1412.

Bibas, S. (2004). Plea bargaining outside the shadow of trial. *Harvard Law Review, 117*, 2463–2547.

Bibas, S. (2011). Regulating the plea-bargaining market: From caveat emptor to consumer protection. *California Law Review, 99*, 1117.

Bibas, S. (2014). The limits of textualism in interpreting the confrontation clause. *Harvard Journal of Law & Public Policy, 37*, 737.

Bjerk, D. (2005). Making the crime fit the penalty: The role of prosecutorial discretion under mandatory minimum sentencing. *The Journal of Law and Economics, 48*(2), 591–625.

Blackwood, H. L. (2009). *A comparison of Miranda procedures: The effects of oral and written administrations on Miranda comprehension* (master's thesis). Denton, Texas. UNT Digital Library. Retrieved August 29, 2018 from https://digital.library.unt.edu/ark:/67531/metadc11057/m2/1/high_res_d/thesis.pdf

Bordens, K. S., & Basset, J. (1985). The plea bargaining process from the defendant's perspective: A field investigation. *Basic and Applied Social Psychology, 6*, 93–110.

Boruchowitz, R. C., Brink, M. N., & Dimino, M. (2009). *Minor crimes, massive waste: The terrible toll of America's broken misdemeanor courts.* Washington, DC: National Association of Criminal Defense Lawyers.

Bowers, J. (2008). Punishing the innocent. *University of Pennsylvania Law Review, 156*, 1117–1179.

Boykin v. Alabama, 395 U.S. 238 (1969).

Brady v. United States, 397 U.S. 742 (1963).

Bureau of Justice Statistics (2013). *Felony defendants in large urban counties, 2009 - statistical tables.* Washington, DC: US Department of Justice.

Bushway, S. D., & Redlich, A. D. (2012). Is plea bargaining in the "shadow of trial" a mirage? *Journal of Quantitative Criminology, 28*, 437–454.

Daftary-Kapur, T., & Zottoli, T. M. (2014). A first look at the plea deal experiences of juveniles tried in adult court. *International Journal of Forensic Mental Health, 13*(4), 323–336.

Eisenstein, J., & Jacob, H. (1977). *Felony justice: An organizational analysis of criminal courts.* Boston, MA: Little, Brown.

Feeley, M. M. (1992). *The process is the punishment: Handling cases in a lower criminal court.* New York, NY: Russell Sage Foundation.

Fellner, J. (2010). *The price of freedom: Bail and pretrial detention of low income nonfelony defendants in New York City.* New York, NY: Human Rights Watch.

Godinez v. Moran, 509 U.S. 389 (1993).

Haigler, K. O., Harlow, C., O'Conner, P., & Campbell, A. (1994). *Literacy behind prison walls: Profiles of the prison population from the national adult literacy survey*, (NCES 94102). Washington, DC: Department of Education.

Heaton, P., Mayson, S., & Stevenson, M. (2017). The downstream consequences of misdemeanor pretrial detention. *Stanford Law Review, 69*, 711–794.

Langbein, J. H. (1992). On the myth of written constitutions: The disappearance of criminal jury trial. *Harvard Journal of Law and Public Policy, 15*, 119–127.

Lynch, T. (2003). The case against plea bargaining. *Regulation, 26*, 24–27.

Kaban, B., & Quinlan, J. C. (2004). Rethinking a "knowing, intelligent and voluntary waiver" in Massachusetts' juvenile courts. *Journal of the Center for Families, Children, and the Courts, 5*, 35–55.

King, N., Soule, D., Steen, S., & Weidner, R. (2005). When process affects punishment: Differences in sentences after guilty plea, bench trial, and jury trial in five guideline states. *Columbia Law Review, 105*, 960–1009.

Kipnis, K. (1976). Criminal justice and the negotiated plea." *Ethics, 86*(2), 93–106.

Malloy, L. C., Shulman, E. P., & Cauffman, E. (2014). Interrogations, confessions, and guilty pleas among serious adolescent offenders. *Law and Human Behavior, 38*, 181–193.

Moskos, P. (2008). *Cop in the hood: My year policing Baltimore's Eastern District.* Princeton, NJ: Princeton University Press.

Nagel, S. S., & Neef, M. G. (1979). *Decision theory and the legal process.* Lexington, MA: Lexington.

Natapoff, A. (2012a). Misdemeanors. *Southern California Law Review, 85*, 1313.

Natapoff, A. (2012b). *Why misdemeanors aren't so minor.* Retrieved July 15, 2014 from www.slate.com/articles/news_and_politics/jurisprudence/2012/04/misdemeanors_can_have_major_consequences_for_the_people_charged_.html

Natapoff, A. (2015). Misdemeanors. *The Annual Review of Law and Social Sciences, 11*, 255–267.

Norris, R. J., Bonventre, C. L., & Acker, J. R. (2018). *When justice fails: Causes and consequences of wrongful convictions*. Durham, NC: Carolina Academic Press.

North Carolina v. Alford, 400 U.S. 25 (1970).

Pirelli, G., Gottdiener, W. H., & Zapf, P. A. (2011). A meta-analytic review of competency to stand trial research. *Psychology, Public Policy, and Law, 17*, 1–53.

Rakoff, J. S. (2014). Why innocent people plead guilty. *The New York Review of Books*. Retrieved from www.nybooks.com/articles/archive/2014/nov/20/why-innocent-people-plead-guilty

Redlich, A. D. (2016). The validity of pleading guilty. In B. H. Borstein & M. K. Miller (Eds.), *Advances in Psychology and Law* (pp. 1–26). New York, NY: Springer.

Redlich, A. D., Bibas, S., Edkins, V. A., & Madon, S. (2017). The psychology of defendant plea decision making. *American Psychologist, 72*(4), 339.

Redlich, A. D., & Bonventre, C. (2015). Content and comprehensibility of adult and juvenile tender-of-plea: Implications for knowing, intelligent, and voluntary guilty pleas. *Law and Human Behavior, 39*, 162–176.

Redlich, A. D., & Shteynberg, R. (2016). To plead or not to plead: A comparison of juvenile and adult true and false plea decisions. *Law and Human Behavior, 40*, 611–625.

Redlich, A. D., & Summers, A. (2012). Voluntary, knowing, and intelligent pleas: Understanding plea inquiries. *Psychology, Public Policy, and Law, 18*, 626–643.

Rhodes, W. (1979). Plea bargaining: Its effect on sentencing and convictions in the District of Columbia. *Journal of Criminal Law and Criminology, 70*, 360–75.

Scott v. Illinois, 440 U.S. 397 (1979).

Schauffler, R., LaFountain, R., Strickland, S., Holt, K., & Genthon, K. (2017). *The Court Statistics Project DataViewer*. Retrieved from http://popup.ncsc.org/CSP/CSP_Intro.aspx

Tor, A., Gazal-Ayal, O., & Garcia, S. M. (2010). Fairness and willingness to accept plea bargain offers. *Journal of Empirical Legal Studies, 7*, 97–116.

Ulmer, J. T., & Bradley, M. S. (2006). Variation in trial penalties among serious violent offenses. *Criminology, 44*, 631–670.

United States v. Ruiz, 536 U.S. 622 (2002).

8

MINOR CRIMES, MAJOR IMPACTS

An Examination of Racially Disparate Outcomes in Misdemeanor Court Processing

Amanda P. Cook

Race is one of the most deliberated predictors of criminal justice outcomes. There is evidence of race impacting outcomes at every level of the criminal justice system, both directly and through its impact on intervening variables (see Spohn, 2000; Zatz, 2000). Even though research on this topic is vast, the majority of it focuses on felony offenses (Chauhan & Travis, 2018). Granted, felonies represent more serious hazards to public safety, but misdemeanors outnumber felonies by an estimation of three to one (Stevenson & Mayson, 2018). Nevertheless, the misdemeanor justice system has largely been ignored by researchers and policymakers, and for that reason, we still know very little about it (Natapoff, 2015; Stevenson & Mayson, 2018).

In this chapter, I will examine misdemeanor court processing, paying particular attention to the impact of race at various decision points. In general, there has been little research aimed at explaining lower court decision-making, and even less that examines the impact of race on those decisions. Previous research has argued that decisions made by prosecutors, defense attorneys, and judges in the lower criminal courts are wrought with more discretion because these actors have fewer restrictions on their decision-making (Feeley, 1979; Nelson, 1994). It is important to examine the extent to which race impacts lower court decisions because misdemeanor court outcomes can have far-reaching implications for offenders. They can impact decisions in future criminal court proceedings in the form of prior arrests, convictions, and sentences (Holleran & Spohn, 2004; Johnson, 2003; Lubitz & Ross, 2001; Spohn, 2000; Ulmer & Johnson, 2004; Zatz, 2000). Also, the invisible punishments associated with misdemeanor processing can have disparate and detrimental effects on people of color, their families, and communities (Smyth, 2005). The effect of race on justice outcomes may be influenced by other factors such as age and gender; this chapter will also explore the relevant findings from studies on the lower courts. Because research on race and misdemeanor court processing is scant, this chapter evaluates the findings from felony research for comparison purposes. By highlighting the relatively few studies that examine race and misdemeanor court outcomes, we will see the importance of expanding research and increasing scrutiny of the misdemeanor justice system.

Race and Misdemeanor Court Processing

A common theme in criminal justice literature is that both legal and extralegal factors impact criminal case processing and outcomes. Generally, legal factors, such as prior criminal record and seriousness of the offense, are the primary determinants of a defendant's sentence (Dixon, 1995;

Gottfredson & Gottfredson, 1988; Hagan, 1974; Kleck, 1981; Kramer & Steffensmeier, 1993; Leiber & Blowers, 2003; Wilbanks, 1987; Zatz, 1987), but evidence also suggests that race and ethnicity impact sentencing outcomes (see Spohn, 2000), especially when dealing with less serious crimes (Crawford, Chiricos, & Kleck, 1998; Munoz & Sapp, 2003; Spohn & DeLone, 2000). In that vein, one would expect to see significant impacts of race and ethnicity at various stages of misdemeanor case processing, from sentencing and pretrial detention decisions to case prioritization and plea offers, given that, by definition, misdemeanors are less serious crimes than are felonies. The research highlighted in the following offers insight into the impact of race on misdemeanor court outcomes.

Race and Misdemeanor Sentencing

Using a sample of females charged with misdemeanors in New York City, Brennan (2006) examined the impact of race on sentencing outcomes. She did not find race/ethnicity to have a direct effect on the likelihood of receiving a jail sentence. Instead, race/ethnicity influenced the likelihood of receiving a jail sentence through its impact on various other factors (class discrimination, pretrial release status, and criminal history). For example, black and Hispanic women charged with misdemeanors were less likely than white women charged with misdemeanors to be high school graduates and employed, and this indirectly improved their odds of receiving a jail sentence. Because black and Hispanic women were less likely to gain pretrial release, due to social class factors, they were ultimately more likely to receive a jail sentence. Also, black females were more likely to have prior convictions than were white females, and prior convictions increased odds of receiving a jail sentence. Brennan (2006) warns that the lack of a direct impact of race/ethnicity on sentencing outcomes is in no way indicative of an unbiased misdemeanor sentencing process and that race/ethnicity impacts sentencing outcomes through a variety of indirect paths.

In addition, Brennan (2006) found that female misdemeanor sentences were influenced by many of the same legal factors that affect felony sentencing decisions. Female misdemeanor offenders with more serious charges and criminal histories, who were in pretrial detention and those who had a documented history of failure to appear were given harsher penalties.

Munoz and Freng (2007) examined the impacts of race, age, and gender on misdemeanor criminal sentencing using a sample of misdemeanor cases from three counties in Nebraska. Munoz and Freng (2007) found that whites are more likely to be convicted of traffic offenses than other misdemeanor offenses, and racial minorities charged with misdemeanors were more likely to be convicted of offenses "other than traffic." Munoz and Freng (2007) also found that the majority of defendants received just a fine, but racial minority individuals, males, and offenders 25 and older were more likely to receive a fine in combination with some other disposition than were whites, females, and younger misdemeanor offenders. Males received slightly higher fines than females, but there were no significant differences between racial/ethnic groups in fine amounts, similar to findings from previous research (Feeley, 1979; Munoz & Martinez, 2001; Nelson, 1994). Findings from research on felony sentencing decisions reveal that younger felony offenders receive harsher sentences than older felony offenders (Steffensmeier, Ulmer, & Kramer, 1998), but findings from Munoz and Freng (2007) suggest young adults (25–29) and adults (30–91) receive higher fines than younger misdemeanor offenders (11–24), and that overall, older white males receive the highest fines for misdemeanor offenses.

Race and Misdemeanor Pretrial Detention

Kim, Chauhan, Lu, Patten, and Smith (2018) examined patterns and predictors of both felony and misdemeanor pretrial readmissions over a ten-year period in New York City. For misdemeanors, non-Hispanic blacks had significantly higher pretrial readmission counts than both non-Hispanic whites and Hispanics, but there was no significant difference between non-Hispanic whites and Hispanics. For felonies, non-Hispanic blacks and Hispanics had higher pretrial readmission counts than non-Hispanic whites, but there was only a marginal difference between non-Hispanic whites and Hispanics. Males had higher readmission counts relative to females for both misdemeanors and felonies. Also, the youngest age group (16–20) had the highest readmission counts compared to all other age groups; however, the 31–35-year-old age group had the second highest readmission counts. For both felony and misdemeanor pretrial readmissions, there was a non-linear relationship with age.

Kim and colleagues (2018) explain that the racial differences in pretrial readmissions could be the result of socioeconomic status. One's socioeconomic status, which is often related to race and ethnicity, is a predictor of whether one can pay bail at arraignment and avoid pretrial detention. Further, both non-Hispanic blacks and Hispanics are more likely to live in poverty in New York City than are non-Hispanic whites. These differences may explain disparities between whites and blacks, but it does not explain the lack of differences between whites and Hispanics. Research argues that Hispanics function fairly well, given their SES, possibly due to stronger social networks (Burchfield & Silver, 2013; Martinez, 2002; Nielson, Lee, & Martinez, 2005; Sampson, 2008; Sampson, Morenoff, & Raudenbush, 2005). This "Latino Paradox" may account for differences in pretrial readmissions (Kim et al., 2018).

Race and Misdemeanor Case Prioritization

The use of prosecutorial discretion and its impact on criminal justice outcomes is understudied by criminal justice researchers, especially in comparison to the multitude of studies focused on sentencing (Baumer, 2013; Bushway & Forst, 2013; Kutateladze, Andiloro, & Johnson, 2016; Shermer & Johnson, 2010; Ulmer, 2012). This is surprising, given that sentencing guidelines that place constraints on judicial decisions have in many ways shifted the power of discretion to prosecutors (Kutateladze et al., 2016; Tonry, 1996; Wilmot & Spohn, 2004). If prosecutorial discretion represents the "black box" of research on courts and sentencing (Shermer & Johnson, 2010, p. 395), then research on prosecutorial discretion for misdemeanors remains elusive within it. This section will highlight research that examines the impact of race on prosecutorial decision-making at various stages for misdemeanor cases.

One way that prosecutors can use discretion in misdemeanor court processing is through their ability to prioritize cases and grant continuances. Using misdemeanor cases from a large county court in a southeastern state, Leiber and Blowers (2003) examined the interaction of race, case seriousness, and other legal factors on misdemeanor decision-making. They found that African Americans were more likely than whites to have their case classified as priority status. Also, African Americans were less likely than whites to be granted a continuance. Although Leiber and Blowers (2003) did not find evidence of a direct effect of race on conviction and incarceration, they found that race indirectly affects these outcomes because blacks are more likely to have their cases classified as priority and are less likely to be granted continuances than are whites. These two factors increase the chances of being convicted and incarcerated.

This research is important because it suggests that the impact of race is more influential in more serious misdemeanor cases than non-serious misdemeanor cases. This is contrary to findings from research on felony court decisions, where race is more influential in non-serious cases than serious cases, where legal factors are better predictors of outcomes (Crawford et al., 1998). This is also important because it indicates that the process of prioritizing cases by prosecutors can produce a biased result in misdemeanor court outcomes.

Race and Misdemeanor Plea-Bargaining

Another way that prosecutors can use discretion, and whereby race can impact decision-making, is in the misdemeanor plea process. Using a sample of misdemeanor marijuana cases from New York City, Kutateladze and colleagues (2016) examined the impact of race/ethnicity on plea bargaining outcomes. Even after accounting for legally relevant factors, racial and ethnic disparities in outcomes remained. Black defendants were significantly more likely to receive plea offers to the current charge (no charge reduction) than were white defendants. Also, black defendants were more likely to receive plea offers that involved jail time than were white defendants. Latinos were also more likely than white defendants to receive plea offers to the current charge and offers that involved spending time in jail. Asian defendants had the most favorable plea offers. These racial disparities in charge offers were greatly reduced when controlling for demographics and legal factors; however, the impact of race and ethnicity remained for pleas involving jail time. Black defendants were more than twice as likely as white defendants to be offered pleas that involved spending time in jail.

In addition, Kutateladze and colleagues (2016) found prior arrest history to be strongly related to race and plea-bargaining outcomes. When prior arrest history was removed from the model, racial and ethnic disparities were exacerbated. This is important because misdemeanor charging guidelines in New York are based on prior arrests, not necessarily prior convictions.

Berdejo (2018) examined racial disparities in the plea-bargaining process using misdemeanor and felony data from Wisconsin Circuit Courts. When controlling for age, gender, type and severity of crime, concurrent convictions, and criminal history, black defendants were more likely to be incarcerated for misdemeanor offenses and to receive longer sentences than white defendants. In misdemeanor cases, white defendants were 45% more likely to see their top charge reduced or dropped in comparison to black defendants. Upon examination of misdemeanor charges that carry the potential for incarceration, white defendants were 75% more likely to have those charges dropped or changed to a lesser charge than were black defendants. White defendants with no criminal history are more likely than black defendants with no criminal history to have their top charge dropped or reduced, and white defendants with no criminal history are 46% more likely than similarly situated black defendants to have charges with potential jail sentences dropped or amended to those carrying no potential for incarceration. Such racial differences in misdemeanor cases are substantially lower when defendants have at least one prior conviction. The Berdejo (2018) research highlights that race may serve as a proxy for potential to commit future crimes and overall dangerousness when no criminal histories are present. Berdejo (2018) suggests the need for greater transparency at the pre-sentencing stages to allow scrutiny of potential prosecutorial biases.

Even with the limited research addressing race and misdemeanor courts, the research highlighted earlier suggests that defendant race can negatively impact misdemeanor court outcomes, particularly for African Americans. Black misdemeanor defendants are less likely to have their charges reduced (Berdejo, 2018) or to be granted continuances (Leiber & Blowers, 2003), and they are more likely to have their cases classified as priority (Leiber & Blowers, 2003) and to be offered plea deals involving jail time (Kutateladze et al., 2016). Black misdemeanor defendants have higher pretrial detention readmissions than do whites and Hispanics (Kim et al., 2018), and older, black males are more likely to receive a fine in conjunction with some of other sanction than are their counterparts (Munoz & Freng, 2007). Also, black misdemeanor defendants receive longer jail sentences than do whites (Berdejo, 2018). Black and Hispanic female misdemeanor offenders are not spared the disparity, being more likely than white females to receive a jail sentence due to factors such as SES, pretrial detention, and criminal histories (Brennan, 2006).

The aforementioned studies suggest that black defendants face disadvantages at every stage of misdemeanor court processing, but it is important to consider discretionary decisions made by criminal justice actors prior to this stage (Kutateladze, Andiloro, Johnson, & Spohn, 2014; Wooldredge, Frank, Goulette, & Travis, 2015). Prior records and pretrial detention, which decrease the odds of charge reduction, are influenced by discretionary decisions of police officers and judges; therefore, less favorable outcomes and plea deals offered to black defendants could be due in part to decisions made earlier in the process (Metcalfe & Chiricos, 2018). If these decisions are based on negative stereotypes and biases, then black defendants may experience "cumulative disadvantage" (Kutateladze et al., 2014; Metcalfe & Chiricos, 2018; Wooldredge et al., 2015).

Theoretical Explanations for Racial Disparities in Misdemeanor Court Outcomes

Due to the relative inattention afforded to the study of misdemeanor justice, generally, explanations for disparate court outcomes are few and insufficient. Several theoretical explanations on racial disparities in court outcomes have been offered, but most serve to explain decisions surrounding more serious offenses. In addition, many of these were developed in order to explain racial disparities in sentencing, and they have since been applied to the plea process (Kutateladze et al., 2014, 2016). One theoretical explanation for why racial differences exist in the plea process revolves around uncertainty avoidance. Albonetti (1990) suggests that black defendants may be less likely to take a plea deal because they distrust a system in which deals are struck behind closed doors. They may be more likely to trust a jury of their peers to determine their guilt or innocence (Frenzel & Ball, 2008). Uncertainty avoidance may also influence prosecutorial decisions when they have little information on which to draw. Prosecutors may rely on implicit bias and stereotypes that label minorities as more dangerous and worthy of punishment (Banaji & Greenwald, 2013; Bridges & Steen, 1998; Kutateladze et al., 2016; Smith & Levinson, 2011; Staats, 2013).

Steffenmeiser and colleagues (1998) describe offender blameworthiness, protection of the community, and practical constraints and consequences as focal concerns of judges when making judicial decisions. Prosecutors may make decisions based on focal concerns that are similar to those of judges (Kutateladze et al., 2014; Spohn, Beichner, & Davis-Frenzel, 2001), but they are also concerned with the likelihood of conviction and the political fallout stemming from charging decisions (Shermer & Johnson, 2010). Shermer and Johnson (2010) argue that prosecutors face less political risk when they reduce charges for offenders who are older, female, and white as compared to those who are young, male, and racial minority.

Findings from several studies suggest that race and sex interact to influence criminal justice outcomes (Brennan & Stohn, 2009; Doerner & Demuth, 2010; Spohn & Beicher, 2000; Steffenmeier & Demuth, 2006). Judges' focal concern about protecting the community from dangerous offenders may only disadvantage minority males and have less of an impact on females (Steffenmeiser & Demuth, 2006). In addition, judges and prosecutors may view females, particularly those with dependent children, as less dangerous, and these stereotypes may explain why minority females are not punished as severely as minority males (Spohn & Beicher, 2000). While scholars can certainly draw inspiration from theoretical explanations discussed here and elsewhere, new theories will be necessary as research on the misdemeanor justice system advances.

Misdemeanors and Invisible Punishments

Most people who are processed through the criminal justice system are there because of interrelated social ills, such as addiction, homelessness, unemployment, and mental illness (Smyth, 2003).

Unfortunately, arrest and conviction only serve to exacerbate the problems that lead to illegal behavior (Travis, 2002). Having to appear in court can cause missed work, which could lead to the loss of jobs (Boruchowitz, Brink, & Dimino, 2009; Smyth, 2003). Misdemeanor arrests and convictions may impact eligibility for student loans and public housing (Boruchowitz et al., 2009; Pinard, 2010; Smyth, 2005). Those convicted of misdemeanors may lose their drivers' licenses and may be unable to apply for particular professional licenses (Boruchowitz et al., 2009; Natapoff, 2015; Smyth, 2015). Misdemeanor convictions may also come with fines and court fees that impact not only the defendant but his or her family (Boruchowitz et al., 2009), and misdemeanor convictions may even lead to deportation (Cade, 2013; Smyth, 2005). Such convictions may also increase the penalties associated with future offending and reduce the likelihood that sentence reductions occur (Boruchowitz et al., 2009). In these ways, minor offenses can have major impacts.

By criminalizing petty social ills, particularly in poor and minority communities, the criminal justice system has created a class of criminals that suffer disproportionately for their behaviors (Thatcher, 2004). And because race and class bias impact nearly every decision-making stage, from arrest, charging decisions, bail, plea offers, and sentencing, minor criminal infractions can have devastating impacts on people, families, and communities of color (Smyth, 2005).

The Future Intersection of Policy, Research, and Race

One potential avenue to reduce the negative impact of misdemeanors is decriminalization. The process of decriminalization serves to reduce the penalties associated with minor offenses, either by reclassifying misdemeanors as civil offenses (imposing fines without creating criminal records) or by eliminating the possibility of jailtime as punishments (Natapoff, 2015). In either scenario, the behavior is still prohibited. According to Natapoff (2015), decriminalization can occur through legislatures or through institutions, and in practice, there are wide-ranging variations. Police can essentially decriminalize certain offenses by issuing citations or summons instead of arresting offenders. Prosecutors can use discretion in choosing not to prosecute at all or they can charge offenders with infractions instead of traditional misdemeanors. Judges can decriminalize offenses by offering alternative forms of sanctions and supervision offered outside of the criminal justice system.

Generally speaking, decriminalization of minor offenses can be beneficial for defendants (by reducing criminal records and incarceration), the state (by reducing expenditures), and the criminal justice system overall (by restoring relationships with minority communities and reducing racial disparity in misdemeanor enforcement) (Butler, 2013; Natapoff, 2015). However, Natapoff (2015) argues that decriminalization could lead to an increasingly racialized criminal justice system. Offenders who are poor and minority may be less able to pay fines and attend programs that are characteristic of a decriminalized system of misdemeanor enforcement. This may explain why minority and poor offenders have little success in drug courts (Bowers, 2008; Natapoff, 2015; O'Hear, 2009). Nonpayment of fines may lead not only to incarceration, but harming credit which reduces the ability to rent an apartment, buy a car, or get a job (Bannon, Nagrecha, & Diller, 2010; Natapoff, 2015). Essentially, a decriminalized system tends to capture poor, minority, and otherwise disadvantaged offenders while allowing white and wealthy offenders to escape relatively unscathed (Natapoff, 2015). Even with its problems, decriminalization has many potential benefits. Having a separate civil administrative system that removes low level violators completely from the realm of criminal justice and diverts them into manageable programs could be beneficial to the violators and the overall criminal justice system (Natapoff, 2015).

Invisible punishments associated with misdemeanor arrests and/or convictions can have disparate impacts on poor and minority offenders. One solution is for defense lawyers to take a holistic or community approach and see their clients as people with complex needs, not just cases with legal issues (Smyth, 2005). By educating prosecutors and judges about the impact of hidden consequences for their clients and their families, defense attorneys have been successful at leveraging that information to obtain more favorable plea bargains and even dismissals (Smyth, 2005). Defendants should be informed by counsel about the devastating impacts of invisible punishments so that they can make informed decisions about plea offers (Chin & Holmes, 2002). This knowledge may lead them to reconsider pleading guilty to misdemeanors, traffic violations, and even non-criminal offenses (Smyth, 2005).

Another suggestion to reduce the racially disparate outcomes associated with court processing is to make post-sentence penalties proportionate and closely related to the particular offense, instead of having a range of penalties applied to all classes of offenders (Pinard, 2010). "Ban the box" initiatives remove the requirement for disclosing a criminal record to potential employers. This allows candidates to move through the hiring process based on qualifications for the job, not prior criminal history. A criminal record should only be relevant if it exposes some level of risk that the applicant could not properly perform the job requirements (Henry & Jacobs, 2007).

Other potential avenues for improving racially disparate outcomes in misdemeanor courts would be to remove the procedure of case prioritization by prosecutors, which negatively impacts black defendants more than white defendants, or create a more structured decision-making process employing race and class neutral criteria (Justice Policy Institute, 2002; Leiber & Blowers, 2003). Also, judges and prosecutors could undergo training to make them more aware of bias involved in court processing decision-making (Leiber & Blowers, 2003). Given that pretrial detention has negative impacts on future charging, detention, and sentencing decisions, misdemeanor justice systems should consider ways to avoid detaining misdemeanor offenders prior to trial and conviction (Chauhan & Travis, 2018; Kim et al., 2018). Kutateladze and colleagues (2016) suggest that revising sentencing guidelines to consider prior convictions instead of prior arrests could significantly reduce any racial and ethnic disparities in misdemeanor plea bargaining outcomes.

Collecting and maintaining data related to misdemeanor charging and sentencing decisions is essential if courts and external groups are to properly scrutinize prosecutorial and judicial discretion to identify racially disparate outcomes (Berdejo, 2018). Such commitment to transparency and accountability can help legitimize a misdemeanor system wrought with opportunities for biased decision-making (Berdejo, 2018; Kutateladze et al., 2014).

Conclusion

The United States is currently in an era of intense scrutiny for disparate criminal justice outcomes for people of color. As this chapter makes apparent, court processing of lower level offenses is also deserving of such focus, even though it has largely been ignored in comparison to the number of studies examining racially disparate outcomes for more serious offenses. Considering just how little we really know about misdemeanor justice in this country, scholarship could benefit from researcher and criminal justice practitioner partnerships dedicated to the study of misdemeanor justice outcomes. A promising example of such collaboration is the Research Network on Misdemeanor Justice, with research partners at John Jay College of Criminal Justice, North Carolina Central University, Seattle University, University of California-Los Angeles, University of Louisville, University of Maryland, University of Missouri-St. Louis, and Mississippi State University. Members of the Network are working with criminal justice practitioners to examine trends in misdemeanor justice in their particular jurisdictions. By working with cross-site partners, analyzing existing data, and working with criminal justice practitioners to improve their data-building capacity, researchers can shed light on the current state of misdemeanor justice, including racially disparate outcomes, and inform policies to address all too often overlooked misdemeanor justice issues.

References

Albonetti, C. A. (1990). Race and the probability of pleading guilty. *Journal of Quantitative Criminology, 6*(3), 315–334.

Banaji, M. R., & Greenwald, A. G. (2013). *Blindspot: Hidden biases of good people.* New York, NY: Delacorte Press.

Bannon, A., Nagrecha, M., & Diller, R. (2010). *Criminal justice debt: A barrier to reentry.* New York University Law School: Brennan Center for Justice. Retrieved from www.brennancenter.org/sites/default/files/legacy/Fees%20and%20Fines%20FINAL.pdf

Baumer, E. P. (2013). Reassessing and redirecting research on race and sentencing. *Justice Quarterly, 30*, 231–261.

Berdejo, C. (2018). Criminalizing race: Racial disparities in Plea-Bargaining. *Boston College Law Review, 59*, 1187–1249.

Boruchowitz, R. C. Brink, M. N., & Dimino, M. (2009). *Minor crimes, massive waste: The terrible toll of America's broken misdemeanor courts.* Washington, DC: National Association of Criminal Defense Lawyers. Retrieved from www.nacdl.org/reports/misdemeanor/

Bowers, J. (2008). Contraindicated drug courts. *UCLA Law Review, 55*, 783–835.

Brennan, P. K. (2006). Sentencing female misdemeanants: An examination of the direct and indirect effects of race/ethnicity. *Justice Quarterly, 23*(1), 60–95.

Brennan, P. K., & Spohn, C. (2009). The joint effects of offender race/ethnicity and sex on sentence length decisions in federal courts. *Race and Social Problems, 1*, 200–217.

Bridges, G. S., & Steen, S. (1998). Racial disparities in official assessments of juvenile offenders: Attributional stereotypes as mediating mechanisms. *American Sociological Review, 63*(4), 554–570.

Burchfield, K. B., & Silver, E. (2013). Collective efficacy and crime in Los Angeles neighborhoods: Implications for the Latino paradox. *Sociological Inquiry, 83*(1), 154–176.

Bushway, S. D., & Forst, B. (2013). Studying discretion in the processes that generate criminal justice sanctions. *Justice Quarterly, 30*(2), 199–222.

Butler, P. (2013). Poor people lose: Gideon and the critique of rights. *Yale Law Journal, 122*, 2176–2204.

Cade, J. A. (2013). The plea bargain crisis for noncitizens in misdemeanor court. *Cardozo Law Review, 34*, 1751–1891.

Chauhan, P., & Travis, J. (2018). Introduction to special issue: Misdemeanor justice project-a focus on criminal justice system responses to lower level offenses. *Criminal Justice Policy Review, 29*(6–7), 527–535.

Chin, G. J., & Holmes, R. W. (2002). Effective assistance of counsel and the consequences of guilty pleas. *Cornell Law Review, 87*(3), 697–742.

Crawford, C., Chiricos, T., & Kleck, G. (1998). Race, racial threat, and sentencing of habitual offenders. *Criminology, 36*(3), 481–511.

Dixon, J. (1995). The organizational context of criminal sentencing. *American Journal of Sociology, 100*(5), 1157–1198.

Doerner, J. K., & Demuth, S. (2010). The independent and joint effects of race/ethnicity, gender, and age on sentencing outcomes in U.S. federal courts. *Justice Quarterly, 27*(1), 1–27.

Feeley, M. (1979). *The process is punishment: Handling cases in a lower criminal court.* New York: Russell Sage Foundation.

Frenzel, E. D., & Ball, J. D. (2008). Effects of individual characteristics of plea negotiations under sentencing guidelines. *Journal of Ethnicity in Criminal Justice, 5*(4), 59–82.

Gottfredson, M., & Gottfredson, D. (1988). *Decision making in criminal justice: Toward the rational exercise of discretion.* Cambridge, MA: Ballinger.

Hagan, J. (1974). Extra-legal attributes and criminal sentencing: An assessment of a sociological viewpoint. *Law and Society Review, 8*, 357–384.

Henry, J. S., & Jacobs, J. B. (2007). Ban the box to promote ex-offender employment. *Criminology & Public Policy, 6*(4), 755–761.

Holleran, D., & Spohn, C. (2004). On the use of total incarceration variable in sentencing research. *Criminology, 42*(1), 211–240.

Johnson, B. (2003). Racial and ethnic disparities in sentencing departures across modes of conviction. *Criminology, 41*(2), 449–489.

Justice Policy Institute. (2002). *Reducing disproportionate minority confinement: The Multnomah County, Oregon success story and its implications.* Washington, DC: The Justice Policy Institute.

Kim, J., Chauhan, P., Lu, O., Patten, M., & Smith, S. (2018). Unpacking pretrial detention: An examination of patterns and predictors of readmissions. *Criminal Justice Policy Review, 29*, 663–687.

Kleck, G. (1981). Racial discrimination in criminal sentencing: A critical examination of the evidence with additional evidence on the death penalty. *American Sociological Review, 46*, 783–805.

Kramer, J., & Steffensmeier, D. (1993). Race and imprisonment decisions. *Sociological Quarterly, 34*, 357–376.

Kutateladze, B. L., Andiloro, N. R., & Johnson, B. (2016). Opening pandora's box: How does defendant race influence plea bargaining. *Justice Quarterly, 33*(3), 398–426.

Kutateladze, B. L., Andiloro, N. R., Johnson, B., & Spohn, C. (2014). Cumulative disadvantage: Examining racial and ethnic disparity in prosecution and sentencing. *Criminology, 52*, 514–551.

Leiber, M. J., & Blowers, A. (2003). Race and misdemeanor sentencing. *Criminal Justice Policy Review, 14*(4), 464–485.

Lubitz, R. L., & Ross, T. W. (2001). *Sentencing guidelines: Reflections on the future. Sentencing and Corrections Issues for the 21st Century Research Brief No. 10.* Washington, DC: U.S. Department of Justice, Office of Justice Programs, National Institute of Justice.

Martinez, R. (2002). *Latino homicide: Immigration violence and community.* New York, NY: Routledge.

Metcalfe, C., & Chiricos, T. (2018). Race, plea, and charge reduction: An assessment of racial disparities in the plea process. *Justice Quarterly, 35*(2), 223–253.

Munoz, E. A., & Freng, A. (2007). Age, racial/ethnic minority status, gender, and misdemeanor sentencing. *Journal of Ethnicity in Criminal Justice, 5*(4), 29–57.

Munoz, E. A., & Martinez, M. R. (2001). Latinas and criminal sentencing: An exploratory analysis. *Voices: A Journal of Chicana/Latina Studies, 3*(1–2), 150–176.

Munoz, E. A., & Sapp, S. G. (2003). Racial/Ethnic misdemeanor sentencing disparities: Additional evidence for contextual discrimination. *Journal of Ethnicity in Criminal Justice, 1*(2), 27–46.Natapoff, A. (2015). Misdemeanor decriminalization. *Vanderbilt Law Review, 68*(4), 1055–1116.

Nelson, J. F. (1994). A dollar a day: Sentencing misdemeanants in New York State. *Journal of Research in Crime and Delinquency, 31*(2), 183–201.

Nielson, A. L., Lee, M. T., & Martinez, R. (2005). Integrating race, place, and motive in social disorganization theory: Lessons from a comparison of black and Latino homicide types in two immigrant destination cities. *Criminology, 43*, 837–872.

O'Hear, M. M. (2009). Rethinking drug courts: restorative justice as a response to racial injustice. *Stanford Law and Policy Review, 20*(2), 463–500.

Pinard, M. (2010). Collateral consequences of criminal convictions: Confronting issues of race and dignity. *New York University Law Review, 85*, 457–534.

Sampson, R. J. (2008). Rethinking crime and immigration. *Contexts,* 7(1), 28–33.

Sampson, R. J., Morenoff, J. D., & Raudenbush, S. (2005). Social anatomy of racial and ethnic disparities in violence. *American Journal of Public Health, 95*, 224–232.

Shermer, L. O., & Johnson, B. D. (2010). Criminal prosecutions: Examining prosecutorial discretion and charge reductions in U.S. Federal District Courts. *Justice Quarterly, 27*, 394–430.

Smith, R. J., & Levinson, J. D. (2011). The impact of implicit racial bias on the exercise of prosecutorial discretion. *Seattle University Law Review, 35*, 795–826.

Smyth, M. (2003). *Bridging the gap: A practical guide to civil-defender collaboration. Clearinghouse Review, 37*(1–2), 56–63. Retrieved from http://povertylaw.org/files/docs/article/chr_2003_may_june_smyth.pdf

Smyth, M. (2005). Holistic is not a bad word: A criminal defense attorney's guide to using invisible punishments as an advocacy strategy. *University of Toledo Law Review, 36*, 479–504.

Smyth, M. (2015). *The consequences of criminal proceedings in New York State: A guide for criminal defense attorneys, civil legal services attorneys, and other reentry advocates.* Retrieved from www.reentry.net/ny/library/item.76898Consequences_of_Criminal_Proceedings_in_New_York_State_August_2014_The_Bron

Spohn, C. (2000). Thirty years of sentencing reform: The quest for a racially neutral sentencing process. In J. Horney (Ed.), *Policies, processes, and decisions of the criminal justice system, Criminal Justice 2000, Vol. 3* (pp. 427–501). Washington, DC: National Institute of Justice.

Spohn, C., & Beichner, D. (2000). Is preferential treatment of female offenders a thing of the past? A multisite study of gender, race, and imprisonment. *Criminal Justice Policy Review, 11*, 149–184.

Spohn, C., Beichner, D., & Davis-Frenzel, E. (2001). Prosecutorial justifications for sexual assault case rejection: Guarding the "Gateway to Justice." *Social Problems, 48*, 206–235.

Spohn, C., & DeLone, M. (2000). When does race matter? An analysis of the conditions under which race affects sentence severity. *Sociology of Crime, Law, and Deviance, 2*, 3–37.

Staats, C. (2013). Implicit bias review 2013. Kirwan Institute for the Study of Race and Ethnicity. Retrieved November 1, 2018, from the Kirwan Institute website: http://kirwaninstitute.osu.edu/docs/SOTS-Implicit_Bias.pdf

Steffensmeier, D., & Demuth, S. (2006). Does gender modify the effects of race-ethnicity on criminal sanctioning? Sentences for male and female, white, black, and Hispanic defendants. *Journal of Quantitative Criminology, 22*, 241–261.

Steffensmeier, D., Ulmer, J., & Kramer, J. (1998). The interaction of race, gender, and age in criminal sentencing: The punishment cost of being young, black, and male. *Criminology, 36*(4), 763–798.

Stevenson, M., & Mayson, S. (2018). The scale of misdemeanor justice. *Boston University Law Review, 98*, 731–777.

Thatcher, D. (2004). Order maintenance reconsidered: Moving beyond strong causal reasoning. *Journal of Criminal Law and Criminology, 94*(2), 381–414.

Tonry, M. (1996). *Sentencing matters*. New York, NY: Oxford University Press.

Travis, J. (2002). Invisible punishment: An instrument of social exclusion. In M. Mauer & M. Chesney-Lind (Eds.), *Invisible punishment: The collateral consequences of mass Imprisonment* (pp. 15–36). New York, NY: The New Press.

Ulmer, J. T. (2012). Recent developments and new directions in sentencing research. *Justice Quarterly, 29*(1), 1–40.

Ulmer, J. T., & Johnson, B. (2004). Sentencing in context: A multilevel analysis. *Criminology, 42*(1), 137–177.

Wilbanks, W. (1987). *The myth of a racist criminal justice system*. Monterey: Brooks/Cole.

Wilmot, K. A., & Spohn, C. (2004). Prosecutorial discretion and real-offense sentencing: An analysis of relevant conduct under the federal sentencing guidelines. *Criminal Justice Policy Review, 15*, 324–343.

Wooldredge, J., Frank, J., Goulette, N., & Travis, L. (2015). Is the impact of cumulative disadvantage on sentencing greater for black defendants? *Criminology and Public Policy, 14*, 187–223.

Zatz, M. S. (1987). The changing forms of racial/ethnic biases in sentencing. *Journal of Research in Crime and Delinquency, 24*(1), 69–92.

Zatz, M. S. (2000). The convergence of race, ethnicity, gender, and class on court decisionmaking: Looking toward the 21st century. In J. Horney (Ed.), *Policies, processes, and decisions of the criminal justice system, Criminal Justice 2000, Vol. 3* (pp. 427–501). Washington, DC: National Institute of Justice.

9

THE FINANCIAL CONSEQUENCES OF MISDEMEANORS

Sean Maddan and Sierra Bell

> There can be no equal justice where the kind of trial a man gets depends on the amount of money he has.
>
> —*Griffin v. Illinois*, 351 U.S. 12 (1956)

Traditionally, misdemeanors have been viewed by both criminologists and the public as less important than felonies due to their classification as petty crimes. As such, most academic work on the courts has focused on "serious" crimes and felony court outcomes, especially relating to determining guilt and imposing sentences. While the most serious crimes and the most serious sanctions deserve emphasis, misdemeanor crimes compose the overwhelming majority of cases processed through the criminal justice system, and the imposed sanctions are not inconsequential (Natapoff, 2015). The failure of academics to fully explore the misdemeanor courts is a failure to examine sanctions that have great impact on many offenders.

Being convicted of a misdemeanor has profound consequences for defendants. For example, in March of 2016, Jeffrey Pendleton was arrested for misdemeanor possession of marijuana in Manchester, New Hampshire. Even though Pendleton had been homeless since 2013, he held a full-time job at the local Burger King and earned minimum wage. Pendleton's bail was $100, which may be meager to most, but not Pendleton. Unable to afford bail, he was forced to stay in jail. Four days after his arrest, Pendleton was found dead of a Fentanyl overdose. The Pendleton case is illustrative of the significant consequences of criminalizing poverty. He was incarcerated for a minor crime and because he was poor, he was unable to post bail to obtain release. As an ironic aside, Pendleton, with the help of the American Civil Liberties Union (ACLU), won a previous lawsuit against the town of Hudson for harassment from repeated panhandling arrests. His case settled for $37,000, but most of the proceeds were paid to his lawyers as fees and costs (Wing, 2016).

While only anecdotal, the Pendleton case is an example of a wider misdemeanor sanctioning problem. According to Natapoff (2015), many states have decreased the use of jailtime for minor offenses; instead, they focus on imposing "nonjail" or "fine-only" sanctions. A nonjail or fine-only punishment includes fines, restitution, and court costs. While these "lesser" sanctions diminish the burden on the misdemeanor offender, his or her family, and community, they can exacerbate short- and long-term financial strain on misdemeanor defendants.

In addition to fines and fees, convictions for misdemeanor offenses may result in loss of employment and housing, as well as liberty. Misdemeanor convictions may be used to increase future sentences or enhance petty crimes to felonies. For example, in the State of Florida, third offenses for driving under the influence, driving on a suspended license, and petty theft may be charged as felonies. This chapter explores the financial sanctions and obligations associated with misdemeanor crimes, particularly focusing on their direct impact and potential hidden or indirect costs.[1]

Forms of Financial Punishments in Misdemeanor Courts

Court processing of misdemeanor cases often takes less than five minutes, and in those minutes, defendants' lives are changed (Smith & Maddan, 2011). Even though misdemeanors are not as serious as felonies, the potential sanctions for these offenses are wide ranging. After determining guilt (through trial or plea), judges may sentence misdemeanor defendants to terms of incarceration in jail, probation, or a combination of sanctions. While a jail sentence has direct impact on defendants, it also results in indirect costs to defendants' financial well-being, including the loss of employment, housing, and the support of friends and families. Imposed fines, court costs, and restitution, likewise, have an immediate, direct impact on the defendants' economic lives, as well as indirect effects. Defendants who cannot afford to pay fines, restitution, and court costs become indebted, which has consequences for defendants' ability to work and pay their bills. For misdemeanor and traffic offending, financial obligations or sanctions are the primary form of punishment (Greenberg, Meredith, & Morse, 2016). These sanctions are explored in the next sections along with their direct and indirect financial impact as well as the effect of community service on defendants, which may be imposed as an alternative to the financial sanctions.

Fines

Fines are one of the oldest sentencing options; English kings found that fines could provide considerable revenue for the government (Steury & Frank, 1996). Today, over a billion dollars is collected in fines each and every year in the United States (Steury & Frank, 1996) and fines are the most prevalent form of punishment imposed by the criminal justice system (Tonry, 1998).

Fines are monetary charges imposed on defendants who are convicted of crimes. Fines are generally paid to the government. As such, fines are the epitome of paying ones' debt to society. Statutory law specifies the maximum number of fines for particular offenses. But, judges hold much discretion and may impose fines from zero to the maximum amount indicated by law. In a survey of financial obligations, Steury and Frank (1996) found that judges tend to "set informal fine amounts," and those amounts are generally small and affordable. Fines-only sanctions are typically imposed in cases involving defendants charged with relatively minor crimes, or those without lengthy records. These include petty and traffic offenses. "Monetary assessments are typically given to low-risk offenders, and the amount of this financial sanction tends to increase with the severity of the crime" (Latessa & Allen, 2003, p. 344). In less serious cases, like misdemeanor offenses, fines are primarily imposed as an alternative to incarceration and probation (Colgan, 2018).

Fines can serve as a deterrent (Sharma, 2016) because they are considered "unambiguously punitive" (McDonald, Greene, & Worzella, 1992, p. 1). In fact, fines are considered more of a deterrent than restitution and court costs because they are normally higher, and often they are used in conjunction with incarceration or probation (McDonald et al., 1992). Additionally, fines may serve as a financial boon to local and state governments. Even if not the intended purpose, fines help to fund state or court systems. As such, fines serve more than a single purpose. They serve as a deterrent and as a way to increase state revenue.

Fines have evolved over the years. Day-fines, a variation on the traditional type of fine that was first promulgated in Sweden in the 1920s, are structured around a defendant's daily income, rather than standardized, statutory scales. As such, day-fines are perceived as proportional and more fair than standardized fine schedules. Since the 1920s, many European countries have adopted this type of financial sanction (McDonald et al., 1992).

Steury and Frank (1996) argued that U.S. courts should adopt the day-fine approach to increase the successful collection of fine monies, which would result in greater revenue for the state and courts than with traditional fine systems. Although Siegel, Schmalleger, and Worrall (2015) asserted that day fines would operate as successful, diversionary strategies, increase the amount of financial payments to the states, result in fewer technical violations and re-arrests than traditional sanctions, they concluded that the day-fine system would be too difficult to implement in the United States because assigning a dollar value based on income would be cumbersome, and it would still leave some offenders unable to pay their fines.

There are, however, inherent, equity problems with fines as a sanction. Steury and Frank (1996) concluded that because fines are consistently low, more affluent defendants are punished less by paying lower fines than they could or should pay.

> If the amount of the fine is commensurate with the seriousness of the offense, with no consideration given to the ability of the offender to pay the fine, then fines will be relatively more burdensome to the poor than to the rich.
>
> *(Hemmens, Brody, & Spohn, 2013, p. 379)*

More affluent defendants may be treated differently in other respects as well. Steury and Frank (1996) indicated that white-collar criminals are likely to receive financial sanctions by administrative rather than criminal laws. Examples of these fines include those imposed for serious securities violations or environmental crimes. In addition to affluent defendants bypassing punishment through the payment of fines, judges are less likely to impose fines in cases involving more serious misdemeanors and felonies because they do not regard fines as a "meaningful alternative to incarceration or probation" (Morris & Tonry, 1990, p. 127).

Despite these inherent problems, fines are widely accepted and implemented in the misdemeanor courts with some success. In fact, Latessa and Allen (2003) indicate that the odds of recidivism are "substantially less" for offenders who receive financial sanctions as opposed to those who receive incarceration sentences. As indicated, the use of proportional day-fines has been shown to have some utility in producing a more equitable administration of justice.

Court Costs

Court costs, also called court fees, are another monetary sanction that are generally imposed to reimburse state or local jurisdictions for the costs associated with processing defendants. Additional court costs or fees that do not relate to offenders' crimes, but are added for the purpose of funding state or local governments and programs are typically called surcharges (Ruback, 2011).

Court costs are also referred to as user fees to represent the intention for defendants, who use the courts, to reimburse the system for its use. Court costs may be imposed at pre-conviction, sentencing, or for supervision (Sobol, 2016). Additional fees may be imposed throughout the criminal justice process, and contrary to popular understanding, court fees are imposed to compensate defense attorneys, prosecutors, prison officials, criminal justice agencies, private companies, or police officers (Sobol, 2016). In many jurisdictions, defendants may have to pay a pre-conviction affidavit or application fee for use of court-appointed counsel (Smith, in press; Wright & Logan, 2006).

In addition to general court costs, defendants may be required to pay additional costs associated with monthly supervision, prosecution and investigatory fees and costs, public defender fees, including application and attorneys' fees, and occasionally other surcharges or expenses. This accumulation of costs and fees poses enormous burdens for defendants, who may be subject to subsequent punishment for failing to pay these costs, and some scholars have questioned the use of court costs and whether these fees serve a legitimate punitive function (Bannon, Nagrecha, & Diller, 2010).

Restitution

Prior to 1982, few state agencies or organizations provided for victim compensation, restitution, and assistance (Goldschied, 2004). The courts, however, essentially ignored victims of crime (Kepple, 1989; Morgan, 1987). President Reagan called for society to address this oversight, appointed a task force to study the problem, and two congressional subcommittees undertook investigations, which brought to light the plight of victims (Kepple, 1989). Shortly thereafter, separate bills were proposed in the House and Senate, and the Victim and Witness Protection Act was passed (Kepple, 1989; 18 U.S.C. § 1512(a) (1982 & Supp. V 1987). "The VWPA ha[d] three major provisions" (Kepple, 1989, p. 89). Under this *federal* law, a pre-sentencing report to assess the "financial, social, psychological and medical impact of the crime upon the victim [is to] be filed with the trial judge" (Kepple, 1989, p. 89; Federal Rule of Criminal Procedure 32(c)(2)). Second, it broadened the definition of who was included as a victim and expanded witness protection beyond those involved in organized crime cases (Kepple, 1989; 18 U.S.C. § 1512(a) (1982 & Supp. V 1987). Third, and relevant here, the Act "authorize[d] restitution for crime victims, but [did] so only when its imposition [would] not unduly complicate or prolong the sentencing process" (Kepple, 1989, p. 90; 18 U.S.C. 3663 and 3663 (d) (Supp. V 1987). The intent of this statute was to ensure that offenders restored victims to their prior state to the extent possible (Kepple, 1989). Under a subsequent Act—the Mandatory Victim Restitution Act—restitution became mandatory in almost all federal cases by 1996 (Haynes, Cares, & Ruback, 2015). Since 1996, most states created statutory provisions that mandate or presumptively require restitution, but these provisions, coverage, and enforcement vary widely (Goldscheid, 2004; Haynes et al., 2015; Office for Victims of Crime, 1998).

Since many offenders do not have the funds to compensate victims, governments have created victim compensation funds. In the United States, California adopted the first victim compensation program in 1964 (Goldscheid, 2004). "Several states quickly followed, and today, all fifty states, the District of Columbia, and the Virgin Islands operate victim compensation programs" (Goldscheid, 2004, p. 182). Congressional adoption of the Victims of Crime Act of 1984 was a "major step toward institutionalizing support for the state programs" (Goldscheid, 2004, p. 183), and the Presidential Task Force of 1982 recommended legislation to fund and assist state crime victim compensation programs (Goldscheid, 2004). These programs provide millions of dollars to nearly 150,000 victims for "expenses related to medical, dental, and mental health expenses; lost wages and loss of support; funeral and burial expenses; crime scene clean up; forensic sexual assault exams; and other expenses" (Goldscheid, 2004, p. 188; see also Bohm & Haley, 2018; Latessa & Allen, 2003). Restitution also serves victims' emotional needs by "legitimizing, in an official manner, that what happened to the victim was wrong and should be rectified" (Haynes et al., 2015, p. 452; National Center for Victims and Crimes, 2011).

Restitution may benefit offenders as well. Supporters and some scholarly findings "claim[] that [restitution] promotes a sense of responsibility and accomplishment in [] offenders, thereby reducing the risk of recidivism" (Haynes et al., 2015, p. 453). Most statutory provisions, including the federal law, require that judges evaluate the financial status of offenders before determining the amount of restitution, the payment schedule, and deadline for satisfaction of the restitution debt (Dickman, 2009). Offenders who have the means to pay restitution, but do not, may be subject to their probation being revoked and even being sentenced to jail or prison (Steury & Frank, 1996).

Despite the wide-spread adoption of victim-restitution statutes, the implementation of and benefits from these provisions have not achieved their aspirational goals (Goldschied, 2004; Haynes, et al., 2015). There are many impediments to victims recovering restitution (Harland & Rosen, 1990). These impediments range from lack of knowledge of the availability of restitution or compensation programs, narrow definitions of recoverable losses, and difficulty in collecting and dispersing restitution (Harland & Rosen, 1990). Some scholarly research has found that victims are unaware of compensation because the courts primarily focus on prosecuting and punishing defendants (Haynes et al., 2015). Even when victims are aware, the strict eligibility requirements deprive many victims who need monetary assistance from getting the help that they need (Haynes et al., 2015). The restrictive eligibility requirements limit access to "innocent" victims—that is, those without a prior history of criminal offending, victims who support and cooperate with law enforcement and prosecutors, and victims who timely file applications for compensation (Goldschied, 2004).

Community Service

"Community service emerged as an alternative sanction in the United States in the 1960s" (Bouffard & Muftic, 2007, p. 171), and it was largely designed to provide an alternative punishment for misdemeanor or first-time offenders (Bouffard & Muftic, 2007). Community service may be imposed instead of or in addition to other penalties (Feeley, Berk, & Campbell, 1992) to "compensate[ ] the community as a whole by requiring the offender to perform service in the community" (Feeley et al., 1992; Steury & Frank, 1996, p. 395). Defendants work in community agencies (hospitals, cleaning up parks or highways, etc.) for a set number of hours established by the sentencing judge. Although community service as an alternative sanction has been implemented for more than 40 years, little research has been conducted to evaluate its effectiveness (Bouffard & Muftic, 2007). Most effectiveness studies have been published in Europe (Bouffard & Muftic, 2007).

One exceptional, but preliminary study in the United States examined the effectiveness of community service as an alternative punishment for misdemeanor offenders (Bouffard & Muftic, 2007). The primary focus of the research by Bouffard and Muftic (2007) was whether community-service sentences reduced recidivism compared to offenders who received a monetary, fine penalty. Bouffard and Muftic (2007) compared the outcomes of 810 adult offenders who were sentenced to community service against a comparison group of 222 adult offenders who were ordered to pay a monetary fine. Although there were weaknesses in the study's design, the preliminary findings demonstrated that even controlling for relevant factors, less serious offenders who participated and *completed* community service were either less likely or similarly likely to recidivate as compared to those who were fined (Bouffard & Muftic, 2007). Community service as an alternative to other forms of punishment may incorporate and serve a restorative justice approach and lead to more positive outcomes for defendants and society (Bazemore & Maloney, 1994). More research is necessary, however, to assess the effectiveness of community service.

Equity in Financial Sanctions

While much research has focused on equity in case processing, very little research has focused on the fairness of imposed financial sanctions. Overall, those who commit serious crimes get more serious punishments, but there are inequities in sentencing, with males, non-whites, and youth being punished more harshly. Likewise, the limited research on financial sanctions has focused predominantly on fines and, similar to sentencing, research found that males receive higher fines than females (Feeley, 1979; Munoz & Martinez, 2001; Nelson, 1994). Other researchers found that younger misdemeanor offenders (ages 11–24) were more likely to receive smaller fines than older misdemeanants, and older white males received the most substantial fines (Munoz & Freng, 2007). In terms of paying fines, Natapoff (2015) found that minority defendants, who may be less able, are less likely to pay fines.

Direct and Indirect Costs of Misdemeanor Convictions

The costs incurred from misdemeanor convictions are most burdensome for those who are poorer. These defendants will have difficulty in paying even the smallest of fines, fees, and restitution. The cost of misdemeanor financial obligations may be split into two categories: direct and indirect. Direct costs are those that impact defendants' finances and, generally, the impact is immediate. Indirect financial costs or consequences are those that defendants generally do not realize until later, and defendants are not advised of these indirect costs at the time of sentencing (Natapoff, 2015).

Direct Costs

In 1979, Feeley outlined the array of direct costs of misdemeanor convictions and financial sanctions. These include bail, attorney's fees, out-of-pocket costs, lost wages, and wasted time. Additionally, the financial sanctions of fines, fees, and restitution are direct costs. If bail is necessary, the defendant, or the defendant's family and friends may post money for bail or pay a bail bondsman a commission. In either instance, the money or collateral must be paid up front. While the money for bail is eventually returned, the money is not accessible to defendants until after their case is concluded. Financial sanctions may be paid in lump sum, or over time. If paid in installments, the defendant typically must pay a surcharge for the processing of those installment payments. These out-of-pocket expenses pose financial burdens on defendants.

Defendants who cannot afford bail, remain incarcerated until trial. Incarceration poses an obvious cost. Even if released, defendants who must attend multiple court proceedings lose wages and potentially their jobs (Kohler-Hausmann, 2018). Defendants, especially in pretrial detention, view the misdemeanor court process as punishment, including travel to court, child care, and other expenses (Feeley, 1979). These direct costs have the most immediate impact on misdemeanor defendants.

Indirect Costs

In addition to direct costs, defendants suffer other consequences for misdemeanor convictions, including added indirect expenses. Misdemeanor arrests and convictions can disqualify defendants from public housing, educational opportunities, professional licensing, and future employment (Natapoff, 2015). Arrests and convictions may impact defendants' credit, leaving them less likely to obtain necessary loans, or paying higher interest rates. Many offenders fall behind in their education due to attending court proceedings, or lose the opportunity to obtain financial support or eligibility for student loans to pursue their education. The consequences of not pursuing their education results in fewer opportunities and lower-wage, unstable jobs.

The Problems with Misdemeanor Financial Punishments

According to Ruback, Hoskins, Cares, and Feldmeyer (2006), misdemeanor financial sanctions are perceived to be "unfair to poor defendants, have no effect on wealthy defendants, and unenforceable because offenders cannot be imprisoned for nonpayment of debt" (p. 1). Impoverished individuals face harsher consequences than more affluent defendants. Poorer offenders are less able to afford the financial sanctions imposed by the courts. The financial sanctions often disparately impact racial and ethnic minorities, which results in the loss of the perceived legitimacy of the criminal justice system. Fairness and equal treatment, not the ability to pay, should be the primary focus of the criminal justice system, especially in misdemeanor courts.

While many categories of debt can be nullified by bankruptcy (e.g., income tax debt can be discharged under certain circumstances), the law prohibits fines, court costs, and restitution from being discharged through bankruptcy. Without any means to dispense with the debt, many defendants do not pay. In fact, the collection rate of financial sanctions is only 50% (Ruback et al., 2006). Ruback and colleagues (2006) surveyed 122 convicted defendants from two Pennsylvania counties who were ordered to pay financial sanctions and evaluated their perceptions of these sanctions. They found that offenders who did not pay their fines, fees, court costs, or restitution most often attributed nonpayment to their inability to afford the payments (Ruback et al., 2006). They also found, however, that defendants did not understand how the fines, fees, and costs were imposed, they did not agree with the reasons for the imposed economic sanctions, and they did not perceive the imposed economic sanctions as fair (Ruback et al., 2006).

Although a burden to defendants, courts are not making money on the imposed financial sanctions. In fact, the amount paid has been outweighed by the costs of collection efforts (Diller, 2010). Defendants who default on their debt may be confronted by several legal mechanisms to recoup the outstanding fines, court costs, and restitution (*Bearden v. Georgia*, 1983). In most states, the first step is to treat the nonpayment as contempt of court or probation violation. After the contempt order is issued or probation violation filed, the court may summon defendants to appear in court. At the hearing, judges must determine whether defendants' failure to pay was willful, in other words, whether defendants had the ability to pay, and did not. If the nonpayment is willful, several actions may be taken. First, and the most severe penalty, is that defendants may be incarcerated for willfully failing to pay their fees, fines, costs, and restitution. Although debtors' prisons were abolished, failing to comply with orders to make financial payments, which were originally implemented to keep offenders out of overcrowded jails or prisons, may result in incarceration (Natapoff, 2015). Another option is that judges revoke community supervision and resentence defendants, impose wage garnishment, or some other sanction. Defendants, who do not have the ability to pay the financial obligations (and therefore have not willfully failed to pay), may be ordered to perform community restitution or service, or, the court may modify the manner or amounts of fines, court costs, and restitution paid.

Conclusion

Recently, the imposition of fines, restitution, and court costs as alternative forms of punishment have become much more typical in the United States. Monetary sanctions are particularly imposed in misdemeanor cases because they are less serious, and the fines and court costs provide additional revenue to the government and courts and keep petty criminals from overcrowding jails.

The range of monetary sanctions, however, is broad and amounts to thousands of dollars (Bannon et al., 2010). These financial obligations are expected to increase due to the high cost of operating the criminal justice system, concern for victim needs, and pressure to alleviate prison and jail overcrowding (Ruback et al., 2006). Despite the perceived benefit of financial sanctions, this chapter has illustrated the problems that result from a financially punitive strategy. The current state of financial sanctions in the United States has been criticized by many organizations and associations, including the American Bar Association, Conference of Chief Justices/Conference of State Court Administrators, National Council of Juvenile Family Courts, National Juvenile Defender Center, and the Juvenile Law Center.

These organizations as well as local and state agencies have advocated for change. For example, Taylor (2016) has urged that California's entire criminal fine and fee system be re-evaluated with a focus on deterrence, proportional punishment, and mitigating the effects of crime. Moreover, Taylor (2016) urged that monetary sanctions be calculated based on defendants' ability to pay and implement alternatives to imposing overwhelming debt by adjusting installment plans, addressing the consequences of nonpayment, and re-assessing the amounts and number of fines and fees. Taylor (2016) and others also assert that financial obligations should not serve to generate revenue for courts or governments. Courts should be fully funded by the government and not reliant on financial sanctions generated by defendants.

A growing number of states and local jurisdictions have either reduced or eliminated various fines, fees, or costs due to the negative impact these financial sanctions have on offenders (Bastien, 2017; Endicott, 2018). Others have implemented promising new strategies (Bastien, 2017). These include requiring an ability-to-pay hearing for all defendants, guidelines for determining defendants' ability-to-pay, adopting flexible and penalty-free payment plans, and eliminating incarceration as a penalty for failing to pay financial obligations (Bastein, 2017). Other reforms include eliminating debt for juveniles and eradicating fees and fines associated with processing fines and court costs (Bastein, 2017). Some county and city reforms have bolstered defendants' rehabilitation by reducing court debt after completing job training and mental health or drug counseling (Bastein, 2017). Other potential reforms may reduce the amount of costs associated with applying for counsel and providing free public defender services for debt hearings (Bastein, 2017).

While limiting financial sanctions is important, courts may also institute reform that provides defendants with the information that they need to make important decisions and ensure greater equity. First, judges should fully inform misdemeanor defendants of the direct and, more importantly, the indirect costs associated with misdemeanor convictions. Additionally, educating courtroom personnel (including judges, lawyers, and other court staff) to achieve more equitable results presents another low-cost, but perhaps impactful reform.

Note

1 Bail decisions are not addressed here; they are covered in Chapter 12.

References

Bannon, A., Nagrecha, M., & Diller, R. (2010). *Criminal justice debt: A barrier to reentry*. New York: Brennan Center for Justice at New York University School of Law. Retrieved from www.brennancenter.org/sites/default/files/legacy/Fees%20and%20Fines%20FINAL.pdf

Bastien, A. (2017, March). Ending the debt trap: Strategies to stop the abuse of court-imposed fines and fees. Retrieved from www.policylink.org/sites/default/files/ending-the-debt-trap-03-28-17.pdf

Bazemore, G., & Maloney, D. (1994). Rehabilitating community service: Toward restorative justice sanctions in a balanced justice system. *Federal Probation, 58*(1), 24–35.

Bearden v. Georgia, 461 U.S. 660 (1983).

Bohm, R. M., & Haley, K. N. (2018). *Introduction to criminal justice* (9th ed). New York, NY. McGraw-Hill Education.

Bouffard, J. A., & Muftic, L. R. (2007). The effectiveness of community service sentences compared to traditional fines for low-level offenders. *Prison Journal, 87*(2), 171–194.

Colgan, B. A. (2018). The excessive fines clause: Challenging the modern debtor's' prison. *UCLA Law Review, 65*(1), 3–77.

Dickman, M. (2009). Should crime pay?: A critical assessment of the mandatory victims restitution act of 1996. *California Law Review, 97*, 1687–1718.

Diller, R. (2010). *The hidden costs of Florida's criminal justice fees.* New York, NY: Brennan Center for Justice. Retrieved from www.brennancenter.org/publication/hidden-costs-floridas-criminal-justice-fees

Endicott, M. (2018, May 23). San Francisco looks to end certain court fees. *U.S. News and World Report.* Retrieved from www.usnews.com/news/best-states/articles/2018-05-23/san-francisco-looks-to-end-certain-court-fees

Feeley, M. (1979). *The process is punishment: Handling cases in a lower criminal court.* New York, NY: Russell Sage Foundation.

Feeley, M., Berk, R., & Campbell, A. (1992). Between two extremes: An examination of efficiency and effectiveness of community service orders and their implications for the U.S. sentencing guidelines. *Southern California Law Review, 66*, 155–207.

Goldscheid, J. (2004). Crime victim compensation in a post-9/11 world. *Tulane Law Review, 79*, 167–233.

Greenberg, C., Meredith, M., & Morse, M. (2016). The growing and broad nature of legal financial obligations: Evidence from Alabama court records. *Connecticut Law Review, 48*, 1079–1120.

Griffin v. Illinois, 351 U.S. 12 (1956).

Harland, A. T., & Rosen, C. J. (1990). Impediments to the recovery of restitution by crime victims. *Violence and Victims, 5*(2), 127–140.

Haynes, S. H., Cares, A. C., & Ruback, R. B. (2015). Reducing the harm of criminal victimization: The role of restitution. *Violence and Victims, 30*(3), 450–469.

Hemmens, C., Brody, D. C., & Spohn, C. C. (2013). *Criminal courts: A contemporary perspective*, (2nd ed.). Thousand Oaks, CA: Sage.

Kepple, D. J. (1989). The victim and witness protection act of 1982: Retroactive application of continuing crimes. *Fordham Law Review, 58*, 87–100.

Kohler-Hausmann, I. (2018). *Misdemeanorland: Criminal courts and social control in an age of broken windows policing.* Princeton, NJ: Princeton University Press.

Latessa, E. J., & Allen, H. E. (2003). *Corrections in the community*, (3rd ed.). Cincinnati, OH: Anderson Publishing Co.

McDonald, D. C., Greene, J., & Worzella, C. National Institute of Justice (U.S.), & Abt Associates. (1992). *Day fines in American courts: The Staten Island and Milwaukee experiments.* Washington, DC: U.S. Dept. of Justice, Office of Justice Programs, National Institute of Justice.

Martin, K. D. (2018). Monetary myopia: An explanation of institutional response to revenue from monetary sanctions for misdemeanors. *Criminal Justice Policy Review, 29*, 630–662.

Morgan, A. M. (1987). Victim rights: Remembering the "forgotten person" in the criminal justice system. *Marquette Law Review, 70*, 572–597.

Morris, N., & Tonry, M. (1990). *Between prison and probation: Intermediate punishments in a rational sentencing system.* New York, NY: Oxford University Press.

Munoz, E. A., & Freng, A. (2007). Age, racial/ethnic minority status, gender, and misdemeanor sentencing. *Journal of Ethnicity in Criminal Justice, 5*(4), 29–57.

Munoz, E. A., & Martinez, M. R. (2001). Latinas and criminal sentencing: An exploratory analysis. *Voices: A Journal of Chicana/Latina Studies, 3*(1–2), 150–176.

Natapoff, A. (2015). Misdemeanor decriminalization. *Vanderbilt Law Review, 68*(4), 1055–1116.

National Center for Victims of Crime (2011). *Making restitution real: Five case studies on improving restitution collection.* Washington, DC: U.S. Department of Justice.

Nelson, J. F. (1994). A dollar a day: Sentencing misdemeanants in New York State. *Journal of Research in Crime and Delinquency, 31*(2), 183–201.

Office of Victims of Crime (1998). *New directions from the field: Victims' rights and services for the 21st century.* Washington, DC: U.S. Department of Justice.

Pennsylvania Department of Public Welfare v. Davenport, 495 U.S. 552, (1990).

Ruback, R. B. (2011). The abolition of fines and fees. *Criminology & Public Policy, 10*(3), 569–581.

Ruback, R. B., Hoskins, S. N., Cares, A. C., & Feldmeyer, B. (2006). Perceptions and payment of economic sanctions: A survey of offenders. *Federal Probation, 70*. Retrieved from www.uscourts.gov/sites/default/files/fed_probation_dec_2006.pdf

Sharma, A. (2016). Fines as a punishment in Indian Penal Code, 1860. *Journal of Contemporary Criminal Justice, 32*(3), 196–204.

Sobol, N. L. (2016). Charging the poor: Criminal justice debt & modern-day debtors' prisons. *Maryland Law Review, 75*(2), 486–540.

Siegel, L. J., Schmalleger, F., & Worrall, J. L. (2015). *Courts and Criminal Justice in America*, (2nd ed.). Boston, MA: Pearson.

Smith, A. (in press). The cost of (in)justice: A preliminary study of the chilling effect of the $50 application fee in Florida's misdemeanor courts. *University of Florida Journal of Law and Public Policy.*

Smith, A., & Maddan, S. (2011). *Three-minute justice: Haste and waste in Florida's misdemeanor courts.* Washington, DC: National Association Criminal Defense Lawyers.

Steury, E. H., & Frank, N. (1996). *Criminal court process.* New York, NY: West Publishing.

Taylor, M. (2016). *Improving California's criminal fine and fee system.* Sacramento, CA: Legal Analyst's Office.

Tonry, M. (1998). *The handbook of crime and punishment.* New York, NY: Oxford University Press.

Wing, N. (2016, March 15). *Homeless man dies in jail after being locked up for marijuana possession [Web log post].* Retrieved from www.huffingtonpost.com/entry/jeffrey-pendleton-death-marijuana_us_56e83dbae4b0860f99da7d42

Wright, R. F., & Wayne, A. L. (2006). The political economy of application fees for indigent criminal defense. *William and Mary Law Review, 47*, 2045–2087.

10

SPECIALTY COURTS AS LOWER CRIMINAL COURTS

Richard D. Hartley

Since the inception of drug courts in the late 1980s, many jurisdictions across the United States have established specialized dockets for certain types of offenses or offenders as an alternative to traditional criminal case processing. These specialized dockets, also referred to as specialty courts or problem-solving courts, operate under a philosophy of therapeutic jurisprudence focusing on the underlying causes of criminal behavior and offender rehabilitation rather than retribution and incapacitation as punishment for criminal offending (Porter, Rempel, & Mansky, 2010). As such, many of the current specialty court programs include, in addition to court conditions and supervision normally required by traditional probation, an intensive treatment component for program participants which they must satisfactorily complete in order to get charges reduced or dropped. The foundation of the specialty court program movement is based on notions that in order to reduce overall recidivism rates and prevent individuals from having future contact with the criminal justice system, the courts must address the underlying causes of the criminal offending. In other words, these courts go beyond traditional supervision and connect offenders to treatments or services that address their criminogenic needs (Baldwin, 2013; Baldwin, Hartley, & Brooke, 2018).

Other differences between traditional criminal court dockets and specialized dockets include that specialty courts utilize a nonadversarial approach where the prosecution and defense work together and view individual cases as problems to be solved rather than engaging in an adversarial process that ends in a formal disposition (Miller & Johnson, 2009). Likewise, instead of a uniform system of punishment or a going rate for a specific offense in any particular jurisdiction, specialty courts take both a more holistic and tailored approach to justice. Supervisory and treatment conditions are therefore based on the unique needs of each individual participant, and the court often partners with outside agencies to take advantage of community expertise in assisting offenders with rehabilitation and reintegration.

Specialty courts operate similar to pretrial diversion, and many of these programs have a pretrial diversion track which essentially diverts certain offenders or cases out of the traditional criminal court process. In practice, prosecutors agree to temporarily stay the prosecution of an offender who then is accepted to participate in the specialty court program; if these offenders successfully complete the requirements of the program, the charges against them will be dismissed (Hartley, Rabe, & Champion, 2018). In some programs and jurisdictions, graduates may also have an opportunity for expungement of their criminal record. If participants do not complete all program requirements, the case will be sent back to a traditional court and the prosecutor will reinstate the original charges.

The ultimate goal of specialty court programs then is rehabilitated offenders and reduced recidivism. Indeed, specialty courts can often be found in jurisdictions where traditional criminal justice processing practices have been ineffective at reducing certain types of crimes, or where certain types of behaviors seem to be especially problematic or habitual. A 2014 National Institute of Justice (NIJ) report which studied more than 400,000 individuals released from prison in 2005 revealed that more than 67% were re-arrested within three years of release, and over 76% were re-arrested within five years (Durose, Cooper, & Snyder, 2014). Obviously, many jurisdictions have recognized that traditional corrections, whether incarceration- or community-based, have not been able to correct individual behavior and the majority of offenders end up re-involved in the justice system. Specialty court programs are an attempt to try something different in dealing with certain types of offenders. Miller and Johnson (2009) put it this way: "Problem solving courts require leaders — judges or judicial officers —willing to exercise an energetic and entrepreneurial spirit with unimpeachable ethical standards and a tolerance for taking risks" (p. 41).

Another reason for the rapid expansion of the problem-solving court model is that treatment-based specialty court programs are often much more cost effective than incarceration (Marlowe, 2010), especially where jails and prisons are simply warehousing offenders until they complete their sentence with no attempt at rehabilitation or provision of treatment or services to inmates. Drug courts are the most prevalent type of specialty court today, numbering well over 3000, but other types of courts include domestic violence courts; mental health courts; driving under the influence (DUI) courts; youth or teen courts; and, more recently, veterans treatment courts. As stated earlier, these specialty court programs are less focused on the offense that has been committed, and more focused on the offender attempting to treat the underlying causes of criminal behavior with the hope of preventing future offending. Although there are some specialty court programs which focus on those arrested for felonies, such as felony drug courts and felony veterans courts, and most of these court programs are lower level misdemeanor courts targeting primarily first-time and nonviolent offenders.

The Specialty Court Model

Specialty court dockets utilize a non-traditional approach where the court and courtroom actors view cases as problems to be solved. Berman and Feinblatt (2005) provide a framework outlining five general components that characterize specialty court programs: 1. *Tailored Justice* - specialty court programs bypass traditional notions of equal justice and instead tailor justice to the needs of each individual case. This requires implementation of a risk need responsivity (RNR) model of recidivism reduction (Andrews & Bonta, 2010) to identify the risk and needs of each program participant via some type of assessment. 2. *Enhanced Accountability*—another component of these types of courts involves a different offender accountability model. These courts employ a much more intensive and frequent approach to monitoring offenders often requiring participants to come to docket and interact with the judge on a weekly or bi-weekly basis in addition to other court conditions (i.e., probation meetings) and treatment and service appointments. Advocates of the specialty court model argue that it is this enhanced accountability that makes these courts more effective than traditional probation or jail (Miller & Johnson, 2009). 3. *Partnering with Outside Agencies* - most specialty court programs partner with other agencies not ordinarily involved in criminal court processing to get participants access to vocational programs, treatment providers, social service agencies, and other community groups which will assist in the rehabilitative process. 4. *Informed Decision-Making* - specialty court team members, because of their partnerships with outside community agencies, are provided with much more information about offenders' supervision and treatment needs and progress thereby allowing them to make more timely and informed decisions about any sanctions that need to be imposed or future treatment provisions that might be necessary. 5. *A Focus on Results*—the last component that differentiates specialty courts is their focus on results. Because specialty court teams receive input on an offender's progress from a number of different sources, they are better able to prevent the risk of relapse or reoffending. In this sense specialty courts, via tailoring treatment, services, and sanctions and incentives to the needs and progress of individual participants, are much more results oriented than punishment based.

The Most Prevalent Types of Specialty courts

Drug Courts

Drug courts have been around for almost 30 years; the first drug court was established in Miami (Dade County) in 1989. Today there are over 3,000 drug courts across all 50 states. According to a 2014 report, a little over half of the drug courts in the United States were adult drug courts, and another roughly 400 serve juveniles, while 300 or so are referred to as family drug courts. About 140 of these courts are in tribal areas, another 30 or so are federal drug courts, and over 300 specifically target driving while intoxicated (DWI) offenders. Finally, although considered a separate type of specialty court, roughly 300 veterans treatment courts are also included in these drug court numbers (National Institute of Justice, 2014). Drug courts specifically target offenders facing drug-related charges, who are drug dependent or drug abusers. Drug courts are the model for other specialty court reincarnations and like those that came after them, operate under a therapeutic approach to justice. The cornerstone of the drug court movement is that drug addiction is at the core of the criminal offending for these individuals (Berman & Feinblatt, 2005). This means that drug court participants are mandated to complete drug treatment requirements, and eventually become abstinent, in addition to adhering to other court conditions, to successfully graduate from the program.

Drug court programs are typically fairly substantial in length, one year or more, and target substance abusers who would otherwise face serious legal punishment (Porter et al., 2010). Mitchell, Wilson, Eggers and Mackenzie (2012) reports that although eligibility requirements differ among the thousands of drug courts, the majority restrict admission to offenders who have not committed violent crimes and who have substance dependence issues (Belenko, 1998).

In 1997, the Office of Justice Programs (OJP) convened a committee of experts to develop and publish ten key components of Drug Treatment Courts. Marlowe (2010) argued that based upon many research studies and numerous evaluations, fidelity to these ten key components is necessary for achieving effective outcomes for both participants and the community. Although not all specialty courts will adhere to all ten key components dependent on the type of court and their mission, and other programs such as Veterans Treatment Courts have modified their own ten key components, the National Association of Drug Court Professionals states that using a multidisciplinary team centered approach along with ongoing judicial interaction, drug testing, and a system of incentives and sanctions in conjunction with evidence-based treatment, are the keys to successful implementation of the problem-solving court model (USDOJ, 1997). The ten key components published by the Office of Justice Programs are as follows:

Key Component #1- Drug courts integrate alcohol and other drug treatment services with justice system case processing
Key Component #2- Using a nonadversarial approach, prosecution and defense counsel promote public safety while protecting participants' due process rights
Key Component #3- Eligible participants are identified early and promptly placed in the drug court program
Key Component #4- Drug courts provide access to a continuum of alcohol, drug, and other related treatment and rehabilitation services
Key Component #5- Abstinence is monitored by frequent alcohol and other drug testing Key Component #6- A coordinated strategy governs drug court responses to participants' compliance
Key Component #7- Ongoing judicial interaction with each drug court participant is essential
Key Component #8- Monitoring and evaluation measure the achievement of program goals and gauge effectiveness
Key Component #9- Continuing interdisciplinary education promotes effective drug court planning, implementation, and operations
Key Component #10- Forging partnerships among drug courts, public agencies, and community-based organizations generates local support and enhances drug court program effectiveness (United States Department of Justice, 1997, p. iii).

Mitchell (2011) and Mitchell and colleagues (2012) specify the typical processes for a drug court treatment program: Those arrested on certain drug offenses are identified and undergo a screening process to determine their eligibility for the program (some programs exclude those with several priors or who have a violent criminal history). If eligible, offenders are accepted into the drug court program (in some jurisdictions, the offender has to plead guilty to the charges in order to be accepted) on conditions that they will adhere to certain requirements in exchange for some form of leniency, either reduced or dropped charges, once they graduate from the program. Drug court programs may have one or more tracks dependent on the type of offense and the drug team or prosecutor's willingness to use pretrial diversion programming. Mitchell et al. (2012, p. 61) refers to these as "pre-plea" and "post-plea" case processing. In the former, offenders waive certain due process rights to enter the program, and if they successfully complete all program requirements, the prosecutor drops the charges against them. In the latter, offenders plead guilty to the charges, and if they complete the program, the judge would sentence them to probation or time served. This is a major criticism of specialty court programs; participants usually have to give up certain due process rights to enter into the program, and if unsuccessful, their case is remanded back to their original court and dealt with in the traditional court process manner. In the case of the pre-plea track, defendants would have their cases processed in the traditional manner, whereas in the post-plea track, the offender would be sentenced to a traditional punishment, most often some jail time and probation.

The drug court movement has been very popular and many jurisdictions across the country have funded these types of programs based on the belief that they will result in lower recidivism rates and provide many benefits for the individuals participating, such as reduced drug abuse, family reunification, including regaining custody of children, increased education and employment, and ultimately prolonged and more productive lives (Berman & Feinblatt, 2005; Office of Justice Programs, 1998). Because of these positive outcomes in many drug court programs, Congress, in 2016, passed the Comprehensive Addiction and Recovery Act or CARA (P.L. 114–198) which authorizes funding for drug courts, veterans treatment courts, as well as increased monies for evidence-based treatment for substance abuse disorders (National Association of Drug Court

Professionals, 1997). More specifically, CARA was the first major federal legislation addressing addiction in over 40 years; it authorized $180 million in federal funding each year to address the opioid epidemic and for specialized treatment courts.

Mental Health Courts

According to the National Alliance on Mental Illness (NAMI), each year two million persons with mental illness are arrested; they also report that mental illness is more prevalent among female arrestees (30%) than male arrestees (15%) (NAMI, 2018). Unfortunately, the majority of jails across the country are not prepared to deal with people who have serious mental health problems; they are not set up to provide mental health services (Wolff, 1998), and inmates with mental illness are less likely to comply with directives from correctional staff. Criminal courts likewise have problems dealing with these offenders because persons with mental health issues are less likely to understand their due process rights, or the sanctions they might be facing for the charges brought against them; they are also less likely to be represented by defense counsel (Hartley et al., 2018).

According to a 2006 Bureau of Justice Statistics report, more than half of jail and prison inmates in 2005 had a recent history or currently had symptoms of mental health issue; this equated to 700,000 prison inmates, almost 80,000 federal inmates, and close to 500,000 jail inmates with mental health problems (James & Glaze, 2006). This report further outlines some of the added concerns that prisoners with mental health issues present for the criminal justice system: State prison inmates with a mental health problem were more likely to have been injured in a fight since being admitted to prison, were more likely to report a past history of physical or sexual abuse, and were more likely to have been homeless in the 12 months prior to their arrest (James & Glaze, 2006).

The broad consequences of persons with mental illnesses in the criminal justice system is the lack of access to adequate treatment; over 80% of inmates with mental health conditions do not have access to the necessary treatment they need which means they will not improve in jail, and in fact may get worse, and be at higher risk for victimization because of their condition (NAMI, 2018).

These statistics make it clear that individuals in society with mental health issues are more likely to come into contact with the criminal justice system than to get the necessary medical help they need. In other words, the criminal justice system has become the de facto mental health hospital of today (Castellano, 2011). Because of the many issues that arise in dealing with inmates with mental health problems as well as the cost incurred related to these inmates, many state and local governments have implemented programs to assist inmates in getting mental health treatment and keeping them out of jail.

One of these alternative programs is the mental health court. From just four programs in 1997 to over 300 court programs across in all 50 states today, mental health courts are a type of specialized court program specifically designed for offenders who have some type of mental illness (Council of State Governments, 2018). These programs link offenders with an array of mental health treatment and services in an attempt to get them stabilized with the ultimate goal of preventing future contact with the criminal justice system. The specific goal on most mental health courts is to decrease an offender's mental health issues and assist them to function independently (Porter et al., 2010). Often those with mental health issues are also dealing with substance abuse issues and therefore it is not uncommon for mental health courts to also provide access to substance abuse treatment. Goldkamp and Irons-Guynn (2000) outline some of the most common features of mental health court programs: offenders must have a demonstrable mental health issue for eligibility, the offense must be low-level, and offenders cannot have a history of violent behavior, most offer community-based treatment in lieu of incarceration, and most strive for early intervention as soon after arrest as possible.

Veterans Courts

The very first veterans treatment court (VTC) was established in 2008 in Buffalo, New York, and since then, VTCs have been one of the fastest growing specialty courts. According to the US Department of Veterans Affairs (VA), as of June 2016, there were 461 VTCs or veterans dockets as part of other existing drug and mental health courts (Flatley, Clark, Rosenthal, & Blue-Howells, 2017). Veterans courts are an amalgam of drug courts and mental health courts as many justice involved veterans suffer dual-diagnoses, including depression, substance abuse and dependence, post-traumatic stress disorder, and traumatic brain injuries stemming from their service in the military (Koetzle Shaffer, 2011). Many veterans of today's era have completed multiple tours of duty and have incurred significant combat related trauma. As such, they are more likely to come into contact with police because of "substance abuse, driving under the influence (DUI), assaults, intimate partner violence (IPV), family conflicts, and homelessness episodes" (Schaffer, 2010, p. 22). Veterans also have higher rates of suicide than the general population, and incarceration increases the likelihood of a suicide attempt (Wortzel, Binswanger, Anderson, & Adler, 2009).

Indeed, one reason for the rapid expansion of VTCs is in response to the increasing number veterans who have become justice involved since returning from the wars in Iraq and Afghanistan (Hartley & Baldwin, 2016). Veterans courts have become an important alternative to traditional case processing as a large number of Iraq and Afghanistan war vets have had trouble adjusting to civilian life again, and become justice involved. VTC target veterans, and in some cases, active duty personnel who are justice involved and connect them to treatments and services they need but which may not have been easily accessed at the VA (Baldwin, 2016; Hartley & Baldwin, 2016). Eligibility requirements in VTCs are often based on military statuses (Baldwin, 2013); these criteria, however, are not usually present in criminal justice data (Baldwin et al., 2018). Most specialty court programs strive to identify potential participants at very early stages in the criminal justice process (i.e., arrest, booking, or bond hearings) but for VTC target populations this is a little more difficult and involved; many program's identification procedures rely on other entities to gather this information and share it with court or criminal justice personnel (Baldwin, 2013; Holbrook & Anderson, 2011).

Despite these additional obstacles to identifying potential participants, many politicians and local leaders across the country believe that helping those who have served get access to the assistance they need is the right thing to do (Haughney, 2010). It also makes a lot of sense economically for jurisdictions to establish a VTC because the Department of Veterans Affairs covers the cost of treatment for veterans who are service connection eligible.

Domestic Violence Courts

Domestic violence courts came about in the 1990s as a response to an offense which is often recurring and where the offender and victim are often linked through marriage and/or children (Gutierrez, Blais, & Bourgon, 2016; Moore, 2009). Domestic violence courts, as opposed to traditional court processes for dealing with these types of cases, are better able to provide consistency in holding offenders accountable for their actions through more frequent supervision, and by mandating treatment such as batterer intervention programs; they also are better advocates for the victim and include provision of treatment and services for them as well (Labriola, Bradley, O'Sullivan, Rempel, & Moore, 2009).

The criminal justice system has traditionally been reluctant to provide a formal response to family and domestic matters (Tsai, 2000; Wolff, 2013), and where the law has been formally invoked, the courts have been criticized that their responses actually make the domestic situation between the victim and offender worse, therefore reoffending is more likely after criminal justice system contact (Hartley et al., 2018; Ostrom, 2006). In that vein, other arguments are that the criminal justice system has not adequately protected the victim from additional violence through ease of access to protection orders, or in cases where the victim is able to secure a protection order, the court's response to violations of it are paltry.

Despite that these courts were established due to increasing caseloads and a previous lack of adequate response to domestic violence by the criminal justice system, like other specialty court programs, the mission of these courts has adapted to focus on underlying problems that cause domestic violence itself (Moore, 2009). The therapeutic jurisprudence court model in domestic violence courts therefore attempts to positively affect victims' lives (Gutierrez et al., 2016; Moore, 2009), and place more attention on the offender to reduce the prevalence of domestic violence (Ostrom, 2006; Porter et al., 2010).

Empirical Status of Specialty Courts

Problem-solving courts tout fidelity to the key components and the team centered holistic approach to justice as elements that enable them to achieve success in reducing recidivism and getting individual lives back on track. Other studies also purport that specialty court programs are more cost effective than incarceration, in the short term, and the continued justice involvement of individuals, in the long term. To date many evaluative studies as well as meta-analytic research has examined the effectiveness of specialty court programs. While the majority of this research concludes a reduction in substance use and criminal involvement (Marlowe, 2010), a few studies are critical of the effectiveness of some of the key specialty court elements (Porter et al., 2010), and question whether eligibility and admission requirements and decisions (target populations) may be more responsible for successful outcomes than the treatment interventions themselves (Wolff, Fabrikant, & Belenko, 2010). Kaiser and Holtfreter (2015) also note that the specialty court movement has continued to expand absent a theoretical framework to explain success; they purport that the procedural justice model might be able to explain offender rehabilitation apart from, or in conjunction with, the therapeutic jurisprudence model that specialty courts claim underpin their success. Belenko, Fabrikand, and Wolff (2011) therefore stress that caution must be exercised when looking at the findings from evaluation research, especially where the results are only from a single specialty court site (Porter et al., 2010).

Most studies of specialty court models reveal that they are more effective at preventing re-offense than traditional court sanctions. Marlowe (2010) in a summary of the results of five meta-analytic reviews concludes that drug courts result in better outcomes than either matched or randomized control groups of drug offenders on regular probation (Wilson, Mitchell, & MacKenzie, 2006); recidivism rates from these five reviews were on average eight to 26% lower for drug court participants. In one of the meta analyses, Koetzle Shaffer (2011) found that 78% of drug courts significantly reduced crime. Lowencamp, Holsinger, and Latessa (2005) found that the very best drug courts had 35%–40% lower recidivism rates. Another multisite study funded by the National Institute of Justice, the *Multisite Adult Drug Court Evaluation*, revealed other beneficial effects of drug courts as well; in addition to significantly lower recidivism rates, drug court participants reported lower rates of alcohol and drug use and better family relationships (Rossman, Green, Rempel, & Downey, 2011).

Studies of juvenile drug courts, however, are not as positive. Findings are mixed; half of the studies show no significant effects, and the others reveal a criminogenic effect where participation in juvenile drug court actually increases recidivism rates (Kralstein, 2008). In this case, the literature reveals that not all specialty court programs are similarly effective (Porter et al., 2010).

Although the research on other specialty courts is not as well developed as the drug court literature, most show positive results in the form of lower recidivism rates. Research also indicates that other specialty court programs attain results that are in line with their overall mission. For example, Casey and Rottman (2003) report that mental health courts are able to tailor mental health treatment plans to individual participant's needs, and provide more mental health services than is available for non-participants. Similarly, domestic violence courts have outcomes that reveal provision of services to a higher percentage of domestic violence victims as well as higher victim satisfaction with court responses than cases processed via traditional court processes (Gover, MacDonald, & Alpert, 2003; Newmark, Rempel, Diffily, & Kane, 2001). Finally, a meta-analysis of 20 domestic violence court studies by Gutierrez et al. (2016) demonstrates that domestic violence courts have a positive impact on lowering recidivism in general, and for domestic violence offending, specifically.

A very limited body of research on Veterans treatment courts limits empirical judgements of their effectiveness (Hartley & Baldwin, 2016). Although VTCs are rapidly expanding, availability of data on them has not surfaced as quickly, as such, only a few studies have examined outcomes for participants of veterans treatment courts (Blonigen et al., 2014). In a national survey of VTCs (N = 79; 69% response rate), Baldwin (2013) reported that 34% of veteran participants had graduated versus only 12% who had been terminated. Another study, which conducted a telephone survey of Veterans Justice Outreach Officers (VJOs) across 168 VTCs, reported that roughly 70% of participants graduated from their programs, while the other 30% were terminated or dropped out (McGuire, Clark, Blue-Howells, & Coe, 2013). Finally, Hartley and Baldwin (2016) conducted a quasi-experimental study which compared a group of VTC participants to a matched control group of VTC eligible probationers in a large urban jurisdiction. Their results revealed that VTC participants, especially those who had graduated from the program, had lower recidivism rates and lower mean numbers of re-arrests compared to the control group at 12–24 and 36-months after program entry.

Many more evaluations of veterans treatment courts are underway as these programs continue to increase each year. Research should evaluate the effectiveness of specialty court programs in general, and of domestic violence, mental health, veterans treatment, and other novel court programs in particular. A very limited number of studies have examined the effectiveness of the specific components of specialty courts on recidivism and other outcomes (Porter et al., 2010). Only a couple studies have attempted to ascertain whether therapeutic jurisprudence is the causal intervention, or whether the procedural justice components of most programs are responsible for positive recidivism results (Kaiser & Holtfreter, 2015). Specifically, there is a dearth of research regarding how programs target populations for participation, or how they determine eligibility of potential participants for program acceptance (Baldwin et al., 2018). Belenko et al. (2011) argue that program procedures related to eligibility requirements result in acceptance of a distinct group of offenders who also self-select into the program. Eligibility and admission processes therefore directly affect what types of offenders will comprise the participants, which could ultimately have an effect on outcomes (Baldwin et al., 2018).

References

Andrews, D. A., & Bonta, J. (2010). The empirical base of PCC and the RNR model of assessment and crime prevention through human service. In D. A. Andrews (Ed.), *The psychology of criminal conduct* (5th ed.). New Providence, NJ: Anderson.

Baldwin, J. M. (2013). Executive summary: National survey of veterans treatment courts. Posted on Social Science Research Network. Retrieved from http://papers.ssrn.com/sol3/papers.cfm?abstract_id=2274138

Baldwin, J. M. (2016). Investigating the programmatic attack: A national survey of veterans treatment courts. *The Journal of Criminal Law and Criminology, 105*, 101–148.

Baldwin, J. M., Hartley, R. D., & Brooke, E. J. (2018). Identifying those who served: Modeling potential participant identification in veterans treatment courts. *Drug Court Review, Winter-2018*, 10–30.

Belenko, S. (1998). Research on Drug Courts: A Critical Review. *National Drug Court Institute Review,* 1, 1–42.

Belenko, S., Fabrikant, N., & Wolff, N. (2011). The long road to treatment: Models of screening and admission into drug courts. *Criminal Justice and Behavior, 38*, 1222–1243.

Berman, G., & Feinblatt, J. (2005). *Good courts: The case for problem solving justice.* New York, NY: Free Press.

Blonigen, D., Bui, L., Elbogen, E., Blodgett, J., Maisel, N., Midboe, A., ... Timko, C. (2014). Risk of recidivism among justice-involved veterans: A systematic review of the literature. *Criminal Justice Policy Review.* doi:10.1177/0887403414562602.

Casey, P. M., & Rottman, D. B. (2003). *Problem-solving courts: Models and trends.* National Center for State Courts; Williamsburg, VA: 2003. Retrieved from www.scribd.com/document/66990782/CASEY-and-ROTTMAN-Problem-Solving-Courts-Models-and-Trends

Castellano, U. (2011). Courting compliance: Case managers as "Double Agents" in the mental health court. *Law & Social Inquiry,* 36, 484–514.

Council of State Governments. (2018). *Mental health courts.* https://csgjusticecenter.org/mental-health-court-project/

Durose, M. R., Cooper, A. D., & Snyder, H. N. (2014). *Recidivism of prisoners released in 30 states in 2005: Patterns from 2005 to 2010.* Washington, DC: United States Department of Justice, Bureau of Justice Statistics.

Flatley, B., Clark, S., Rosenthal, J., & Blue-Howells, J. (2017). *Veterans court inventory 2016 update: Characteristics of and VA involvement in Veterans Treatment Courts and other Veteran-focused court programs from the Veterans Justice Outreach specialist perspective.* Washington, DC: US Department of Veterans Affairs, Veterans Health Administration.

Goldkamp, J. S., & Irons-Guynn, C. (2000). *Emerging judicial strategies for the mentally ill in the criminal caseload: Mental health courts in Fort Lauderdale, Seattle, San Bernardino, and Anchorage.* Washington, DC: Bureau of Justice Statistics. Retrieved from www.ncjrs.gov/pdffiles1/bja/182504.pdf

Gover, A. R., MacDonald, J. M., & Alpert, G. P. (2003). Combating domestic violence: Findings from an evaluation of a local domestic violence court. *Criminology and Public Policy, 3*, 109–132.

Gutierrez, L., Blais, J., & Bourgon, G. (2016). Do domestic violence courts work? A meta-analytic review examining treatment and study quality. *Justice Research and Policy, 17*, 75–99.

Hartley, R. D., & Baldwin, J. M. (2016). Waging war on recidivism among justice involved veterans: An impact evaluation of a large urban veterans treatment court. *Criminal Justice Policy Review.* doi:10.1177/0887403416650490

Hartley, R. D., Rabe, G. A., & Champion, D. J. (2018). *Criminal courts: Structure, process and issues.* Boston, MA: Pearson.

Haughney, K. (2010, October 20). Senate report suggests veterans court. *The St. Augustine Record,* October 20.

Holbrook, J., & Anderson, S. (2011). Veterans courts: Early outcomes and key indicators for success. *Widener Law School Legal Studies Research Paper Series no. 11–25.* Retrieved from https://papers.ssrn.com/sol3/papers.cfm?abstract_id=1912655

James, D. J., & Glaze, L. E. (2006). *Mental health problems of prison and jail inmates.* Washington, DC: United States Department of Justice, Bureau of Justice Statistics.

Kaiser, K. A., & Holtfreter, K. (2015). An integrated theory of specialized court programs: Using procedural justice and therapeutic jurisprudence to promote offender compliance and cooperation. *Criminal Justice & Behavior.* doi:10.1177/0093854815609642.

Koetzle Shaffer, D. (2011). Looking inside the black box of drug courts: A meta-analytic review. *Justice Quarterly, 28*(3), 493–521.

Kralstein, D. 2008. *Evaluation of the Suffolk County juvenile treatment court: Process and impact findings.* New York, NY: Center for Court Innovation. Retrieved from www.courtinnovation.org/sites/default/files/Suffolk_JTC.pdf

Labriola, M., Bradley, S., O'Sullivan, C. S., Rempel, M., & Moore, S. (2009). *A national portrait of domestic violence courts*. Washington, DC: National Institute of Justice, Center for Court Innovation.

Lowencamp, C. T., Holsinger, A. M., & Latessa, E. J. (2005, Fall). Are drug courts effective? A meta-analytic review. *Journal of Community Corrections, 15*(1), 5–28.

Marlowe, D. B. (2010). *Research update on adult drug courts*. National Association of Drug Court Professionals. Retrieved from https://ndcrc.org/resource/need-to-know-research-update-on-adult-drug-courts

McGuire, J., Clark, S., Blue-Howells, J., & Coe, C. (2013). An inventory of involvement in veterans courts, dockets and tracks. Retrieved from www.justiceforvets.org/sites/default/files/files/An%20Inventory%20of%20VA%20involvement%20in%20Veterans%20Courts.pdf

Miller, J., & Johnson, D. C. (2009). *Problem solving courts: A measure of justice*. Lanham, MD: Rowman & Littlefield.

Mitchell, O. (2011). Drug and other specialty courts. In M. Tonry (Ed.), *Oxford handbook of crime and criminal justice* (pp. 843–871). New York, NY: Oxford University Press.

Mitchell, O., Wilson, D. B., Eggers, A., & Mackenzie, D. L. (2012). Assessing the effectiveness of drug courts on recidivism: A meta-analytic review of traditional and non-traditional drug courts. *Journal of Criminal Justice, 40*, 60–71.

Moore, S. (2009). *Two decades of specialized domestic violence courts: A review of the literature*. The Center for Court Innovation. Retrieved from www.courtinnovation.org/sites/default/files/DV_Court_Lit_Review.pdf

National Alliance on Mental Illness. (2018). *Jailing people with mental illness*. Retrieved from www.nami.org/Learn-More/Public-Policy/Jailing-People-with-Mental-Illness

National Association of Drug Court Professionals. (1997). *Defining drug courts: The key components*. Alexandria. Retrieved from www.ncjrs.gov/pdffiles1/bja/205621.pdf

National Institute of Justice. (2014). *Drug courts*. Department of Justice. National institute of Justice. Retrieved from www.nij.gov/topics/courts/drug-courts/pages/welcome.aspx

Newmark, L., Rempel, M., Diffily, K., & Kane, K. M. (2001). *Specialized felony domestic violence courts: Lessons on implementation and impacts from the Kings County Experience*. Washington, DC: Urban Institute.

Ostrom, B. J. (2006). Domestic violence courts. *Criminology and Public Policy, 3*, 105–108.

Porter, R., Rempel, M., & Mansky, A. (2010). *What makes a court problem-solving? Universal performance indicators for problem-solving justice*. The Center for Court Innovation. Retrieved from www.courtinnovation.org/sites/default/files/What_Makes_A_Court_P_S.pdf

Rossman, S. B., Green, M., Rempel, M., & Downey, P. M. (2011). Do adult drug courts reduce drug use? In S. B. Rossman, J. K. Roman, J. M. Zweig, M. Rempel, & C. H. Lindquist (Eds.), *The multi-site adult drug court evaluation: The impact of drug courts—final report*. Urban Institute.

Schaffer, B. (2010). Veterans Courts and Diversion Alternatives. *American Jails*, XXIII, (6), January/February, p. 21–24.

Tsai, B. (2000). The trend toward domestic violence court: Improvements on an effective innovation. *The Fordham Review, 68*, 1285–1327.

United States Department of Justice. (1997). *Defining drug courts: The key components*. Washington, DC: Office of Justice Programs.

United States Department of Veterans Affairs (2017). *Veterans court inventory, 2016 update: Characteristics of and VA involvement in veterans treatment courts and other veteran-focused court programs from the veterans justice outreach specialist perspective*. Washington, DC: US Department of Veterans Affairs.

Wilson, D., Mitchell, O., & MacKenzie, D. L. (2006). A systematic review of drug court effects on recidivism. *Journal of Experimental Criminology, 2*, 459–487.

Wolff, N. (1998). Interactions between mental health and law enforcement systems: Problems and prospects for cooperation. *Journal of Health, Politics, Policy and Law, 23*, 133–174.

Wolff, N. (2013). Domestic violence courts: The case of lady justice meets the Serpents of Caduceus. In R. L. Wiener & E. M. Brank (Eds.), *Problem solving courts* (pp. 83–112). New York, NY: Springer.

Wolff, N., Fabrikant, N., & Belenko, S. (2010). Mental health courts and their selection processes: Modeling variation for consistency. *Law and Human Behavior, 35*, 402–412.

Wortzel, H. S., Binswanger, L. A., Anderson, C. A., & Adler, L. E. (2009). Suicide among incarcerated veterans. *Journal of American Academy of Psychiatry and the Law, 37*, 82–91.

SECTION 3

Recommendations for Reforming the Lower Courts

11

THE PROSECUTOR IN THE MISDEMEANOR COURTROOM

Nudging Culture Change in Policy and Practice

Julian Adler, Sherene Crawford, and Tia Pooler[1]

> [G]iven the prosecutor's ability to determine which offenders are subject to criminal punishment in the first place, changing the hearts and minds of prosecutors who make these judgements is essential to any reform agenda.
>
> —Wright & Levine, 2014, p. 1126

In ways that are often informal, interstitial, and discretionary, prosecutors wield an outsized influence on the trajectories of the roughly 13.2 million misdemeanor cases filed each year in the lower criminal courts (Stevenson & Mayson, 2018). Since precious few of these cases will ever make it to trial, the prosecutor-judge-defender troika—commonly described as the courtroom workgroup—is largely informal in its operations and focuses most of its energies on making discretionary decisions about bail and plea bargains (Alexander, 2012; Feeley, 1992; King, 2011; Kohler-Hausmann, 2018; Natapoff, 2012; Natapoff, 2016; Primus, 2013). An abundance of scholarship over the last four decades makes clear that the workgroup's business as usual in most misdemeanor courtrooms in the United States leads to a dismal array of outcomes—variously characterized as "assembly-line justice," "McJustice," and "plea mills" (Barrett, 2017; Bohm, 2007; Boruchowitz, Brink, & Dimino, 2009; Feeley, 1992; Natapoff, 2012; National Legal Aid and Defender Association [NLADA], 2008). The results are staggering: 75% of the individuals held in jail are either facing charges or serving sentences for nonviolent traffic, property, drug, or public order crimes (Subramanian, Delany, Roberts, Fishman, & McGarry, 2015, p. 5). Even in lieu of jail time, misdemeanor convictions often trigger legal financial obligations and enduring collateral consequences (Boruchowitz et al., 2009; Natapoff, 2012; Natapoff, 2016).

While we are cautious not to generalize about courtroom culture across jurisdictions, recent analysis finds a "surprising degree of uniformity in misdemeanor trends… suggest[ing] that the misdemeanor system may have a deeper and more uniform structure than we anticipated" (Stevenson & Mayson, 2018, p. 738). At the same time, recent scholarship also observes a reigning cultural norm that is often a far cry from justice:

> Unfortunately, the practices of many misdemeanor courts leave much to be desired. There are courts where innocent people are convicted of crimes they did not commit;

> where defendants plead guilty without understanding important consequences of their conviction or without the benefit of counsel; and where defendants are detained because they cannot afford bail.
>
> *(Roth, 2018, p. 104)*

We argue that any meaningful attempt to reengineer this misdemeanor courtroom culture toward fairer and more humane outcomes must first disrupt the default settings on the courtroom workgroup. To this end, we propose starting with prosecutors.

Why Prosecutors?

Observers of the American criminal justice system tend to agree that prosecutors exert tremendous power on court proceedings, generally, and on the use of incarceration, specifically (Albonetti, 1987; Gershowitz, 2016; Kerstetter, 1990; Pfaff, 2017; Sklansky, 2018; Thomas & Fitch, 1976). On this point, a recent *New York Times* op-ed (Rice, 2017) does not mince words: "America incarcerates more people than any other country, and it is prosecutors who are largely responsible" (para. 14). While judges and defenders wield considerable influence in the courtroom workgroup, and as Fordham University law professor John Pfaff (2017) concludes, prosecutors are inarguably "the most powerful actors in the criminal justice system" (p. 133). While the misdemeanor courtroom is no exception, the informal influence or power of the prosecutor merits more attention.

To this end, this chapter explores two fundamental questions: How might we better immunize the misdemeanor courtroom workgroup against what Stanford law professor David Alan Sklansky (2018) terms the prosecutor's "punitive ideology" (p. 458)? More ambitiously, how might we flip the script and galvanize prosecutors to serve as affirmative agents of misdemeanor justice?

Making a foray into behavioral economics, we first suggest a strategy of acknowledging the prosecutor's "anchoring effect" in bail and plea determinations and taking steps to either mitigate it outright or redirect its influence toward alternatives to incarceration. We then argue that a critical correlate to this strategy is a willingness to counteract "young prosecutors' syndrome" by rethinking the typical assignment and training of less-experienced prosecutors (Wright & Levine, 2014). "With great power comes great responsibility," and we are quite concerned that less-experienced prosecutors may be falling short in great number—with a disproportionate impact on the misdemeanor population. Both of these ideas are pragmatically feasible and neither requires a seismic influx of resources to realize in practice. Combined, we argue they hold the potential to begin to transform the machinery of the misdemeanor courtroom workgroup in relatively short order.

Anchoring Effects

The prosecutor sets the courtroom dynamic in motion. In New York City, a groundbreaking 2004 study found that the prosecutor's bail request was the most influential factor in criminal court judges' release and bail decisions at arraignment (Phillips, 2004). Controlling for charge severity, researchers discovered that the higher the prosecutor's requested bail amount, the lower the likelihood of the judge releasing a defendant on recognizance. Moreover, the actual bail amount requested by the prosecutor closely resembled that ultimately set by the judge. Observing that judges rarely made decisions that were "harsher than the prosecutor's request," the researchers described the prosecutors as "establish[ing] boundaries that judges are reluctant to exceed" (Phillips, 2004, p. 7).

Subsequent experimental research on sentencing decisions suggests that defense attorneys may be similarly susceptible to a prosecutor's initial request. In a 2005 study, legal experts, assuming the role of defense attorneys, unwittingly adopted the prosecutor's position as a reference point from which to adjust their counter-position, thereby contributing to a steeper final sentencing decision. Underscoring how the prosecutor always goes first in presenting arguments before the court, the authors warned that "the standard procedural sequence in court may place the defense at a distinct disadvantage" (Englich, Mussweiler, & Strack, 2005, p. 41). This matters in judgement-making scenarios, as evidence has long suggested that people are generally biased toward information that is presented first in a sequence or narrative (Asch, 1946; Nahari & Ben-Shakhar, 2013). Somewhat ironically, "by granting the defense attorney the right of the last word," researchers caution that "the legal system simultaneously grants the prosecutor the right of the first word" (Englich et al., 2005, p. 718).

In the parlance of behavioral economics, the prosecutor's bail or sentencing request functions as an "anchor" or an initial value that biases all subsequent estimates and decisions (Englich & Soder, 2009; Marti & Wissler, 2000; Strack & Mussweiler, 1997; Tversky & Kahneman, 1974). As Richard Thaler and Cass Sunstein (2009) explain in their seminal text, *Nudge: Improving Decisions about Health, Wealth, and Happiness*, even though decision-makers will subsequently "adjust in the direction [they] think is appropriate... [t]he bias occurs because the adjustments are typically insufficient" (p. 23). Put another way, "anchoring and adjustment" describes an automatic human tendency to remain tethered to the first data point presented (Tversky & Kahneman, 1974).

Strikingly, this cognitive bias is so hardwired that it has been shown to persist in laboratory settings even when the decision-maker is told that the anchor in question is arbitrary (Wilson, Houston, Etling, & Brekke, 1996). For example, in a 2006 experiment, researchers found that legal experts adjusted their final sentencing decisions based on initial demands (anchors) even when they were told the demands had come from irrelevant sources or had been randomly generated. Notably, neither judicial expertise nor experience mitigated this robust anchoring effect (Englich, Mussweiler, & Strack, 2006). A 2007 study found a similar effect when judges were asked to determine monetary damages in civil matters. The researchers (Guthrie, Rachlinski, & Wistrich, 2007) described the anchor's "powerful influence on judgment... [even] when the anchor bore essentially no relation to the magnitude of the claim and when the judges knew full well that they were supposed to ignore the anchor" (p. 21). They concluded that the anchor "triggered intuitive, automatic processing that the judges were unable to override" (p. 21).

Beyond bail, Thaler and Sunstein (2009) offer insight into how a prosecutor's anchoring effect might further sway the plea-bargaining process, that is, the primary mechanism by which most misdemeanor cases reach their conclusion. "Clever negotiators often get amazing deals for their clients by producing an opening offer that makes their adversary thrilled to pay half that very high amount," (Thaler & Sunstein, 2009, p. 24). This is particularly troubling in light of Pfaff's (2017) finding that "[n]early 95 percent of the cases that prosecutors decide to prosecute end up with the defendant pleading guilty" (p. 132). In the misdemeanor courtroom, this likely contributes to a culture of "plea now and go home today," often in lieu of a searching inquiry into factual guilt versus innocence (Luna & Wade, 2012; Sklansky, 2018). A comprehensive national report (Boruchowitz et al., 2009) on the misdemeanor court system offers the following account of this culture:

> Often, prosecutors put pressure on defendants to plead guilty at the first court appearance by offering a more favorable plea bargain if, and only if, the client pleads guilty *that day*. Time and time again, defenders reported getting plea bargain offers just before the first

> hearing that would allow the client to go home, if they accepted the plea that day. Such plea offers place enormous pressure on the clients, who, as noted above, want nothing more than to go home.
>
> *(Boruchowitz et al., 2009, p. 33, our emphasis)*

Furthermore, the prosecutor's anchoring effect may persist throughout what can often be a protracted pretrial period. Although it involved a felony-level charge of stealing a backpack, Kalief Browder's now high-profile experience is a case in point. As the *New York Times* reported, "he insisted on his innocence, refusing several offers from prosecutors to take a plea deal, including one that would have allowed him to be released immediately" (Schwirtz & Winerip, 2015, para. 12). His refusal to plead guilty, combined with glaring case processing inefficiencies that are not uncommon in lower criminal courts, resulted in three years of pretrial incarceration on Rikers Island, New York City's notorious jail complex. Prosecutors eventually dropped the charges.

Raising the Anchor

Although it seems rather modest, the first step toward mitigating prosecutors' anchoring effect may simply be to acknowledge it and remain vigilant—if not hypervigilant—against its unconscious influence, especially when courtroom workgroups are managing heavy dockets (we are hardly the first to point to the high volume of cases in a typical misdemeanor courtroom as a major contributing factor to a host of procedural insufficiencies) (Boruchowitz et al., 2009; King, 2011; Natapoff, 2012; Roberts, 2013; Roth, 2018).

More affirmatively, elected prosecutors can establish office policies to redirect prosecutors' anchoring influence. For example, Brooklyn District Attorney Eric Gonzalez recently instituted a default policy of not asking for money bail on misdemeanor cases (Manhattan District Attorney's Office, 2018). "As part of my commitment to making criminal justice fairer and more equitable in Brooklyn, I instructed our Assistant District Attorneys that our policy is to not ask for bail in most misdemeanor cases," he explained. "Bail shouldn't be requested when we don't intend to seek jail time and must never be used as leverage to obtain a guilty plea" (Manhattan District Attorney's Office, 2018, para. 6). Contrary to customary plea-bargaining practice, Philadelphia District Attorney Larry Krasner (2018) went so far as to explicitly direct assistant district attorneys to make plea offers on most cases "below the bottom end of the mitigated range" (Plea Offers section, para. 2), requiring a supervisor's approval for anything higher.

Beyond policy, elected prosecutors can also establish practices that leverage the anchoring power of the prosecutor in positive ways. A 2018 national study of prosecutor-led programs strongly suggests that diversion strategies can be effectively customized to suit the particular needs and preferences of the office and the local court culture, including whether charges are formally filed before defendants are admitted to the program and the intensity of the mandates (Labriola et al., 2018). Notably, across jurisdictions, the study largely found "inclusive planning processes involving both public defenders and the court… consistent dismissals for diversion completion (limiting collateral consequences for defendants); and generally positive perceptions, as articulated by staff, stakeholders, and program participants themselves" (Labriola et al., 2018, executive summary, p. xi).

Elected prosecutors are not the only actors in a position to influence the anchoring behavior of line prosecutors on misdemeanor matters. Our experience in New York City suggests that prosecutors will integrate alternatives to incarceration into their standard offer practice if surrounded with the right resources. In this capacity, behavioral economists might describe justice reformers as "choice architects," influencing the behavior of prosecutors by "organizing the context in which [they] make decisions" (Thaler & Sunstein, 2009, p. 3).

For example, the Midtown Community Court was established in 1993 in Manhattan's Times Square neighborhood to provide a range of alternative sentencing options for defendants charged with misdemeanors. Despite open resistance from the District Attorney's Office at the time (Hoffman, 1993), research shows that line prosecutors availed themselves of the alternative sentencing options at the Midtown Community Court—and to a statistically significant degree. Cases arraigned at the Midtown Community Court were more likely to receive an alternative sanction (community service or social services) when compared to similar cases seen at the traditional downtown criminal court (76% versus 55%) and less likely to receive a jail sentence (Hakuta, Soroushian, & Kralstein, 2008).

Another New York City initiative, established in 2005, confirms this finding. Unlike the Midtown model, Bronx Community Solutions offers alternative sentencing options to line prosecutors arraigning cases in the centralized criminal courthouse in the Bronx. In 2007, a fifth (20.3%) of all convicted misdemeanors in the Bronx received a jail sentence; fast-forward to 2017, and this proportion has dropped to just over 10% (10.5%) (New York State Division of Criminal Justice Services, 2007–2017). Instead, prosecutors and judges have embraced alternative sentencing; in 2017, over 6,000 misdemeanor cases were mandated to programming at Bronx Community Solutions (including drug treatment, mental health counseling sessions, community service, and job training workshops) as an alternative to traditional sentencing (Center for Court Innovation, 2018, p. 17).

Of course, the idea of nudging line prosecutors toward more equitable plea practice and the increased utilization of alternatives to incarceration presupposes some willingness and ability to rethink prosecution as usual. This may prove quite challenging.

Young Prosecutors' Syndrome

In many prosecutors' offices across the country, the newest, least-experienced prosecutors are assigned misdemeanor cases, while felony matters are reserved for more seasoned practitioners. This practice may help to explain the suboptimal dynamics of the courtroom workgroup. Writing in the *Arizona Law Review,* Ronald F. Wright and Kay L. Levine (2014) diagnose what they term "Young Prosecutors' Syndrome," which entails "the early collection of beliefs and attitudes about the importance of every case, the constant quest for trials, and the aggressive posturing with defense attorneys" (p. 1068). In misdemeanor cases, the challenge for prosecutors is to distinguish between cases that should probably be diverted or dismissed outright against more serious matters, that is, to operate with a scalpel rather than a one-size-fits-all sledgehammer.

In their 2014 study, Wright and Levine analyzed over 200 in-person interviews and surveys with prosecutors across eight offices. Their findings suggest that the effects of professional experience are particularly significant at the plea-offer stage: Compared to their junior counterparts, senior prosecutors were less committed to trials and convictions and more willing to calibrate their approach to each case. And this willingness is important: Research suggests that more experienced, "syndrome free" prosecutors are more inclined to make reasonable plea offers and to consider case resolution through diversion (Wright & Levine, 2014).

The Work of Culture Change

Not surprisingly, one way to cure this syndrome is to diversify case assignments so that new prosecutors are less concentrated on the misdemeanor docket. With time and experience, Wright and Levine (2014) posit that prosecutors acquire confidence, the ability to better differentiate between serious and minor cases, and "prosecutorial empathy" (p. 1111) that will result in more restrained and proportionate offers. Taking a step back, Wright and Levine (2014) also suggest that law schools can do more to cultivate less adversarial, less punitive, and more humane mindsets among aspiring prosecutors (p. 1124).

Short of rethinking case assignments, Wright and Levine proffer some practical strategies that can be applied in the here and now. Elected prosecutors can provide training programs that simulate real courtroom practice experience (e.g., plea bargaining rather than trial practice), while emphasizing the value of the defense and the costs of incarceration (Wright & Levine, 2014, p. 1117). In fact, there are many efforts underway, including the Institute for Innovation in Prosecution at John Jay College of Criminal Justice and Fair and Just Prosecution, to offer progressive prosecutors the training and tools they need to change practice. For example, Prosecutor Impact, an organization led by former Boston prosecutor Adam Foss, has established a platform and a space to rethink how to effectively train new prosecutors as they join the line. Foss's training is premised on three core ideas: (1) prosecutors' offices need to improve educating and preparing new prosecutors for the untidy realities of the work; (2) prosecutors are hired with little or no exposure to the communities and people most impacted by the criminal justice system; and (3) new prosecutors are largely unprepared for the high-pressure environment of the courtroom (Prosecutor Impact, n.d.). With an eye toward humanizing defendants and tempering prosecutorial discretion, Foss proposes such activities as "taking [new prosecutors] from inside the courtroom and their offices out to the communities — visiting a jail, a homeless shelter, a mental health facility — and understanding what it's like in the community" (Connolly, 2017, para. 1).

Beyond training, Wright and Levine highlight the value of mentorship—both informal and formal. This can be accomplished by creating teams that reflect various levels of professional experience. Strategic caseload assignments can serve to ensure new and seasoned prosecutors work closely together on the same team (Wright & Levine, 2014, p.1070). Even simple physical working proximity with other offices and agencies could change the way prosecutors comport themselves in the workgroup. A study in Pennsylvania looked at the effects of judge and district attorney sharing an office building on sentencing practice and found that workgroups with greater proximity were less likely to mete out incarceration sentences (Haynes, Ruback, & Cusick, 2008).

Of course, all the training in the world will prove insufficient if "Young Prosecutors' Syndrome" is in fact symptomatic of deeper, more entrenched institutional values. As a former prosecutor who practiced in a self-identified "progressive" office describes, her early efforts to eschew incarceration and to approach the work more humanely were thwarted by her supervisors. "They would call me soft," she recounts, when she started asking questions about defendants' lives and struggles. "I would start to ask those questions, and I found that that was very unpopular. My bosses didn't want to hear that. They started to tease me and say, 'You sound like a defense attorney'" (Anonymous interview, January 18, 2018). Similarly, in *Let's Get Free: A Hip Hop Theory of Justice*, former prosecutor and Georgetown law professor Paul Butler (2010) underscores the primacy of office culture in shaping and tempering prosecutorial discretion. "I did not start right in calling the defendant's 'cretins' and 'douche bags'" (p. 116), he writes of his own negative transformation as a prosecutor. "[T]he workplace ethos of many prosecutor's offices is overly combative, overly cynical, and dismissive of defendants' interests," adds Stanford law professor David Alan Sklansky. "Those attitudes can be transmitted through and reinforced by the casual use of language that consciously or unconsciously indulges in racial, ethnic, and sexist tropes" (Sklansky, 2017, p. 39; Van Cleve, 2016).

Similarly, if new prosecutors are promoted based solely or primarily on traditional metrics like trial statistics and conviction rates, there may be little-to-no incentive for prosecutors to change their behavior. In truth, careers have been built on racking up these numbers.

"What prosecutors have in common with most other lawyers is that they are competitive and ambitious," observes Butler.

> We all like to win. For prosecutors, that means getting a tough sentence and defeating defendants' claims that the police violated their constitutional rights. Getting promoted, and maintaining the professional regard of your peers, requires keeping your eyes on the prize.
>
> *(Butler, 2010, p. 116)*

A blue-ribbon panel was tasked in 2014 with developing "a blueprint for federal prosecutors to establish a new set of priorities to better reduce crime and reduce incarceration, while modernizing criminal justice" (Eisen, Fortier, & Chettiar, 2014, p. 1). The panel recognized the need to move away from the traditional metrics of success, promoting metrics such as the percentage of the community feeling safe, the reduced percentage of individuals sentenced to incarceration compared to previous years, and the increased frequency of recommended downward departures. Sklansky (2017) proffered similar metrics:

> You can and should evaluate the attorneys in your office in part based on how scrupulous they are in honoring constitutional rights, how thoughtful they are in crafting fair plea bargains, and how measured they are in exercising their discretion.
>
> *(p. 30)*

The upshot: Culture change demands a thorough revaluation of how prosecutors conduct business, how prosecutors are evaluated, and how their behavior is explicitly and implicitly reinforced.

Toward a New Business as Usual

Although we emphasize the role that prosecutors might play in anchoring a new culture of misdemeanor justice, they obviously cannot—and should not—go it alone. Defenders and judges wield considerable influence in the courtroom workgroup and should be held accountable as such for its improvement.

In the 2010 case of *Padilla v. Kentucky*, for example, the United States Supreme Court formally acknowledged that guilty pleas can carry significant collateral consequences (559 U.S. 356 2010). "Until today," Justice Samuel Alito noted in his concurrence, "the longstanding and unanimous position of the federal courts was that reasonable defense counsel generally need only advise a client about the *direct consequences* [emphasis added] of a criminal conviction" (559 U.S. 356, 2010). Of course, this wasn't news to defense attorneys practicing in misdemeanor courtrooms, who have and will continue to carry the primary responsibility for humanizing and advocating for their clients; this necessarily means acknowledging the lasting effects of misdemeanor convictions, no matter how indirect or delayed. Some even argue that defense attorneys should be responsible for understanding and recommending any available alternatives to incarceration (Clarke, 2002; Gideon & Sung, 2010; Porter, Lee, & Lutz, 2002; Winick, 1999). "Great defense attorneys need to help iron out the wrinkles in young prosecutors' angular understanding," argues defense attorney Ibrahim Awad. "How can this seemingly impossible feat be accomplished? Simple. Humanize the defendant" (Awad, 2014, para. 4).

With respect to judges and culture of the misdemeanor courtroom, for example, there is a growing body of research that shows how treating criminal defendants with respect and decency—in addition to being humane—may enhance perceptions of their legitimacy, thereby increasing law-abiding behavior (Farley, Jensen, & Rempel, 2013; Gottfredson, Kearley, Najaka, & Rocha, 2007; Rossman, Roman, Zweig, Rempel, & Lindquist, 2002). Known as procedural justice, the empirical literature strongly suggests that judges have the greatest influence on defendants' overall perceptions of fairness in court proceedings (Abuwala & Farole, 2008; Farley et al., 2013; Frazer, 2006; Lee et al., 2013; Rossman et al., 2011). On this score, it stands to reason that the judge's influence could also extend to the behavior of prosecutors and defenders.

Ultimately, the importance of reform in the lower criminal courts cannot be overstated. "There is a misdemeanor crisis in the United States," writes American University law professor Jenny Roberts (2013). "Although mass incarceration continues to plague states around the nation, the current criminal justice crisis is more aptly characterized as one of mass misdemeanor processing" (p. 1091). The courtroom workgroup can either be an accelerant of this crisis or a potential vehicle for its resolution. Prosecutors are in the best position to tip that balance.

Note

1 We would like to thank Hayley Setear and Isabella Banks for providing research support.

References

Abuwala, R., & Farole, D. J. (2008). *The effects of the Harlem housing court on tenant perceptions of justice.* New York, NY: Center for Court Innovation.

Albonetti, C. A. (1987). Prosecutorial discretion: The effects of uncertainty. *Law & Society Review, 21,* 291–314.

Alexander, M. (2012, March 11). Go to trial: Crash the justice system [Letter to the editor]. *The New York Times.* Retrieved from www.nytimes.com/2012/03/11/opinion/sunday/go-to-trial-crash-the-justice-system.html

Anonymous interview, January 18, 2018 (on file with the first author).

Asch, S. E. (1946). Forming impressions of personality. *Journal of Abnormal and Social Psychology, 41,* 258–290.

Awad, I. J. (2014, March 16). *Humanize the defendant [Weblog].* Retrieved from www.theawadlawfirm.com/single-post/2014/03/16/Humanize-the-Defendant

Barrett, C. J. (2017). Adjudicating "broken windows": A qualitative inquiry of misdemeanor case processing in the New York City's lower criminal courts. *Criminology, Criminal Justice, Law & Society, 18*(2), 62–79.

Bohm, R. M. (2007). "McJustice": On the McDonaldization of criminal justice. *Justice Quarterly, 23*(1), 127–146.

Boruchowitz, R. C., Brink, M. N., & Dimino, M. (2009). *Minor crimes, massive waste: The terrible toll of America's broken misdemeanor courts.* Washington, DC: National Association of Criminal Defense Lawyers.

Butler, P. (2010). *Let's get free: A hip hop theory of justice.* New York, NY: The New Press.

Center for Court Innovation. (2018). *Annual Report 2017.* Retrieved from www.courtinnovation.org/sites/default/files/media/documents/2018-03/annual_report_2017.pdf

Clarke, C. (2002). Problem-solving defenders in the community: Expanding the conceptual and institutional boundaries of providing counsel to the poor. *Georgetown Journal of Legal Ethics, 14*(2), 401–458.

Connolly, M. (2017). *Former prosecutor Adam Foss speaks out on how to fix our criminal justice system.* Washington, DC: Aspen Institute. Retrieved from www.aspeninstitute.org/blog-posts/former-prosecutor-adam-foss-speaks-fix-criminal-justice-system/

Eisen, L., Fortier, N., & Chettiar, I. (2014). *Federal prosecution for the 21st century.* Retrieved from Brennan Center for Justice website: www.brennancenter.org/sites/default/files/analysis/Federal_Prosecution_For_21st_Century.pdf

Englich, B., Mussweiler, T., & Strack, F. (2005). The last word in court – A hidden disadvantage for the defense. *Law and Human Behavior, 29*(6), 705–722.

Englich, B., Mussweiler, T., & Strack, F. (2006). Playing dice with criminal sentences: The influence of irrelevant anchors on experts' judicial decision making. *Personality and Social Psychology Bulletin, 32*(2), 188–200.

Englich, B., & Soder, K. (2009). Moody experts – how mood and expertise influence judgmental anchoring. *Judgment and Decision Making, 4*(1), 41–50.

Farley, E., Jensen, E., & Rempel, M. (2013). *Improving courtroom communication: A field test in Milwaukee.* New York, NY: Center for Court Innovation.

Feeley, M. M. (1992). *The process is the punishment: Handling cases in a lower criminal court* (2nd ed.). New York, NY: Russell Sage Foundation.

Frazer, M. S. (2006). *The impact of the community court model on defendant perceptions of fairness: A case study at the Red Hook community justice center.* New York, NY: Center for Court Innovation.

Gershowitz, A. M. (2016). Consolidating local criminal justice: Should prosecutors control the jails? *Wake Forest Law Review, 51.* Retrieved from: https://ssrn.com/abstract=2858462

Gideon, L., & Sung, H. (2010). *Rethinking corrections: Rehabilitation, reentry, and reintegration.* Los Angeles, CA: SAGE Publications Inc.

Gottfredson, D., Kearley, B., Najaka, S., & Rocha, C. (2007). How drug treatment courts work: An analysis of mediators. *Journal of Research in Crime and Delinquency, 44,* 3–35.

Guthrie, C., Rachlinski, J. J., & Wistrich, A. J. (2007). Blinking on the bench: How judges decide cases. *Cornell Law Review, 93*(1), 1–43.

Hakuta, J., Soroushian, V., & Kralstein, D. (2008). *Do community courts transform the justice response to misdemeanor crime? Testing the impact of the Midtown Community Court.* New York, NY: Center for Court Innovation.

Haynes, S. H., Ruback, B., & Cusick, G. R. (2008). Courtroom workgroups and sentencing: The effects of similarity, proximity, and stability. *Crime & Delinquency, 56*(1), 126–161.

Hoffman, J. (1993, October 1). A user-friendly experiment in justice; community court aims at saving time and money in dealing with minor offenses. *The New York Times.* Retrieved from www.nytimes.com/1993/10/01/nyregion/user-friendly-experiment-justice-community-court-aims-saving-time-money-dealing.html

Kerstetter, W. (1990) Gateway to justice: Police and prosecutorial response to sexual assaults against women. *Criminology,* 81, 267–313.

Krasner, L. (2018, February 15). *New policies announced February 15, 2018* [Memo]. Retrieved from https://assets.documentcloud.org/documents/4415817/Philadelphia-DA-Larry-Krasner-s-Revolutionary-Memo.pdf

King, J. D. (2011). *Procedural justice, collateral consequences, and the adjudication of misdemeanors.* Washington & Lee Public Legal Studies Research Paper No. 2011–19.

Kohler-Hausmann, I. (2018). *Misdemeanorland: Criminal courts and social control in an age of broken windows policing.* Princeton, NJ: Princeton University Press.

Labriola, M., Reich, W., Davis, R. C., Hunt, P., Rempel, M., & Cherney, S. (2018). *Prosecutor-led pretrial diversion: Case studies in eleven jurisdictions.* New York, NY: Center for Court Innovation.

Lee, C., Cheesman, F., Rottman, D., Swaner, R., Lambson, S., Rempel, M., & Curtis, R. (2013). *A comprehensive evaluation of the Red Hook community justice center: A community court grows in Brooklyn.* Williamsburg, VA: National Center for State Courts.

Luna, E., & Wade, M. (2012). *The prosecutor in transnational perspective.* Oxford, UK: Oxford University Press.

Manhattan District Attorney's Office. (2018, January 9). Manhattan and Brooklyn district attorney's offices end requests for bail in most misdemeanor cases [Press release]. Retrieved from www.manhattanda.org/manhattan-and-brooklyn-district-attorneys-offices-end-requests-bail-most-misdemeanor/

Marti, M. W., & Wissler, R. L. (2000). Be careful what you ask for: The effects of anchors on personal injury damages awards. *Journal of Experimental Psychology: Applied, 6*(2), 91–103.

Nahari, G., & Ben-Shakhar, G. (2013). Primacy effect in credibility judgements: The vulnerability of verbal cues to biased interpretations. *Applied Cognitive Psychology, 27*(2), 247–255.

Natapoff, A. (2012). Misdemeanors. *Southern California Law Review, 85,* 101–163.

Natapoff, A. (2016). *Criminal misdemeanor theory and practice.* Oxford Handbooks Online. doi:10.1093/oxfordhb/9780199935352.013.9

National Legal Aid and Defender Association. (2008). *A race to the bottom: Speed & savings over due process: A constitutional crisis*. Washington, DC. Retrieved from www.nlada.net/sites/default/files/mi_racetothebottomjseri06-2008_report.pdf

New York State Division of Criminal Justice Services. (2007–2017). *Dispositions of adult arrests by county and region: Bronx* [Data file]. Retrieved from www.criminaljustice.ny.gov/crimnet/ojsa/dispos/index.htm

Padilla v. Kentucky, 559 U.S. 356 (2010).

Pfaff, J. (2017). *Locked in: The true causes of mass incarceration and how to achieve real reform*. New York, NY: Basic Books.

Phillips, M. T. (2004). *Release and bail decisions in New York City*. (Research Brief No. 6.) New York, NY: New York City Criminal Justice Agency.

Porter, R., Lee, S., & Lutz, M. (2002). *Balancing treatment and punishment: Alternatives to incarceration in New York City*. New York, NY: Vera Institute of Justice.

Primus, E. (2013). Our broken misdemeanor justice system: Its problems and some potential solutions [Review of Misdemeanors by A. Natapoff]. *Southern California Law Review Postscript, 86*, 80–87.

Prosecutor Impact. (n.d.). *The current role of the prosecutor*. Retrieved from https://prosecutorimpact.com/the-role-of-the-prosecutor/

Rice, J. D. (2017, October 16). Cyrus Vance and the myth of the progressive prosecutor. *The New York Times*. Retrieved from www.nytimes.com/2017/10/16/opinion/cy-vance-progressive-prosecutor.html

Roberts, J. (2013). Crashing the misdemeanor system. *Washington & Lee Law Review, 70*(2), 1089–1131.

Rossman, S., Roman, J., Zweig, J., Rempel, M., & Lindquist, C. (2002). *The multi-site adult drug court evaluation*. Washington, DC: Urban Institute.

Rossman, S. B., Rempel, M., Roman, J. K., Zweif, J. M., Lindquist, C. H., Green, M., … Farole, D. J. (2011). *The multi-site adult drug court evaluation: The impact of drug courts*. Washington, DC: Urban Institute.

Roth, J. (2018). The culture of misdemeanor courts. *Hofstra Law Review*, Forthcoming, Cardozo Legal Studies Research Paper No. 531. Retrieved from https://ssrn.com/abstract=3103314

Rudes, D. S., & Portillo, S. (2012). New roles in the courtroom workgroup: Developing federal problem solving courts. Law & Policy, 34(4). Retrieved from www.academia.edu/865168/New_Roles_in_the_Courtroom_Workgroup_Developing_Federal_Problem_Solving_Courts

Schwirtz, M., & Winerip, M. (2015, June 8). Kalief Browder, held at Rikers Island for 3 years without trial, commits suicide. *The New York Times*. Retrieved from www.nytimes.com/2015/06/09/nyregion/kalief-browder-held-at-rikers-island-for-3-years-without-trial-commits-suicide.html

Sklansky, D. A. (2017). The progressive prosecutor's handbook. *UC Davis Law Review Online, 50*, 25–42.

Sklansky, D. A. (2018). The problems with prosecutors. *Annual Review of Criminology, 1*, 451–469.

Stevenson, M. T., & Mayson, S. G. (2018). The scale of misdemeanor justice. *Boston University Law Review, 98*, 731–777.

Strack, F., & Mussweiler, T. (1997). Explaining the enigmatic anchoring effect: Mechanisms of selective accessibility. *Journal of Personality and Social Psychology*, 73, 437–446.

Subramanian, R., Delany, R., Roberts, S. Fishman, N., & McGarry, P. (2015). *Incarceration's front door: The misuse of jails in America*. New York, NY: Vera Institute of Justice.

Thaler, R. H., & Sunstein, C. R. (2009). *Nudge: Improving decisions about health, wealth, and happiness*. New York, NY: Penguin Books.

Thomas, C. W., & Fitch, W. A. (1976). Prosecutorial decision making. *American Criminal Law Review*, 13, 507–559.

Tversky, A., & Kahneman, D. (1974). Judgment under uncertainty: Heuristics and biases. *Science, 185*(4157), 1124–1131.

Van Cleve, N. G. (2016). *Crook county: Racism and injustice in America's largest criminal court*. Redwood City, CA: Stanford University Press.

Wilson, T. D., Houston, C. E., Etling, K. M., & Brekke, N. (1996). A new look at anchoring effects: Basic anchoring and its antecedents. *Journal of Experimental Psychology General, 125*(4), 387–402.

Winick, B. J. (1999). Redefining the role of the criminal defense lawyer at plea bargaining and sentencing: A therapeutic jurisprudence/preventive law model. *Psychology, Public Policy, and Law, 5*(4), 1034–1083.

Wright, R. F., & Levine, K. L. (2014). The cure for young prosecutors' syndrome. *Arizona Law Review, 56*(4), 1065–1128.

12

BAIL AND PRETRIAL DETENTION REFORM IN THE LOWER COURTS

Reveka V. Shteynberg and Alissa Pollitz Worden

Court systems across the United States are in the midst of what some describe as the third wave of bail reform. The first wave is usually attributed to the Congressional Bail Reform Act of 1966, which directed federal courts to release defendants on recognizance (or an unsecured bond), absent evidence that the defendant was a flight risk, in part to reduce defendants' peremptory guilty pleas (Goldkamp & Gottredson, 1979). By 1984, amid public concern about rising crime rates, Congress adopted new legislation that directed federal courts to continue such release practices, except in cases in which release posed a "serious risk" to the safety of individuals or the community. This expansion of discretion, marking the second wave of reform, permitted courts to consider the nature of the offense charged, as well as assessments of the circumstances of the case, in making pretrial detention decisions (Johnson & Johnson, 2012).

At both times, many states followed the federal lead, pivoting first from a more elastic standard for imposing bail to, later, a more restrictive one. More than three decades hence, the questions that prompted reform—questions about the legitimate objectives, effectiveness, efficiency, and fairness of bail practices—remain unresolved. A bit of recent history sets the stage for today's dilemmas, marking the third wave of reform.

The first decade of this century witnessed three developments that prompted doubts about existing pretrial detention and release practices. First, beginning in the early 1990s property and violent crime rates began a dramatic decline (Truman & Morgan, 2018). By the 2000s, this decline had caught the attention of researchers as well as policymakers (Zimring, 2007). Second, the marked incarceration increases that resulted from many states' policies and practices in the 1980s and 1990s became cause for growing alarm during the Great Recession of 2008, as states struggled to reconcile punishment policies and practices with decimated tax bases and competing economic needs. Third, at about the same time, researchers and advocates began to systematically document the links between the earliest decision points of adjudication, and the long-term implications of those decision points for case outcomes and collateral consequences for defendants and communities. Arraignment and bail hearings, long overlooked and often characterized as perfunctory and routinized proceedings, became the target for investigation, criticism, and reform initiatives. In addition to an increased emphasis on pretrial due process, the focus on bail and pretrial detention reforms have been further spurred by the fact that pretrial detainees account for a costly two-thirds of jail inmates and 95% of the jail population growth in the last two decades (Minton & Zeng, 2015).

This chapter examines bail policies and practices in the lower courts—those courts responsible for adjudication of misdemeanors and minor violations and, often, initial hearings in felonies. We consider the challenges of establishing fair and efficient pretrial policies in these courts, whose practices, policies, constraints, and resources differ from those in felony jurisdiction courts (King, 2013). In the following pages we address (1) the evolution of state policies governing bail decisions, (2) research on courthouse practices and customs in lower courts' bail decisions, (3) critiques of contemporary bail and pretrial detention practices in these courts, and finally (4) the prospects and challenges to reforming bail in misdemeanor proceedings.

State Policies Governing Bail in the Lower Courts

In the English common law system, bail emerged during medieval times as a means of ensuring that those accused of crimes did not flee before their trials. Some historians believe that the accused, obliged to post bail to secure physical freedom pending trial, would balance the loss of money against the likely severe punishment upon conviction, and sensibly depart the jurisdiction; hence bail also conveniently served, retroactively, as a punitive fine, to be retained by the government if a defendant absconded (Schnacke, Jones, & Brooker, 2010; Schnacke, 2014). Today, the use of money bail and bond—a deposit of money in exchange for freedom pending a verdict and the securing of a bond by a third party as an alternative—is justified as insurance of defendants' return for court proceedings.

Bail has also been justified as a way to reduce defendants' opportunity for additional offending, a justification known as preventive detention. By this logic, bail protects complainants and witnesses from intimidation or further victimization, and the public from new crimes. Despite lively contemporary debates on bail policy and practice, little is known about how effectively either of these objectives is achieved in most courts.

The structures of bail policies are made by the states, but national authorities also advocate for standards in practices as well as policies. The American Bar Association's guidelines for pretrial release and setting of bail define these purposes narrowly:

> The purposes of the pretrial release decision include providing due process to those accused of crime, maintaining the integrity of the judicial process by securing defendants for trial, and protecting victims, witnesses and the community from threat, danger or interference. The judge or judicial officer decides whether to release a defendant on personal recognizance or unsecured appearance bond, release a defendant on a condition or combination of conditions, temporarily detain a defendant, or detain a defendant according to procedures outlined in these Standards. *The law favors the release of defendants pending adjudication of charges.*
>
> *(American Bar Association, 2007, p. 1; italics added)*

The criteria on which judges should base these judgements are broad, and they are not easily defined or applied in a consistent manner. For example, New York law directs judges to consider defendants' "character, reputation, habits, and mental condition" as well as employment, local family ties, prior adult and juvenile record, previous violations of protective orders, ownership or use of firearms, and the "weight of evidence" on the current charges (New York Consolidated Laws, Criminal Procedure Law CPL § 510.30, 2018). Inevitably, broad edicts such as these create wide parameters around judicial discretion and feed the emergence of local practices that serve local values and needs.

Bail Practices and Customs in Misdemeanor Courts

There is no national clearinghouse on misdemeanor bail data, and little is known about decisions and outcomes of bail hearings beyond the fact that practices vary across jurisdictions. We consider three common practices governing pretrial release decisions: (a) bail schedules, (b) bail surety bonds, and (c) pretrial bond and detention fees.

Bail Schedules

To standardize bail setting within jurisdictions, many courts created bail schedules, which assign dollar amounts or ranges to specific charge categories based on the severity of the offenses (Subramanian, Delaney, Roberts, Fishman, & McGarry, 2015). Although some states promulgate uniform bail schedules for their courts, most states have patchworks of schedules across local jurisdictions. In New Mexico, for instance, a study of 22 jurisdictions revealed that each had its own schedule (Cathey & Vallejos, 2014). Bail schedules also vary in their specificity. For example, the standard bail amount for the majority of B class misdemeanors in Utah is listed as $583.00 (Administrative Office of the Courts, 2018). In Alabama, a class B misdemeanor can result in bail ranging from $300 to $3,000 (Alabama Rules of Criminal Procedure, Rule 7.2). Of course, similar criminal acts are classified differently in state laws; for example, harassment may be classified as a violation in one state and a high-level felony in another. But even when charges are comparable in scope and charge level, the bails prescribed by schedules vary considerably.

In many jurisdictions, law enforcement has the authority to release misdemeanor arrestees directly from the station house using a bail schedule, a practice often referred to as desk bail or jailhouse bond. Officers can use this schedule to assign bail in misdemeanor cases when a person is arrested without a warrant. These practices can save costs associated with the time that judges, bailiffs, and attorneys would spend on bail hearings in court and, in jurisdictions where courts do not hold evening and weekend arraignment sessions, they can reduce the number of defendants who are detained for a few hours or a few days pending their first appearance.

Bail Surety Bonds

Most states permit the use of surety bonds: issuance of bonds for which third parties, often commercial entities, guarantee payment of the defendant's assigned monetary amount if he or she fails to appear in court. Typically, those entities require a deposit, often 10%, for this service; an amount that is usually non-refundable. According to a 2013 study, four states prohibited commercial bondsmen (Widgery, 2013), and in the remainder of states there is considerable variation in how bail bond agencies are regulated. Depending on local conventions, the disparities among defendants' opportunities for pretrial release can be stark. For example, a recent California study found that in Mono County someone arrested for a misdemeanor would likely face $250 bail, but next door in Mariposa County, the cost of pretrial release on that case would be $10,000 bail or 10% bond ($1000) to obtain release (Krupnick, 2017).

Fees

Even when defendants post bail with the courts rather than bond agencies, and comply with court hearing dates, they may forfeit some of their reimbursement. Until 2018, for example, Philadelphia courts were allowed to keep 3% of the total bail that defendants posted, regardless of their failure to appear (FTA) rates or ability to comply with the conditions of the bond. This bail fee produced $3 million for the city each year (D'Onofrio, 2018). Moreover, in many lower courts, defendants are obliged to pay fees beyond those associated with bail or bond. In Denver courts, in addition to bond fees, defendants may also be charged a $50 booking fee to complete the paperwork to process their bail refunds; the revenue from these fees offsets the jail's $70 per day cost of housing an inmate (American Civil Liberties Union, 2018). Although there have been recent efforts to reform county pretrial booking, detention, supervision, and release fees, the extent of the use of these additional fees is not well documented, and hence, not well regulated.

Intended and Unintended Consequences of Bail Practices Ensuring Compliance and Preventing Crime

Do bail setting practices have the intended effects of (1) ensuring that defendants appear in court, and (2) preventing new offenses? While these would seem to be the most pressing policy questions, given the patchwork of misdemeanor courts' practices and the lack of multi-jurisdictional data on these courts' defendants, these questions elude straightforward answers. For example, defendants who fail to appear for court dates may not be absconders, but rather, simply people who lack transportation or child care that would enable them to get to court; in courts where this is not uncommon (particularly in areas with limited public transportation), judges (especially if alerted by defense attorneys or family members) may simply adjourn the case to another date rather than treat it as an FTA and issue a warrant. Further, if in theory the purpose of setting bail is to create a financial incentive to return to court, there is little if any published research on cost-benefit analyses defendants might make at these points in the legal process.

We also know little about judges' cognitive processes as they make decisions, nor is there much empirical evidence on the extent to which they rely on recommendations of prosecutors or defense attorneys (when they are present). Karnow (2008) observed that setting bail at effective levels is a more challenging task in misdemeanor than in felony cases inasmuch as judges are likely to have less information on defendants' backgrounds and prior records, and defendants charged with lesser crimes, such as prostitution or petty theft, may be likely to reoffend (albeit with similar petty offenses) if released. Observational research across multiple states suggests that in many lower courts judges seldom take more than five minutes to complete an individual bail hearing (Injustice Watch Staff, 2016; National Center for Access to Justice, 2013; Smith & Maddan, 2011; Stevenson, 2018), suggesting very limited inquiry into defendants' circumstances. And one cannot overlook the likely bias in this decision process: A *detained* defendant will almost surely make it to his next court appearance, and he will almost surely not commit another offense (at least, outside of jail). Hence, it would not be surprising to learn that judges erred on the side of making false positive judgments when estimating risks of bad outcomes and setting bail.

That said, detention is expensive. Release on recognizance saves the costs of booking and detaining defendants, which entail seldom considered processes for obtaining mugshots, fingerprinting, inventories of possessions, and usually health and mental health screenings, as well as making accommodations for visits from attorneys and family members. Defendants released under probation supervision require far fewer tax dollars; for example, in New York State, the average annual cost per inmate in New York City jail is $76,229; the average annual cost of probation services per probationer is approximately $4,000 (Human Rights Watch, 2010).

Collateral Consequences: Due Process Deficits

Notwithstanding the limits of empirical evidence about the efficacy of bail practices, researchers are compiling persuasive evidence that many lower courts' pretrial processes embody failures of due process that have repercussions for defendants and communities. The context of decisions made at the defendant's first appearance in court can set off a cascade of consequences that are not easily reversed. These include (1) the absence of counsel at critical early appearances, (2) the qualifications and expertise of lower court judges who make bail decisions in misdemeanor, and often felony, cases, and (3) the compromised positions in which detained defendants are placed as they contemplate plea offers.

First, legal representation is critical during initial appearances (which typically are also first bail hearings). Defendants are not well positioned to make accurate, relevant, and well-articulated arguments for their own release. In *Lafler v. Cooper* (2012) and *Missouri v. Frye* (2012), the Supreme Court asserted that the loss of a favorable plea bargain opportunity can constitute a lack of effective counsel. The impact of critical decisions can be fixed at the earliest court appearance, with consequences for defendants' outcomes. Particularly in misdemeanor charges, rushed or uninformed judicial rulings on pretrial detention have the potential to place defendants, without compelling justification, in pretrial detention. Once jailed, defendants' motivation to return to their homes and families may lead them to accept guilty plea agreements that they would not have accepted were they in less coercive circumstances (Gerstein, 2013).

In some states, such as South Carolina and Florida, defendants are rarely represented by defense counsel at first appearance in lower courts; in fact, there may be no lawyers in the courtroom at all as their initial fates are decided. According to a recent study in South Carolina lower courts, approximately 25% of the defendants' cases were disposed without legal counsel. In addition, Solicitors—the South Carolina term for a prosecutor—were seldom present. Instead, the arresting officers serve as both prosecutor and witness as cases were disposed (NACDL, 2017; Price, Tvedt, Andersson, & Greene, 2016; Smith, Maddan, Price, & Tvedt, 2017). In a study of Florida's lower courts, efficiency trumped due process concerns, particularly in larger counties. Approximately 70% of the defendants accused of misdemeanors resolved their cases at the first hearing (the arraignment) and without a lawyer present, with the overwhelming majority pleading guilty. Those who were in custody and without counsel were the most likely to plead guilty (Smith & Maddan, 2011).

Second, in some states, the courts where neither prosecutors nor defenders are present are also courts in which judges' professional credentials do not mandate legal training. In twenty-two states, including New York and South Carolina, elected local judges, who are not required to have law degrees or admission to the state bar, are authorized to sentence defendants to a range of penalties, including jail, for misdemeanor charges; they also make bail decisions in cases involving felonies and misdemeanors.

In fourteen of these states, a defendant has the right to seek a new trial before a legally trained judge if they receive a jail sentence from a nonlawyer judge. But defendants in the eight other states—Arizona, Colorado, Montana, Nevada, New York, South Carolina, Texas, and Wyoming—do not have the same opportunity (Ford, 2017). The presence of nonlawyer judges varies by state. In Montana, for example, where the use of nonlawyer judges came about in 2003 as a cost-saving measure, they are only allowed to practice in rural or sparsely populated counties (Ford, 2017). In New York, although city judges must be lawyers, approximately 70% of the judges in the 1,200 towns and villages outside of the state's 61 cities and New York City are nonlawyers (New York State Office of Court Administration, 2006).

Third, understandably, nonlawyer judges making pretrial detention and sentencing decisions in these lower courts may raise concerns about due process and the Sixth Amendment right to a fair trial—or a fair plea agreement. In the words of Stuart Banner, a law professor, "What's the point of having a legally-trained lawyer if the judge can't understand what they're saying?" (Ford, 2017, para 6). Since nonlawyer judges do not have formal legal training, they may not be prepared to make judgments about flight risk and public safety guided by ABA standards.

Nonlawyer judges may fail to adequately or appropriately advise defendants of rights, may have little information about defendants' circumstances, may accept a premature guilty plea, may concede to the whims of the prosecutor or defense counsel, may not be able to appropriately assess whether a defendant is making a "voluntary, knowing, and intelligent" plea decision, and may fail to advise defendants of the possible collateral consequences of guilty pleas, such as loss of employment, loss of social services, and deportation.

Collateral Consequences: Long-term Barriers to Reintegration

When bail is not set at affordable levels, defendants await their dispositions in local jails. According to the U.S. Federal Reserve, almost half of U.S. families do not have immediate access to $400 in the case of an emergency expense. Approximately three fourths of these families simply could not cover the expense and the remainder would need to borrow the money, sell something, or purchase it on their credit card and pay it off over time (Board of Governors of the Federal Reserve System, 2016). This would suggest that even low bails may be insurmountable for many defendants.

Unsurprisingly, pretrial detention is associated with a greater likelihood of conviction and a lower likelihood of dismissal or acquittal (Devers, 2011; Dobbie, Goldin, & Yang, 2018). Pretrial detention is also associated with less favorable plea deals. Even brief pretrial detention can have implications for defendants and their families, including loss of employment, custody of children, access to social services such as housing, eligibility for student loans, or even deportation (Boruchowitz, Brink, & Dimino, 2009).

An individual's inability to pay bail bond fees or fines can result in direct and collateral consequences, including having bail revoked and being sent back to jail for violating a condition of release. It can also result in suspension of license to drive, which can cascade into unemployment and inability to pay for court-mandated fines; failure to pay fines can convert to civil judgements, which in turn can lower credit scores and further enmesh individuals in a cycle of poverty and disadvantage.

Toward Policy Reform

As the current wave of reform proposals continues to develop, one must ask: Will reforms that work in city courts and urban jurisdictions transfer well to lower courts, particularly rural and small town courts? The first issue to consider is demography. Where courts are staffed during business hours and have standby personnel at other times, implementing reforms may just be a matter of coordination among agencies. But many limited jurisdiction courts are distant from centralized court administration, and those in small communities may meet only once or twice a week, making it more difficult for members of the courtroom workgroup to gather for bail hearings after arrests. These courts may also be distant from probation and pretrial services programs, as well as rehabilitative and diversion opportunities. A second issue, equally important, is availability of resources and staff to implement new bail practices. In most states, limited jurisdiction courts—those that handle most arraignments—are partially or completely funded by local governments, and therefore may not have sure access to state judicial system funding opportunities.

The following sections identify current initiatives that could change the way bail and pretrial release decisions are made, beginning with changes in local justice organizations such as courts themselves, prosecution, and indigent defense programs, and law enforcement. At the community level, grassroots groups have worked with these authorities to advocate for inventive community-based initiatives. The third wave of court reform also includes ambitious proposals, at both the state and federal levels, that would rebuild the structure of pretrial bail and detention altogether.

Reforms: Local Initiatives

Locally implemented bail reform issues include early access to counsel, the use of pretrial risk assessment instruments (PRAIs), the use of video arraignments, and efforts to reduce FTA rates through use of notification system, and increased use of pretrial services for release under supervision (RUS) and diversion opportunities. Early access to counsel, particularly at the first bail appearance, is an important due process right and safeguard against excessive bail/bond setting. It is more difficult to ensure that counsel is present in many lower courts because they are not routinely staffed by public defenders, and they may be located far from the public defender's office. When present, attorneys can present a narrative about the client's prospects for release by supplying information on his community ties and employment, and may be able to facilitate RUS, far more effectively than a defendant might do on his own. But ensuring counsel is present, and arraignments are prompt, requires some creative thinking in limited jurisdiction courts, particularly those presided over by part-time judges. Across the state of New York many counties are addressing this need by coordinating police, public defenders, and judges into centralized arraignment sessions that consolidate travel time to centrally located courthouses, conserving time and resources; and public defense administrators have sought funding to ensure that they have attorneys to assign to these hearings (Worden, Morgan, Shteynberg, & Davies, 2018; New York Office of Indigent Legal Services, n.d.).

Pennsylvania is one of several states that has expanded the use of video-conferenced arraignments, linking district court judges to arrestees who are held in booking centers and jails. The legislature justified its support for this initiative as a matter of efficiency as well as public safety. Of the more than 15,700 video conferences conducted in Pennsylvania state courts, more than half were for preliminary arraignments and bail hearings. This saved the state's lower courts an estimated $1.7 million per month (Danzig, 2011). But videoconferencing is controversial, particularly if it is imposed without defendants' consent and if it compromises their ability to privately confer with their attorneys.

Historically, judges have set bail with limited information: At the initial bail hearing they might have a prosecutor's recommendation, possibly a rap sheet, and whatever they learn from questioning the defendant. One of the most widely adopted bail reforms, the adoption of PRAIs, reduces judges' discretion by applying a tested protocol to each defendant, with a fixed set of questions (Moraff, 2016; Stevenson & Mayson, 2017; The Pretrial Justice Institute, 2012). The information produced by the answers—information about age, charge type, prior record, and prior FTA, for instance—are weighted and summed, producing scale scores that are statistical estimates of that defendant's FTA or new criminal activity. Judges' decisions, in these models, would be guided by risk scores.

Evaluations of PRAIs' implementation and effectiveness are, so far, mixed. Under a 2011 law that made risk assessment a mandatory step in the pretrial release decision, Kentucky courts adopted the Laura and John Arnold Foundation's Public Safety Assessment (PSA). An evaluation of this PRAI in that state found that judges did indeed release more arrestees under the new protocol (although the effects eroded somewhat over time as judges reclaimed their discretion), but some jurisdictions experienced increases in FTA and rearrests (Stevenson, 2018). In New Orleans, a pilot project found that people released under a risk assessment algorithm returned to court at approximately the same rate as those released, although the re-arrest rate for defendants released based on the algorithm were higher than rates for those whose fates were at the judge's discretion (Shen, 2017). More recently, when San Francisco courts started using the PSA, pretrial release rates doubled (Ewing, 2017). The enthusiasm surrounding PRAIs is tempered somewhat by these findings, but also by concerns about whether the underlying algorithms reflect the variation in community populations (they have been mostly tested in urban areas, often on samples charged with felonies), and their limited capacity to take into account the conditions under which defendants will be released (Koepke & Robinson, 2018).

It is important to note that PRAIs are intended to reduce two very different behavior risks: (1) FTA and (2) offending behavior pending disposition. It is not clear that any single risk assessment instrument can accurately predict both. Recognizing that the first problem may have less to do with deliberate efforts to avoid the courts than with forgetfulness or with practical difficulties in getting to the courthouse, new initiatives have emerged, mostly in cities, that generate alerts of impending court dates, usually via text messages and email reminders. In 2005, an early adopter, Mulnomah County, Oregon (80% of whose population resides within Portland city limits), experienced a reduction in FTA rates from 29% to 16% (Elek, Sapia, & Keilitz, 2017). Courts in Colorado and West Virginia have adopted three-day telephone reminders as well (Elek et al., 2017). Notably, New York City's text-message reminder program reportedly reduced FTA rates by 26% (The Official Website of the City of New York, 2018). The promise of this seemingly simple innovation is likely replicable in urban areas with reliable public transportation, and future research should investigate how well those successes map onto outlying courts where practical barriers to making it to the courthouse, such as lack of transportation, is the more problematic cause for missed appearances.

Beyond the bench, law enforcement agents have initiated programs intended to reduce the number of bail hearings altogether. Following a 2008 City Council ordinance, The New Orleans Police Department increased its reliance on citation and release in arrests involving municipal ordinance offenses (with the next court appearance written on the ticket), with a resulting increase in summonses from 40 to 70% (Subramanian et al., 2015). Outside cities like New Orleans, this approach might be particularly efficient in reducing arresting officers' travel time and the coordination among judges and attorneys to accomplish a just bail hearing.

Another popular law enforcement initiative is intended to divert arrestees away from the courts altogether. In October 2011, the Law Enforcement Assisted Diversion (LEAD) program in King County, Washington began identifying individuals arrested for low-level drug and prostitution offenses and diverting them into community-based services to keep them out of the criminal justice system (LEAD Law Enforcement Assisted Diversion, n.d.). In 2015, the city of Albany, New York started a LEAD program intended to divert low-level drug offenders suffering from mental illness, addiction, and poverty, rerouting them toward medical and mental health care (LEAD, n.d.). These initiatives may have promise for replication, although only if the services available to clients can be replicated across the diverse jurisdictions of the lower courts.

Finally, in a handful of jurisdictions, prosecutors have taken the initiative in rolling back local bail practices. Philadelphia's current District Attorney, for example, recently announced that he will instruct his attorneys not to seek cash bail decisions from judges in misdemeanor and nonviolent felony cases, a move that has proven controversial among his staff and law enforcement (Palmer, 2018).

Reforms: State and Federal Initiatives

Philadelphia's prosecutorial initiative illustrates a local version of a broader trend in state policy reform: calls for the reduction or elimination of the use of cash bail in pretrial decisions. Such reforms, it is thought, would create a clearer distinction between defendants who are truly at risk of flight, or reoffending, and those who could safely go about their lives pending the disposition of their cases. Not surprisingly therefore, these calls have often paired the use of risk assessments with the elimination of cash bail; adequate risk assessments would relieve the court of its obligation to maintain a financial grip on released defendants.

New Jersey sharply curtailed the use of cash bail in a bipartisan reform in 2014, opting instead for routine use of the PSA pretrial risk assessment protocol, followed by pretrial supervision of released arrestees. Since then, other states have experimented with similar legislation, but consensus on the elimination of cash bail appears to be blocked by uncertainty about how accurately algorithms (or judges) can really predict defendants' behavior. This may be further complicated by the salience of undesirable release outcomes to different constituencies. Judges and other court actors are reasonably concerned about FTA since staff in multiple agencies must contribute to efforts to ensure appearance (indeed, it is estimated that an FTA accrues approximately $1000 in staff time and effort when a warrant is issued) (Elek et al., 2017). The more problematic possibility in judges' and prosecutors' imaginations, however, is the potential for reoffending, particularly violent reoffending, when in the eyes of the public, the court had—but declined—the opportunity to incarcerate the offender after the initial arrest.

Alaska and California have recently faced controversy over similar initiatives. Legislation, passed in 2018, that all but eliminated cash bail for misdemeanors in Alaska (in favor of risk assessments and pretrial supervision) was effectively reversed six months later, by new laws that reinstated judges' prerogative to require cash bail (Kitchenman, 2018). In the same year, the California governor supported a bill that abolished cash bail in favor of PRAIs (following that state's appellate court's decision to declare the cash bail system unconstitutional). The new legislation, which reportedly would not have required most misdemeanor defendants to be assessed (Exstrum, 2018), was almost immediately challenged by a ballot initiative that would reverse the new policy. As a final example, New York's governor announced, in January 2018, an ambitious list of public policy reforms, and he capped his list of 22 proposals with a bold proposal to eliminate cash bail for misdemeanor and nonviolent felony charges throughout the state (State of the State Proposals, 2018). At the time of this writing, however, no bills that would actualize this initiative had advanced through the state legislature.

Finally, despite the staunchly federalist nature of crime and justice policy in the United States, Congress has been presented with at least two proposals that would create financial incentives for states to overhaul their bail practices. Vermont Senator Bernie Sanders introduced the No Money Bail Act in July 2018 to the Senate to accompany California Representative Ted Lieu's H.R. 1437 No Money Bail Act introduced in the House (Haynes, 2018). This bill would (1) end cash bail in federal criminal proceedings, (2) provide grants to states that end money bail and implement alternative pretrial practices, (3) withhold Department of Justice grant funding from states that continue to use money bail systems, and (4) ensure that the new systems do not lead to disparate detention rates by requiring an evaluation of the law's impact after three years This bill was endorsed by a number of organizations, including the American Civil Liberties Union (American Civil Liberties Union, 2018).

In a related effort, Democratic California Senator Kamala Harris and Republican Kentucky Senator Rand Paul jointly drafted a bill titled the Pretrial Integrity and Safety Act to amend the Omnibus Crime Control and Safe Streets Act of 1968 and to require the Department of Justice to make grants to (1) replace bail systems using money payment as a condition of pretrial release in criminal cases, and (2) implement a National Pretrial Reporting Program that would collect data on the processing of defendants at the state and local court levels (Harris & Paul, 2017; Senate1593 Pretrial Integrity Safety Act of 2017).

The Realpolitik of Bail Reform Initiatives in Lower Courts

In May 2018, Google's director for Global Product Policy publicly announced that the tech giant had adopted a "new policy to prohibit ads that promote bail bond services from our platforms" (Graff, 2018, para. 2) The announcement went on to add that bail bond providers made their profits from disadvantaged communities, when they were at "their most vulnerable" (Graff, 2018, para. 2). This statement not only underscored the new public salience of an historically obscure stage in the criminal justice process, the bail decision; it also unveiled the role of commercial and other financial interests in the complex arena of criminal justice reform. The resistance to California's bail reform, noted earlier, was fueled by an industry interest group, the American Bail Coalition, that organized signature collections in favor of a repeal referendum. Despite the homespun names of local bail bond offices, the industry is overwhelmingly the stepchild of national insurance organizations, who wield significant influence in state and federal legislation. Bail reform has become a matter of mainstream policy debate, and the focus of organized and powerful commercial interests.

At the same time, grassroots efforts to reinvent bail processes have captured the public imagination. An organization called SONG (Southerners on New Ground) conducted fund-raising and networking to bail out 30 detainees in a project called "Black Mamas' Bail Out Action" (Rankin, 2018). A similar effort, The Bail Project, was launched in Tulsa, Oklahoma, and St. Louis, Missouri, with hopes of extending its use of donors' money to create a revolving fund that would pay the bail for low-income defendants (Rappleye, Breslauer, & Atalla, 2018). While one cannot know how successful these efforts might be, the fact that they have attracted public interest and sympathy suggests some degree of momentum behind reforms.

One can only conclude that bail reform efforts are not easily reduced to spirited arguments about the rights of the accused, contrasted with concerns about public safety and court efficiency. Indeed, some reforms that appeared, at first glance, to favor the interests of accused defendants were later resisted by organizations that reliably favor due process protections. For example, the American Civil Liberties Union expressed doubts about California's bail reform efforts, due in part to concerns about whether the PRAI that would, in a sense, replace judges' discretionary power would prove to be racially tinged (Exstrum, 2018).

As proponents rally behind reform legislation, it is important for policymakers to remember that the challenges of implementation of such reforms may be substantially different in the lower courts. As Jessica Roth (2017, p. 235) observed, "[n]owhere are the structural disincentives and barriers to innovation and effective judicial leadership more daunting" than in misdemeanor courts. Misdemeanor courts are the most varied in terms of organizational structure and jurisdiction, which results in a lack of accountability and inconsistent enforcement of best practices (Roth, 2017). As the contemporary debates about bail policy sort themselves out, it is essential that reformers and researchers be mindful of Malcolm Feeley's observation about criminal courts:

> The criminal court is a political agency, a public service institution that operates within the constraints of scarce resources and faces conflicting and competing demands from a multiplicity of publics and the organizational exigences of its own personnel. Perhaps its most visible quality is fragmentation: it is fragmented in its organizations, its operations, and its goals.
>
> *(Feeley, 2013, p. 6)*

In judging lower courts' capacity to adapt to new expectations for the purposes and limitations of bail, and the constraints on pretrial detention and release, reformers would be wise to pay close attention to the resources, political expectations, and capacities of those who work in, and with, those courts.

References

Administrative Office of the Courts. (2018, May 9). *Uniform fine/bail forfeiture schedule.* Retrieved from www.utcourts.gov/resources/rules/ucja/append/c_ fineba/FineBail_Schedule.pdf

Alabama Rules of Criminal Procedure, Rule 7.2.

American Bar Association. (2007). *ABA standards for criminal justice third edition: Pretrial release.* Retrieved from www.americanbar.org/content/dam/aba/publications/ criminal_justice_standards/pretrial_release.authcheckdam.pdf

American Civil Liberties Union. (2018, July 25). *ACLU endorses senate bail reform bill.* Retrieved from www.aclu.org/news/aclu-endorses-senate-bail-reform-bill

American Civil Liberties Union. (2018, October 10). *ACLU sues Denver for jailing man who could not pay $50 fee.* Retrieved from www.aclu.org/news/aclu-sues-denver-jailing-man-who-could-not-pay-50-fee

Board of Governors of the Federal Reserve System. (2016). *Report on the economic well-being of U.S. households in 2015.* Washington, DC: Federal Reserve Board. Retrieved from www.federalreserve.gov/2015-report-economic-well-being-us-households-201605.pdf

Boruchowitz, R. C., Brink, M. N., & Dimino, M. (2009). *Minor crimes, massive waste: The terrible toll of America's broken misdemeanor courts.* Washington, DC: National Association of Criminal Defense Lawyers. Retrieved from www.nacdl.org/reports/misdemeanor/

Cathey, D., & Vallejos, I. (2014, June). *New Mexico bail bond schedules: A comparison of Bernalillo County's bond schedule to 21 New Mexico jurisdictions.* New Mexico: Bernalilli County Public Safety Division. Retrieved from http://isr.unm.edu/reports/2014/new-mexico-bail-bond-schedules-a-comparison-of-bernalillo-countys-bond-schedule-to-21-new-mexico-jurisdictions.pdf

Danzig, C. (2011, June 17). *Video arraignments save money and make judges feel safer.* New York, NY: Above the Law. Retrieved from https://abovethelaw.com/2011/06/video-arraignments-save-money-and-make-judges-feel-safer/

Devers, L. (2011). *Plea and charge bargaining: Research summary.* Washington, DC: U.S. Bureau of Justice Assistance.

Dobbie, W., Goldin, J., & Yang, C. (2018). The effects of pre-trial detention on conviction, future crime, and employment: Evidence from randomly assigned judges. *American Economic Review, 108*, 201–240.

D'Onofrio, M. (2018, October 11). Philly's courts to stop withholding bail fee. *The Philadelphia Tribune.* Retrieved from www.phillytrib.com/news/philly-s-courts-to-stop-withholding-bail-fee/article_3830412f-1e50-5d96-b565-3ba0bfc9aaaa.html

Elek, J., Sapia, S., & Keilitz, S. (2017). *Use of court date reminder notices to improve court appearance rates* (Pretrial Justice Brief 10). Williamsburg, VA: National Center for State Courts' Pretrial Justice Center for Courts.

Ewing, M. (2017, December 25). A judicial pact to cut court costs for the poor. *The Atlantic.*

Exstrum, O. (2018, August 27). California is about to abolish cash bail: Criminal justice advocates aren't happy. *Mother Jones.* Retrieved from www.motherjones.com/ crime-justice/2018/08/california-preventive-detention-cash-bail-risk-assessment/

Feeley, M. (2013). *Court reform on trial: Why simple solutions fail.* New Orleans, LA: Qui Pro Quo Books.

Ford, M. (2017, February 5). When your judge isn't a lawyer. *The Atlantic.* Retrieved from www.theatlantic.com/politics/archive/2017/02/when-your-judge-isnt-a-lawyer/515568/

Gerstein, C. (2013). Plea bargaining and the right to counsel at bail hearings. *Michigan Law Review, 111*(8), 1513–1534.

Goldkamp, J. S., & Gottfredson, M. R. (1979). Bail decision making and pretrial detention: Surfacing judicial policy. *Law and Human Behavior, 3*(4), 227–249.

Graff, D. (2018, May 7). *Google bans ads for bail bond services.* Retrieved from www.blog.google/products/ads/google-bans-ads-for-bail-bonds-services/

Harris, K. D., & Paul, R. (2017, January 20). To shrink jails, let's reform bail. *The New York Times.* Retrieved from www.nytimes.com/2017/07/20/opinion/kamala-harris-and-rand-paul-lets-reform-bail.html

Haynes, C. (2018, August 29). *Bernie Sanders introduces bill to eliminate cash bail. Equal justice under law.* Retrieved from https://equaljusticeunderlaw.org/ thejusticereport/2018/8/22/bernie-sanders-introduces-bill-to-eliminate-cash-bail

Human Rights Watch. (2010, December 2). The price of freedom: Bail and pretrial detention of low income nonfelony defendants in New York City. *Human Rights Watch*. Retrieved from www.hrw.org/report/2010/12/02/price-freedom/bail-and-pretrial-detention-low-income-nonfelony-defendants-new-york#

Injustice Watch Staff. (2016, October 14). *Change difficult as bail system's powerful hold continues punishing the poor*. Retrieved from http://injusticewatch.org/interactives/bent-on-bail

Johnson, M., & Johnson, L. A. (2012). Bail: Reforming policies to address overcrowded jails, the impact of race on detention, and community revival in Harris County, Texas. *Northwestern Journal of Law & Social Policy, 7*, 42–86.

Karnow, C. E. (2008). Setting bail for public safety. *Berkeley Journal of Criminal Law, 13* (1), 1–30.

King, N. (2013). Three directions for future research into sentencing discretion. *Justice Quarterly, 30*(2), 223–230.

Kitchenman, A. (2018, July 4). New law gives judges more discretion when setting bail. *Alaska Public Media*. Retrieved from www.alaskapublic.org/2018/07/04/new-law-gives-judges-more-discretion-when-setting-bail/

Koepke, J., & Robinson, D. (2018, March 17). *Danger ahead: Risk assessment and the future of bail reform*. Retrieved from www.americanbailcoalition.org/wp-content/uploads/2018/06/Danger-Ahead.pdf

Krupnick, M. (2017, September 20). Bail roulette: How the same minor crime can cost $250 or $10,000. *The Guardian*. Retrieved from www.theguardian.com/us-news/2017/sep/20/bail-disparities-across-the-us-reflect-inequality-it-is-the-poor-people-who-suffer

Lafler v. Cooper, 132 S. Ct. 1376 (2012).

LEAD Law Enforcement Assisted Diversion. (n.d.). About LEAD. Retrieved from http://leadkingcounty.org/about/

LEAD. (n.d.). What is LEAD? *The Official Site of the City of Albany, New York*. Retrieved from www.albanyny.gov/Government/Departments/PoliceDepartment/ LEAD.aspx

Minton, T. D., & Zeng, Z. (2015, June). *Jail inmates at midyear 2014*. Washington, DC: Bureau of Justice Statistics. Retrieved from www.bjs.gov/content/pub/pdf/jim14.pdf

Missouri v. Frye, 566 U.S. 134 (2012).

Moraff, C. (2016, March 24). U.S. cities are looking for alternatives to cash bail. *Next City*. Retrieved from https://nextcity.org/daily/entry/cities-alternatives-cash-bail

National Association of Criminal Defense Lawyers. (2017, January 18). *Report: Nation's criminal defense bar documents "Sixth Amendment-free" proceedings in South Carolina Courts*. Retrieved from www.nacdl.org/RushToJudgement_Release/

National Center for Access to Justice. (2013, January 25). *Length of a bail hearing in North Dakota: 3 Minutes*. Retrieved from http://ncforaj.org/2013/01/25/length-of-a-bail-hearing-in-north-dakota-3-minutes

New York Consolidated Laws, Criminal Procedure Law CPL § 510.30 (2018).

New York State. (2018). *2018 State of the state: Restoring fairness in New York's criminal justice system*. Retrieved from www.ny.gov/programs/restoring-fairness-new-yorks-criminal-justice-system

New York State Office of Court Administration. (2006). *The twenty-ninth annual report of the chief administrator of the courts for calendar year 2006*. New York, NY: New York State Unified Court System.

New York State Office of Indigent Legal Services (n.d.). *Counsel at first appearance*. Retrieved from www.ils.ny.gov/content/counsel-first-appearance

Palmer, C. (2018, February 22). For some crimes, Philadelphia says goodbye to cash bail. *Governing the states and localities*. Retrieved from www.governing.com/topics/public-justice-safety/tns-philadelphia-cash-bail.html

Price, D. D., Tvedt, C. Andersson, E., & Greene., T. (2016). *Summary injustice: A look at constitutional deficiencies in South Carolina's summary courts*. Washington, DC: National Association of Criminal Defense Lawyers and the American Civil Liberties Union.

Rankin, K. (2018, May 7). National black mama's bail out seeks to reunite families for mother's day. *Colorlines*. Retrieved from www.colorlines.com/articles/national-black-mamas-bail-out-seeks-reunite-families-mothers-day

Rappleye, H., Breslauer, B., & Atalla, M. (2018, September 2). *'It always comes down to money:' How a nonprofit is changing lives by paying bail. NBC News*. Retrieved from www.nbcnews.com/news/crime-courts/it-always-comes-down-money-how-nonprofit-changing-lives-paying-n905221

Roth, J. A. (2017). The culture of misdemeanor courts. *Hofstra Law Review, 46*(1), 215–252.

Schnacke, T. R. (2014, September). *Fundamental of bail: A resource guide for pretrial practitioners and a framework for American pretrial reform*. Retrieved from https://s3.amazonaws.com/static.nicic.gov/Library/028360.pdf

Schnacke, T. R., Jones, M. R., & Brooker, C. M. B. (2010, September 24). *The history of bail and pretrial release*. Rockville, MD: Pretrial Justice Institute. Retrieved from https://b.3cdn.net/crjustice/2b990da76de40361b6_rzm6ii4zp.pdf

Senate 1593 Pretrial Integrity Safety Act of 2017. (2018, July 2017). Retrieved from www.congress.gov/bill/115th-congress/senate-bill/1593

Shen, A. (2017, October 19). New Orleans' great bail reform experiment. *CityLab*. Retrieved from www.citylab.com/equity/2017/10/new-orleanss-great-bail-reform-experiment/543396/

Smith, A., & Maddan, S. (2011). *Three-minute justice: Haste and waste in Florida's misdemeanor courts*. Washington, DC: National Association of Criminal Defense Lawyers. Retrieved from www.nacdl.org/reports/threeminutejustice/

Smith, A., Maddan, S., Price, D., & Tvedt, C. (2017). *Rush to judgment: How South Carolina's summary courts fail to protect constitutional rights*. Washington, DC: National Association of Criminal Defense Lawyers.

Stevenson, M. (2018). Distortion of justice: How the inability to pay bail affects case outcomes. *Journal of Law, Economics & Organization, 34*(4), 511–542.

Stevenson, M. T., & Mayson, S. G. (2017). Pretrial detention and bail. *Reforming Criminal Justice, 3*, 21–47. Retrieved from http://academyforjustice.org/wp-content/uploads/2017/10/2_Reforming-Criminal-Justice_Vol_3_Pretrial-Detention-and-Bail.pdf

Subramanian, R., Delaney, R., Roberts, S., Fishman, N., & McGarry, P. (2015, February). *Incarceration's front door: The misuse of jails in America*. New York, NY: Vera Institute of Justice. Retrieved from www.vera.org/publications/incarcerations-front-door-the-misuse-of-jails-in-america

The Official Website of the City of New York. (2018, January 24). *New text message reminders for summons recipients improves attendance in court and dramatically cuts warrants*. Retrieved from www1.nyc.gov/office-of-the-mayor/news/058-18/new-text-message-reminders-summons-recipients-improves-attendance-court-dramatically

The Pretrial Justice Institute. (2012). *Rational and transparent bail decision making: Moving from a cash-based to a risk-based process*. Rockville, MD: The Pretrial Justice Institute.

Truman, J., & Morgan, R. (2018). *Criminal victimization, 2015*. Washington, DC: Bureau of Justice Statistics.

Widgery, A. (2013, April 23) *Bail bond agent business practices*. Washington, DC: National Conference of State Legislatures. Retrieved from www.ncsl.org/research/civil-and-criminal-justice/bail-bond-agent-business-practices.aspx

Worden, A. P., Morgan, K. A., Shteynberg, R. V., & Davies, A. L. (2018). What difference does a lawyer make? Impacts of early counsel on misdemeanor bail decisions and outcomes in rural and small town courts. *Criminal Justice Policy Review, 29*(6–7), 710–735.

Zimring, F. E. (2007). *The great American crime decline*. New York, NY: Oxford University Press.

13

NECESSARY BUT NOT SUFFICIENT

A Reexamination of Procedural Justice in the Lower Courts (and Beyond)

Julian Adler, Rachel Swaner, and Michael Rempel[1]

When researchers from the National Center for State Courts first set out to evaluate the Red Hook Community Justice Center back in 2009, they evinced a healthy skepticism about what they might find. Located in an isolated corner of Brooklyn, New York, the Justice Center is a community court that handles misdemeanor cases from three police precincts. Wherever possible, the Justice Center offers defendants the opportunity to complete community service and short-term social or clinical services in lieu of jail and fines. Compared to the approach taken on cases routed through the centralized criminal court, the researchers expected to see reduced use of punitive sanctions—and, indeed, only 1% of misdemeanor defendants, who pled guilty, in Justice Center cases were sentenced to jail, compared to 15% of cases in a matched comparison group (Lee et al., 2013).[2] Considering the limited duration of community or social service interventions—often a mere two or three days—the researchers cautioned, however, that it was unlikely that the new approach to sentencing would reduce recidivism.

When it came time to analyze the data a few years later, the researchers were pleasantly surprised: "A defendant whose misdemeanor case was processed at the Red Hook Community Justice Center is 20 percent less likely to be re-arrested than a similar defendant whose case was processed in a traditional criminal court" (Lee et al., p. 153). Furthermore, the researchers noted that this recidivism reduction was "comparable to other proven criminal justice interventions, many of which are of long duration" (Lee et al., p. 176).

Despite these positive effects, the researchers struggled to square the empirical findings with their hypothesized theories of change. Going in, the assumption had been that any detectable impact on recidivism would, at least in part, reflect the therapeutic impact of social and clinical services or the use of evidence-based deterrence strategies, with the latter seen in the Justice Center's close monitoring of defendant compliance with service mandates and regular use of sanctions for noncompliance. However, quantitative analysis did not provide support for these hypotheses. Instead, relying heavily on qualitative findings from interviews with offenders and observations in the Red Hook and the downtown criminal courts, the researchers turned to a third explanation: "procedural justice [was] the most plausible alternative explanation for the observed reduction in recidivism among [Justice Center] defendants" (Lee et al., p. 139).

In retrospect, not all of the qualitative data supported this procedural justice hypothesis. For example, respondents cited "leniency"—hinting that less punitive *outcomes* mattered more than a fair *process*—as the primary difference between the Red Hook and downtown courts, ranking "respect" thereafter. A number of respondents quite explicitly tied their greater overall perceptions that they were treated fairly at the Justice Center, not to better interpersonal interactions, but to the kinds of sentences they received at the end of the day—less often "jail" and more often an order to attend a "class." As one respondent summarized, "[They] explained to me that I had a choice, did I want to go on or take the class? That experience was something new to me" (Lee et al., 2013, p. 39). A subtle, but fascinating, element contained in the preceding quoted excerpt is that it actually evokes both outcome and process fairness. The respondent praises the Justice Center for offering a sentence to a class in lieu of jail (better outcome) and for affording the respondent input (a "voice") into whether this kind of alternative was preferable (better process). Another cautionary note contained in the qualitative data was that, despite the positive perceptions that Red Hook respondents had of the Justice Center, there was no significant difference between the percentage of Red Hook and downtown court users who self-reported that they would continue to do the things that sent them to court in the first place—and those saying their behavior would not change was high (three quarters of respondents). Indeed, the respondent quoted earlier went on to state: "I still walk my dog off the leash."

Finally, in the conclusion of the qualitative report, the researchers evoked the larger context of any court's efforts to promote procedural justice, emphasizing the role of the Justice Center in mitigating "some of the damage done by law enforcement and act[ing] as a check and balance against the potentially capricious exercise of power by the police" (Lee et al., 2015, p. 49). This last theme, that the impact of procedural justice in court may be mediated or constrained by negative experiences with the police or other negative experiences during case processing, is explored further in the following.

To summarize, it is not entirely clear that procedural justice in the courtroom best captured the entirety of defendants' experiences of the system or truly explained their subsequent actions, after considering the totality of findings in the Justice Center evaluation. These complexities notwithstanding, many readers took the National Center for State Courts' evaluation as a largely unqualified endorsement of procedural justice. Comparing Red Hook to a similar approach being taken on misdemeanor cases across the river at Newark Community Solutions in New Jersey, *The Guardian* went so far as to proclaim procedural justice to be "[t]he simple idea that could *transform* US criminal justice" (Rosenberg, 2015, Article Title, our emphasis).

Popularized through the work of Yale law professor Tom Tyler, procedural justice has come to represent the idea that the way defendants are treated in court can matter as much as—if not more—to them as the substantive outcome (Tyler, 1984). It challenges traditional frameworks for evaluating case outcomes, shifting from a calculus of "wins and losses" to an emphasis on the interpersonal treatment of defendants and the overall quality and integrity of court procedures. Although there is some variation, scholars typically operationalize the experience of procedural justice as defendants' perceptions of five key elements: voice (the opportunity to tell your side of the story); respect (being treated with dignity); neutrality (decision makers acting without bias); understanding (comprehending what is happening and the implications of decision made); and helpfulness (having your personal needs and situation taken into account) (Frazer, 2006; Malangone, 2017; Tyler, 1990). Ultimately, as with the evaluation of the Red Hook Community Justice Center, proponents of procedural justice argue that the way defendants are treated in the courtroom has tremendous bearing on whether they will comply with court orders in the present and the law in the future (Schulhofer, Tyler, & Huq, 2011). In other words, the experience of procedural justice *legitimizes* the authority of the criminal justice system and thereby elicits voluntary compliance with the law.

But as political philosopher John Rawls cautions in his seminal text *A Theory of Justice* (1971), the substantive preconditions for this "pure" view of procedural justice require a "just basic structure, including a just political constitution and a just arrangement of economic and social institutions" (p. 76). Similarly, researchers working outside of the criminal justice context (Bauman & Skitka, 2011; Brockner & Wiesenfeld, 1996; Mayer, Greenbaum, Kuenzi, & Shteynberg, 2009; Mullen & Skitka, 2006) have suggested that boundary conditions exist for procedural justice, including when people's outcome preferences represent strong moral convictions (i.e., something is right or wrong, moral or immoral) and when an outcome violates a central aspect of one's personal identity.

We hypothesize that similar limits also extend to applications of procedural justice in criminal courts, generally, and in lower courts, specifically. Recent research (Swaner, Ramdath, Martinez, Hahn, & Walker, 2018; Swaner, White, Kralstein, & Lyons 2019) suggests that, in fact, defendants may often have positive perceptions of procedural justice in the courtroom, but still maintain negative views of the court system, overall. This may help to explain why criminal justice researchers have struggled thus far to make a consistent empirical case for procedural justice's efficacy in changing future behavior (Farley, Jensen, & Rempel, 2014). Ostensibly, marked asymmetries between fair process and fair outcome may limit—though certainly not obviate—the utility of procedural justice as a tool for criminal justice reform.

Taking an intensive look at this recent research, we argue for a more nuanced and modest view of procedural justice in the criminal court setting. Viewing procedural justice in the courtroom as both a useful tool for advancing reform and a legitimate end in itself, we caution against overreliance on it as a decontextualized and ahistorical means for legitimizing the courts and the broader criminal justice system. We conclude on a cautionary note about overselling procedural justice as a means for increasing compliance with court orders and the law.

New Research

The Center for Court Innovation recently conducted two separate studies that suggest that while procedural justice can be a useful tool for improving the experiences of criminal court users, positive perceptions of procedural justice in court do not necessarily translate into believing in the overall fairness and legitimacy of the court system. In the first study, researchers chose two mid-sized cities (Newark, New Jersey and Cleveland, Ohio) to conduct an exploratory study of procedural justice. Outside of the Newark and Cleveland Municipal Courts, researchers conducted 800 closed-ended surveys with justice-involved people to determine their perceptions of procedural justice and overall feelings of fairness and legitimacy related to multiple criminal justice actors and agencies. Additionally, researchers conducted 100 open-ended interviews with people who had extensive justice system involvement to learn about how they operationalized concepts of procedural justice and what impacts their overall perceptions of legitimacy (Swaner et al., 2018).

In the second study, criminal justice reformers implemented a two-pronged intervention in a New York City criminal court to determine if physical changes to a courthouse and courtroom (e.g., deep cleaning; improved audibility; signage related to wayfinding, rules, court processes and defendant rights) and attempted improvements in judicial behaviors (e.g., using a script to explain the process at the beginning of each session, questions to ask of each defendant) impacted defendant perceptions of procedural justice and overall attitudes towards the court system. As part of a quasi-experimental evaluation of the intervention, Swaner et al. (2019) administered surveys to over 1,100 defendants, the majority of whom were in court on misdemeanor or lesser charges.

The current procedural justice theory in a court setting is that more positive perceptions lead to greater views of the court system as legitimate, which in turn leads to increased compliance with court mandates and law-abiding behavior. Findings from these studies—particularly that positive perceptions of procedural justice did not necessarily lead to greater generalized feelings of legitimacy—point to the limits of the current and popular conceptualization of procedural justice as a means to an end.

The Limits of a Decontextualized and Ahistorical Concept

Participants in both studies provided their overall views of the court system, and their experiences suggest at least three reasons why a more modest and contextualized concept of procedural justice may be appropriate: Their overall perceptions of the court system were informed by (1) their full continuum of experiences across the criminal justice system, (2) witnessing inconsistencies in processes and outcomes, and (3) the historical and political significance and resonance of the court system in their lives.

The Continuum of Experiences Across the Criminal Justice System

As one Newark participant stated: "It's one thing to be treated on a surface level with respect... but I think the true respect comes in how the whole process treats you from beginning to end and the sentence."[3] Indeed, while people may have positive interactions with any number of court actors (e.g., judges, court officers, defense attorneys) who are acting in a procedurally just way, the "process" includes a number of additional components: transportation to the court, the amount of bail set and ability to pay, and the consequences of spending a day in court. One Newark participant described his experience going to court from a local jail:

> I didn't tell you about the transportation process to court. They get you up 3:00 or 3:30 in the morning.... They going to put y'all in holding cells. ... They got like 4–5 holding cells. It's going to be like 80 people in each room. Sometimes it's standing room only. You're going to stay there until about 7:30. The sheriff's department is going to come and get you. You get a band on your arm. They going to look at your band, they going to tell you where you go in court, now they're going to hook you up to a four-man chain. ... They going to put you on a bus, they going to transport you to the courthouse. You're going to go downstairs to the big ... Essex County courtroom bullpens, they only have like two or three cells so they can only take like six people up at a time, eight people up at a time. Mind you, you've been up since 3:00–3:30 this morning. You might not get back to the jail until like 3:00–4:00pm. The whole thing is, you might go through all of that and get canceled.

That many people go to court and wait many hours for their case to be heard—or, as in the previous case, rescheduled—factors into defendants' views of their experience in court. As one Cleveland participant noted,

> I don't think it's fair how you can inconvenience my whole life and then find me not guilty and that's just it. What about all them hours I missed at work? What about all the gas I used getting back and forth?

Missed work was an oft-cited unintended consequence of the court process itself, not only for time spent in court on any given day, but for jail time served when fines or bail could not be paid. As another Cleveland participant explained,

> Going to court pushed a lot back, because you can go to court, and they want you to pay. If you can't pay, they send you into a cell. You miss out on a lot. ... I lost a job because of court before.

Similarly, others felt that even convictions of low-level offenses impacted their lives, as this New York City participant stated:

> I had half a blunt. I see many here sitting all day, spending a day in court over something that is supposed to no longer be a crime. Now I have lost income from work, [and have] an arrest on my record.

In addition to frequently citing the repercussions of time spent travelling to and waiting in court, many participants pointed to their initial interactions with law enforcement at the very start of their case—before any court involvement—as critical in shaping their overall experience. Indeed, in the New York study, when asked what accounts for the difference in their positive perceptions of procedural justice during court that day and their overall negative views of the court system, people responded with answers about the police: "problems with police officers being unjust, but less [the] court"; "in society today, people are judged before they get to the judge, a lot of times by the police"; and "the problem is the police, not the court system itself, but it feeds into the system."

Similarly, quantitative data from the survey component of the study in Newark and Cleveland showed that satisfaction with the criminal justice system (including prosecutors, defense attorneys, judges, and the court system, in addition to police and jail administrators) was significantly higher for people who had positive perceptions of procedural justice during their most recent police stop or arrest, those who had positive general perceptions of local police, those who viewed their last court outcome as fair, and those who felt that judges are generally fair in their decisions. Having positive perceptions of procedural justice during most recent court appearance, on the other hand, was *not* a significant predictor of global satisfaction with the criminal justice system.

Inconsistencies in Processes and Outcomes

Many defendants charged with low-level misdemeanors cycle in and out of the court system, and their views of the court's legitimacy are often based on multiple experiences, with the most recent and possibly "positive" experience not necessarily obliterating the memory or impact of prior negative ones. Indeed, some participants pointed to the ways they or people close to them had been treated in court on previous occasions—"Even as a juvenile, I got caught with two bags of weed, and they tried to really roast me for that" stated one Newark participant—as the reason why they had overall negative views of the court. They often cited how their *process* experiences differed by the demeanor and tone of the judge. Another Newark participant explained:

> I've been in the courtroom quite a few times and ... you can tell when the judge is kind of over it or when he's going to be lenient or extra hard. I've been in a courtroom to where the judge was like, "Stand up. Tuck your sweater in your pants. Don't come here like this." What are you talking about tuck my sweater in? You get some judges like that, but then you've got some judges that are just kind of cool and they work with you like, "Listen, I'll give you some time. If you don't have money, just make a payment plan." You've

> got some judges that be like, "Listen. You've got to come up with $500 right now." … You can tell people just kind of be like, "Alright. What judge do I got? What mood is the judge going to be in?" He was just like, "Relax. I'm just trying to get you guys in and out. I don't want to waste anybody's time or have you in here any longer than you should be." Some judges will keep you there until the end just for the hell of it.

This very inconsistency—that one might appear before a procedurally just judge but, for random reasons that cannot be controlled, one might alternatively appear before an altogether uncaring judge—is itself an element of procedural unfairness that is fully perceived by this respondent.

Other participants pointed to inconsistency in *outcomes* for different groups—particularly divided along race and class lines—as a reason for questioning the legitimacy of the court, even if they had had positive experiences themselves. As one Cleveland participant explained:

> Since [I was in court for] just a traffic warrant, I didn't feel the need to need an attorney … the guys with the lawyers go first and whoever doesn't have a lawyer … go after everybody else. I get to sit back and I watch … how the judge is actually dictating the penalties to these cases. In a lot of the cases, for the same offense, you can see a clear difference. You hate to make it a white and black thing but it was just so prevalent in your face as you're sitting there. I'm saying to myself, "She just gave this guy probation and then this guy did the same thing and you're sending him to jail for six months." … I saw it a lot as I was sitting there.

Similarly, one New York City participant pointed to the racial differences in sentencing outcomes for drug crimes: "[The court is] biased because [the] crack epidemic hit. It hit people of color. Now that white people are addicted, they want to give them treatment as an alternative to jail."

Recently, the vast and random inconsistencies seen in defendant outcomes was illustrated in a study of bail decision-making in New York City (Barry-Jester, 2018). In all five boroughs of the city, it was found that based on the identity of the judge who happened to be presiding, similar defendants could have significantly different probabilities of receiving release on recognizance (without conditions) or having to pay bail at arraignment—and that, among cases facing bail, the bail amounts also significantly differed by judge. For instance, in felony cases, bail-setting rates ranged from 30% to 69% across different judges. Whether through first-hand experience across multiple cases that were each handled differently, or by hearing from family members or friends with justice involvement, it makes sense to assume that even if defendants themselves lack the hard data produced in this type of study, they still experience and are fully aware of the inconsistency in decision-making that this study reveals. In this context, defendants, may appreciate when they do appear before a judge whose interpersonal interactions and explanations in court seem comprehensible and respectful, but it may not be so credible to expect deeper attitudes about the legitimacy of the justice system to change significantly.

Historical and Political Context

Finally, the research makes a case for a contextualized view of procedural justice and its limits to improving overall legitimacy of the courts by highlighting that defendants sometimes see the court—particularly because of its sentencing power—as perpetuating a racist American history. As one Cleveland participant stated,

> Every time I think about [the criminal justice system], I just think about the 13th amendment. … The one that got rid of slavery and involuntary servitude *except as punishment for a crime if duly convicted*. Like what the fuck? (emphasis added).

A Newark participant clearly situated the power of the court within a racial and political context: "Let's look at the facts. Black man get conviction, black man can't vote. That's the bottom line."

Necessary but Not Sufficient

Without question, the totality of the extant research literature points to procedural justice as a necessary component of court reform. In fact, the literature is not without studies that make a clear empirical case for procedural justice impacting defendants' future behavior. For example, a national study of 23 drug treatment courts from across the country found that the drug courts with judges who scored medium-to-high on procedural justice attributes produced significantly greater recidivism *reductions* than other drug courts—after controlling for other policy, practice, and defendant characteristics across programs (Rossman, Roman, Zweig, Rempel, & Lindquist, 2011). Yet this very study also illustrates the importance of outcomes as well as process, because drug courts come from a starting point of creating less punitive and more therapeutic outcomes, meaning that the most successful drug courts are not changing behavior through process changes alone.

To be clear, even where outcomes or the larger context of procedural justice is more challenging to impact than in a drug court, the literature still by no means discounts classic conceptions of procedural justice. Indeed, in our recent studies in Newark, Cleveland, and New York City, many participants described procedural justice concerns—how they felt disrespected by court actors, how they did not understand essential legal rights and judicial processes, how they felt they did not have a voice, how they perceived judges to be biased against people who could not afford lawyers or who had criminal histories, and how they wished the courts had been more understanding of their situations and personal needs (Swaner et al., 2018). However, study participants also pointed to ways in which factors other than procedural justice impact perceptions of the legitimacy of the court system, including the view that the court metes out excessive punishment for low-level crimes, particularly those that defendants do not even believe should be crimes.

Views of Misdemeanor Crimes

Participants who had been charged with misdemeanors often felt courts "worry a lot about small crimes when the focus should be on big crimes" (as one New York City participant stated) and "should let go of petty things and use resources for more important criminal offenses and prevention" (as another New York City participant noted). Moreover, some felt that there was a lack of proportionality when it came to low-level drug offenses. As one Cleveland participant said,

> [For] severe crimes, maybe they're fair. But the minor ones, the lower-level crimes, I think a lot of times they could try to rehabilitate you more, give you some help or treatment to make sure you're not coming back in a year or a few years or something.

One Newark participant made an explicit connection between low-level crimes and court legitimacy, showing why procedural justice might not make a difference in overall attitudes:

> People who have been involved with courts for drug possession and drug dealing, they tend to think badly of the courts because they don't think that what they're doing is really a crime. People that have a bad opinion of it are the ones that have an issue with the laws, not with the judge.

This sentiment underscores the notion that some people think certain misdemeanor crimes are not actually criminal. As one Cleveland participant stated: "Morally, personally, I don't think that I did anything wrong, just because I had a little bit of a substance that I don't really feel is very detrimental." And, as the aforementioned Newark participant described, it may be the case that if they do not believe the law to be legitimate, the institution that applies the law (i.e., the court) may also be perceived as problematic.

Moving Forward

When asked about why fellow judges should prioritize procedural justice, Hennepin County, Minnesota District Judge Kevin Burke offered a twofold response: "The first reason is that procedural fairness is the right thing to do. But the [other] [sic] good reason is that procedural fairness increases compliance with orders" (Center for Court Innovation, 2017, p. 19). In the days ahead, we urge justice reformers to double-down on the former but to seriously consider doubling-back on the latter.

We agree that procedural justice is the right thing to do in the courtroom, and as argued, it must extend—in all directions—beyond the courtroom to stand a chance at legitimizing local criminal justice systems. Even a strong dose of procedural justice when a case is heard in the courtroom may be insufficient to overcome its glaring absence at other procedural stages—seen most notably in oftentimes negative interactions with police as well as in real and perceived adverse life impacts of repeated trips to court and long waiting times, let alone, in some cases, perceived unjust and/or arbitrary incarceration in jail. Ultimately, the aforementioned research strongly suggests that the practice of procedural justice will prove ineffective if judges and other courtroom actors are not willing to back it up with substantively fair decision-making.

The upshot? As researchers continue to test the impact of procedural justice in courtrooms and other corners of the criminal justice system, reformers and practitioners alike should consider adapting a more modest posture toward its efficacy and more honest posture toward its relationship to *actual* fairness.

Notes

1 We would like to thank Elise Jensen and Hayley Setear for providing research support.
2 The Red Hook evaluation ultimately found that 11% of Justice Center and 17% of comparison cases received a sentence to jail, although nearly all of the jail sentences imposed by the Justice Center were actually "re-sentences" after a defendant first received an alternative to jail but was noncompliant with its terms, for example by repeatedly failing to show up to perform assigned community service.
3 All quotations from the two studies are drawn from unpublished interview transcripts.

References

Barry-Jester, A. M. (2018). *You've been arrested. Will you get bail? Can you pay it? It may all depend on your judge*. Retrieved from https://fivethirtyeight.com/features/youve-been-arrested-will-you-get-bail-can-you-pay-it-it-may-all-depend-on-your-judge/

Bauman, C. W., & Skitka, L. J. (2011). Moral disagreement and procedural justice: Moral mandates as constraints to voice effects. *Australian Journal of Psychology, 61*(1), 40–49.

Brockner, J., & Wiesenfeld, B. M. (1996). An integrative framework for explaining reactions to decisions: Interactive effects of outcomes and procedures. *Psychological Bulletin, 120*(2), 189–208.

Center for Court Innovation. (2017). *To be fair: Conversations about procedural justice.* New York, NY: Center for Court Innovation.

Lee, C., Cheesman, F., Rottman, D., Swaner, R., Lambson, S.H., Rempel M., & Curtis, R. (2013). *A community court grows in Brooklyn: A comprehensive evaluation of the Red Hook Community Justice Center.* Williamsburg, VA: National Center for State Courts. Submitted to the U.S. Department of Justice.

Farley, E., Jensen, E., & Rempel, M. (2014). *Improving courtroom communication: A procedural justice experiment in Milwaukee.* New York, NY: Center for Court Innovation.

Frazer, S. M. (2006). *The impact of the community court model on defendant perceptions of fairness.* New York, NY: Center for Court Innovation.

Malangone, D. (2017). *Integrating procedural justice in domestic violence cases: A practice guide.* New York, NY: Center for Court Innovation.

Mayer, D. M., Greenbaum, R. L., Kuenzi, M., & Shteynberg, G. (2009). When do fair procedures not matter? A test of the identity violation effect. *Journal of Applied Psychology, 94*(1), 142–161.

Mullen, E., & Skitka, L. J. (2006). Exploring the psychological underpinnings of the moral mandate effect: Motivated reasoning, group differentiation, or anger? *Journal of Personality and Social Psychology, 90*(4), 629–643.

Rawls, J. (1971). *A theory of justice.* Cambridge, MA: Belknap Press of Harvard University Press.

Rosenberg, T. (2015, June 23). *The simple idea that could transform US criminal justice. The Guardian.* Retrieved from www.theguardian.com/us-news/2015/jun/23/procedural-justice-transform-us-criminal-courts

Rossman, S. B., Roman, J. K., Zweig, J. M., Rempel, M., & Lindquist, C. H. (2011). *The multi-site adult drug court evaluation.* Washington, DC: The Urban Institute.

Schulhofer, S. J., Tyler, T. R., & Huq, A. Z. (2011). American policing at a crossroads: Unsustainable policies and the procedural justice alternative. *The Journal of Criminal Law and Criminology, 101*(2), 335–374.

Swaner, R., Ramdath, C., Martinez, A., Hahn, J., & Walker, S. (2018). *What do defendants really think? Procedural justice and legitimacy in the criminal justice system.* New York, NY: Center for Court Innovation.

Swaner, R., White, E., Kralstein, D., & Lyons, L. (2019). *Procedural justice at the Manhattan Criminal Court.* New York, NY: Center for Court Innovation.

Tyler, T.R. (1984). The role of perceived injustice in defendants' evaluations of their courtroom experience. *Law and Society Review, 18*, 51–74.

Tyler, T.R. (1990). *Why people obey the law.* New Haven, CT: Yale University.

14

THE FUTURE OF DRUG, HOMELESS, AND VETERANS COURTS

Mai E. Naito

Since 1989, specialty courts or problem-solving courts have become part of the American criminal justice system to address individualized treatment for specific groups of offenders. Criminal defendants with alcohol or substance addiction and/or homelessness oftentimes become trapped in the revolving doors of the criminal justice system without adequate assistance to address the underlying cause of illegal behavior. Also, some veterans enter the justice system due to untreated traumatic experiences from their military service. Berman and Feinblatt (2001) recognized that specialty courts "broaden the focus of legal proceedings, from simply adjudicating past facts and legal issues to changing the future behavior of litigants and ensuring the future well-being of communities" (p. 126).

Therapeutic jurisprudence became a prevalent legal theory in the early 1990s to address the underlying issues of drug addictions through the courts. Slobogin (1995) defined therapeutic jurisprudence as "the use of social science to study the extent to which a legal rule or practice promotes the psychological and physical well-being of the people it affects" (p. 196). Therapeutic jurisprudence put into action the non-adversarial approach of specialty courts, which gained traction in combatting problems of prison overcrowding and high recidivism rates by defendant population who required special attention. The purpose of specialty courts is "holding offenders accountable and providing rehabilitation through effective treatment" (Atkin-Plunk & Armstrong, 2016, p. 525). As an alternative to incarceration for nonviolent offenders, specialty courts such as drug courts were created to respond to the increase in drug arrests. Now, there are over 4,000 drug courts across the United States and other specialty courts such as homeless and veteran courts have also emerged.

Long court dockets and continued issues of prison overcrowding are familiar problems of the justice system. According to the National Center for State Courts, there has been 17.8 million criminal caseloads to include felonies, misdemeanors, criminal appeals from limited jurisdiction trial courts, and other criminal cases in 2016. An overwhelming number of prison sentences were from drug convictions (Lurigio, 2008). In turn, it is estimated that over 4.5 million adults are under correctional supervision in the community (i.e., probation, parole, etc.), which is an "estimated one in 55 adults in the United States" (Kaeble, 2018, p. 1). Rather than focusing on the root causes of individuals committing vice crimes, many are oftentimes pushed in and out of the criminal justice system without proper medical or psychological care that "causes further victimization and crime, hurts the offender and his or her family, and costs taxpayers millions of dollars a year" (Alm, 2015, p. 1666). Observations at a micro-level to understand day-to-day operations of specialty courts and identify the effective procedures through performance measures is important as the macro-level observations of how the criminal justice system and the community-based treatments are affecting society as a whole (Burns, 2010; Rubio, 2008). As state legislators and policymakers are faced with limited budgets for criminal justice resources and growing prison populations, there is a need for reducing sentences for nonviolent drug crimes (Patten, Messer, & Candela, 2015). When making decisions due to limited funding, it is imperative to examine the effectiveness of specialty courts to be established or maintained, as well as explore innovative options to better accommodate and supervise offenders. This chapter extends the discussion of research on the specialty courts from Chapter 10 and provides a discussion of the future policy direction of drug courts, veterans courts, and homeless courts.

Drug Courts

Since drug courts were the first of the specialty courts to be established, there is much history and evolution to the current model to target various populations. The first drug court was established in Miami, Florida in 1989 as an experiment for handling the rise in drug-related offenses (Belenko, 1998). Since its success, the Drug Courts Standards Committee of the National Association of Drug Court Professionals (NADCP) released a report in 1997 with ten key components to be used as a framework or guidance in implementing a successful drug court. It is important to note that not all drug courts operate the same with program design and implementation (Henry, 2018). Some drug courts have been established in response to move drug-related cases to a separate docket solely to expedite case processing rather than therapeutic jurisprudence; therefore, the key components from NADCP may not be applicable to all drug courts. To recommend further actions to improve specialty courts, it is important to understand what prior literature has shown regarding the effectiveness of drug treatment courts.

Much of the research in the last decade has focused on the effectiveness of non-traditional courts, recidivism, and behavioral changes. Meta-analyses that examined over 100 drug court evaluation found that drug courts were more effective than traditional probation and reduced recidivism (Mitchell, Wilson, Eggers, & MacKenzie, 2012; Shaffer, 2011). Further studies have found support for the effectiveness of drug courts in decreases in alcohol/drug dependence as well as decreases in recidivism (Belenko, 2001; Cissner & Rempel, 2005; Goldkamp, 2003; Gottfredson, Kearley, Najaka, & Rocha, 2007; Harrell, 2003; Marlowe, DeMatteo, & Festinger, 2003; Marlowe, Heck, Huddleston, & Casebolt, 2006; Roman, Townsend, & Bhati, 2003; Wilson, Mitchell, & Mackenzie, 2006) and "significant decreases in primary drug use, arrest, and incarceration" (Evans, Li, Urada, & Anglin, 2014, p. 925). Gallagher (2014) also found that graduates of drug courts were 11 times *less* likely to reoffended in comparison to individuals who were terminated from drug court programs.

Findings on race/ethnicity, age, and level of education of the drug court participants have been mixed. Some studies found that Whites were more likely to graduate or complete drug court treatment than non-Whites (Butzin, Saum, & Scarpitti, 2002; Gray & Saum, 2005; Miller & Shutt, 2001; Schiff & Terry, 1997; Sechrest & Shicor, 2001; Senjo & Leip, 2001; Wolf, Sowards, & Wolf, 2003) while others did not find significance with race/ethnicity on successful program completion (Evans, Li, & Hser, 2009; Hickert, Boyle, & Tollefson, 2009; Mateyoke-Scrivner, Webster, Stanton, & Leukefeld, 2004; Rempel & DeStefano, 2001; Roll, Predergast, Richardson, Burdon, & Ramirez, 2005; Shannon, Jones, Newell, & Neal, 2018).

In term of age of the participants, some studies found that older participants were more likely to be successful in drug court programs (Atkin-Plunk & Armstrong, 2016; Brown, 2010;

Hickert et al., 2009; Mateyoke-Scrivner et al., 2004; Rempel & DeStefano, 2001; Wolf et al., 2003; Young & Belenko, 2002), while others did not find age significant (Butzin et al., 2002; Gallagher, 2014; Gray & Saum, 2005; Miller & Shutt, 2001; Roll et al., 2005; Schiff & Terry, 1997; Sechrest & Shicor, 2001). Also, participants with higher levels of education were more likely to be successful in drug courts (Brown, 2010; Butzin et al., 2002; Cissner & Rempel, 2005; Mateyoke-Scrivner et al., 2004; Peters, Haas, & Murrin, 1999; Schiff & Terry, 1997; Shannon et al., 2018) while other studies did not find any significance between education and drug court completion (Gray & Saum, 2005; Rempel & DeStefano, 2001; Roll et al., 2005; Sechrest & Shicor, 2001; Senjo & Leip, 2001). Although the results are mixed, it is important to note that not all drug courts are designed, implemented, and operated in the same way. More research is needed to better understand the effective aspects of drug treatment courts within each state by counties or judicial circuits that track participants beyond program completion.

Another division of drug courts operates in conjunction with child welfare. Family Treatment Drug Court (FTDC) addresses the needs of parents with substance use disorder and the goal of family reunification. The combination of the two has grown since 1995 (Cosden & Koch, 2015; Rodi et al., 2015). Cosden and Koch (2015) examined a single six-month intensive treatment program to determine behavioral changes of families participating in FTDC. In the sample of 76 adults, 115 children from 62 families, they found that successful parents in FTDC had "reductions in substance use disorders and positive 0-to-5-year-old child development" (Cosden & Koch, 2015, p. 104). In addition, it was found that successful participants had a greater likelihood of reunification as well as improved family communication and parenting abilities. Similar to the study by Cosden and Koch (2015), Rodi and colleagues (2015) studied targeted interventions with 2,596 adults, 4,245 children from 1,940 families across 12 FTDCs. The FTDC was designed to include "an evidence-based intervention focused on parenting, child and parent trauma, parent-child relationships, or parental recovery" (Rodi et al., 2015, p. 207). With treatment, they found that "children seem to be subject to less neglect and abuse, stays in out-of-home care are shorter, families are more stable, and family functioning appears to be improved" (Rodi et al., 2015, p. 230).

While research has shown that FTDCs have successful outcomes, more research is needed to further assess specific needs of the participants. Cosden and Koch (2015) indicated that additional research is needed to "identify those aspects of treatment that are associated with behavior change and to determine other methods of obtaining positive changes for older children and adolescents within these families" (p. 104). Further evaluation is necessary on how to "best match FTDC service arrays with participant needs and characteristics, establish clearer models to predict which families are best served by FTDCs, and estimate the cost and benefits of those interventions" (Rodi et al., 2015, p. 231).

While it is important to observe how drug court works in conjunction with child welfare offices, it is also important to explore participants' perspectives about drug courts. One study found that drug court participants' perception of procedural justice or fairness of the process did not significantly influence their graduation from the program or recidivism (Atkin-Plunk & Armstrong, 2016). Other focus groups provided more information about what the participants or treatment staff recommend from their experience. For example, motivations for completing a treatment program were explored and the most common responses were: avoid incarceration, commit to a sober life, and/or become a responsible parent (Farole & Cissner, 2005; Goldkamp, White, & Robinson, 2002; Patten et al., 2015). Farole and Cissner (2005) found through their focus groups that previous drug court participants suggested a need for more treatment providers partnering with the court, flexible scheduling of classes, access to education and job training, and travel accommodations and the staff recommended more treatment services for women, non-English speakers, and dually diagnosed as well as more training about addiction to judges, attorneys, and other legal staff (Farole & Cissner, 2005).

With the large population of drug-related arrests and convictions, it is not a surprise that many have multiple co-occurring disorders. Dually diagnosed offenders oftentimes have co-occurring mental health problems, but are placed in drug court programs (Belenko, 2001; Peters, Wexler, & Lurigio, 2015; Zettler, 2018). One study found successful outcomes with dually diagnosed offenders. In the drug court participants studied by Baughman, Tossone, Singer, and Flannery (2018), "substance use, mental health symptoms, and risky sexual and needle-sharing behaviors decreased from intake to discharge" (p. 11). Other research indicates that dually diagnosed offenders require more resources and supervision. Zettler (2018) found that dually diagnosed offenders "may pose a higher risk of reoffending shortly following program participation, and have different risk factors associated with recidivism than other court participants" (p. 389). The need for more knowledge and understanding about mental health and dually diagnosed offenders is significant. More research on this population is warranted for "both justice processing and behavioral development" (Zettler, 2018, p. 364).

While it is important to understand attributes of drug court participants and participants' perspectives, it is significant to observe the attributes of the judge who presides over the drug treatment court. The judge is the central figure of the drug court whose role is to closely supervise both the treatment and the offender (Driscoll, 2018). Goldkamp and colleagues (2002) found that the level of involvement by the judge is key to effective treatment. Positive judicial attributes include being respectful, fair, attentive, enthusiastic, consistent, predictable, caring, and knowledgeable (Rossman & Zweig, 2012). Burns (2010) also identified that some judges are "gifted in therapeutic, persuasive, and interpersonal skills" (p. 78). An example of judicial leadership to address absences at hearings includes a drug court judge who arranged "child care services for mothers participating in the court program so they would not miss treatment appointments because of child care obligations as the custodial parent" (Burns, 2010, p. 79).

Since the judge is a critical component of drug courts, it is imperative that judges receive continued and consistent education and training that helps in building rapport with clients and providing a better understanding of the needs of drug court participants (Atkin-Plunk & Armstrong 2016; Farole & Cissner, 2005). As the authority figure in the process, judges must be both aware and responsive to the "highly personal struggles of the defendant who are coping with stigmatizing conditions and complex, multi-faceted problems" (Burns, 2010, p. 76). Building a rapport between the judge and defendant is not as common in a criminal trial, but it is a major component in drug treatment courts. Trainings are recommended to have more experienced drug court judges to "model how to nurture and persuade defendants to facilitate treatment while also understanding and honoring the client's distinctive issues, concerns, and culture" (Burns, 2010, p. 80). Also, it is important to be open to innovative methods to accommodate the large population on drug court participants through limited resources. In order for effective drug treatment court operation, it is suggested that leadership from judges, administrators, and specialty court advocates be up-to-date on realistic implementation strategies (Griller, 2011).

It is also important to examine the population of clients who were terminated from the drug court program. As previously hypothesized, participants who were terminated were more likely to recidivate than those who successfully completed the drug court program (Gibbs, Lytle, & Wakefield, 2018). Studies that examined motivations for drug court participants found that rather than focusing on the underlying issues associated with alcohol and drug use, participants were terminated from the program listed prison avoidance as their main reason for entering drug court (Fulkerson, Keena, & O'Brien, 2012; Patten et al., 2015). Drug court admission should indicate whether the drug arrest was due to a chronic problem rather than an isolated incident that does not require rehabilitation (Griffin, Griffin, Copes, & Dantzler, 2018). The focus of drug treatment courts should be on "chemical dependency issues among habitual offenders" (Gibbs et al., 2018, p. 1). Improved evaluations to determine a participants' need is crucial in recommending treatment services and filter out individuals who do not need medical services. Griffin and colleagues (2018) found that "many of the participants did not have charges that were indicative of a need for drug rehabilitation" (p. 394).

In moving forward, scholars have recommended that drug court intake/admission criteria should be revised to better recommend treatment for those who truly benefit from behavioral changes rather than avoiding legal consequences. Also, studies have recommended that drug courts should accommodate more serious offenders (Huddleston, Marlowe, & Casebolt, 2008; Rossman & Zweig, 2012). Huddleston et al. (2008) found that "78% of adult drug courts nationwide have a probationary or post-plea condition, suggesting that drug courts are working more often with a higher risk and higher need offender population" (p. 5). There is a disconnect between the population eligible for drug court not needing the treatment and population who is not eligible for drug court due to previous criminal history, but could benefit from treatment. More research on drug court admission and clinical screening is needed. In addition, closer examination of specific populations such as veterans and homeless offenders is warranted.

Veteran and Homeless Courts

Veterans who suffer from substance use disorder, mental health conditions, or trauma may become involved in the criminal justice system upon returning to society as a civilian. Transitioning to reenter civilian lifestyle may be different than the structure and camaraderie found in the military which may put some veterans at risk of criminal behavior. Moreover, many veterans are also homeless, which creates yet another barrier for veterans to reentry. It is established that veterans with combat experience report post-traumatic stress disorder (PTSD) at a higher rate than civilians. To accommodate veterans with their specific training and combat experience, special treatment for the veteran population is recommended, usually services not available through other specialty courts.

Veteran Courts or Veteran Treatment Courts (VTC) were first introduced in 2008, and as of 2016, the U.S. Department of Veterans Affairs (VA) estimated that over 450 veteran-focused court programs are currently in operation. The purpose of VTC is to divert individuals to rehabilitation rather than incarceration, or court-ordered treatment sessions to allow veterans to have a second chance. Collaboration between the VA and the criminal justice system is one of the unique characteristics of VTC (Douds, Ahlin, Howard, & Stigerwalt, 2017). Several resources and services have been created to help address the needs of justice-involved veterans. The VA created the Health Care for Re-entry Veterans (HCRV) services that includes outreach and assessment for incarcerated veterans and referrals for social services and case management assistance for recently released veterans.

Due to untreated trauma, veterans may risk an increase in criminal justice involvement such as alcohol/drug addiction and domestic violence. Studies have shown that veterans may experience homelessness, unemployment, relationship problems, and aggressive behaviors (Tsai & Rosenheck, 2015; Yerramsetti, Simons, Coonan, & Stolar, 2017). Justice for Vets is a division of the National Association of Drug Court Professionals which helped establish over 200 veteran treatment courts nationally.

Studies have examined that veterans who were exposed to trauma during their military career may require special attention that traditional drug courts do not provide. Knudsen and Wingenfeld (2016) examined 86 veterans enrolled in a Veterans Treatment Court program and found that participants "experienced significant improvement in PTSD, depression, substance abuse, overall functioning, emotional wellbeing, relationships with others, recovery status, social connectedness, family functioning, and sleep" (p. 127). Support for effectiveness of VTC was found in several studies. One study found that "veterans particularly improved when provided a combination of trauma-specific treatment, peer mentor services, and medication" (Knudsen & Wingenfeld, 2016, p. 131). After comparing two VTCs in Kentucky, Shannon et al. (2017) found various effective themes of "services, referrals, partnerships, and program components offered the veterans a sense of accountability and a second chance at life" (p. 64). Moreover, examination of the Harris County Veterans Court found that the "integrated care approach employed in VTCs is important and appropriate, addressing issues such as mental health and substance use treatment, housing, and employment in one multifaceted program" (Yerramsetti et al., 2017, p. 519). An examination of a single VTC in Pennsylvania showed that graduates showed positive responses in their testimonies and their perspectives on the program effectiveness.

Continued research on veterans and VTC is necessary for better understanding the population and implementing effective programs and treatments. VTCs must incorporate mentorship and understanding of the military/veteran culture as studies have indicated that veterans benefitted from trauma-specific therapy and positive peer role models (Knudsen & Wingenfeld, 2016). Mentorship is a key aspect of VTC that provides guidance as "veterans faced unique challenges with family and community reintegration that were not easily addressed in the traditional criminal justice venue" (Douds et al., 2017, p. 757).

Another consideration is responding to the needs of women veterans that often do not have the same support as their male counterparts. The U.S. Department of Justice estimated that veterans made up about 10% of those serving time in state and federal prisons and women veterans made up about 1% of this population—or approximately 1,400 women. The National Resource Center for Justice Involved Women (NRCJIW) addressed that "issues facing women veterans in the justice system may be complex as a result of untreated trauma, mental illness, substance abuse, and their unique military experiences" (p. 2). According to the U.S. Department of Defense (DOD), there are currently over 200,000 women in the armed forces and it was estimated in 2015 that two million veterans are women, but only account for 9% of the total veteran population (Veterans Affairs, 2015). In addition, female veterans are more likely to experience sexual assault than male veterans (Zinzow, Grubaugh, Monnier, Suffoletta-Maierle, & Frueh, 2007). The combination of military trauma and military sexual assault has a long-term effect on women veterans where ongoing treatment is recommended to prevent decline into "substance abuse, unemployment, homelessness, or criminal justice involvement" (NRCJIW, 2013, p. 4). As the number of women serving in the military continues to increase after the DOD opened military occupations and specialties previously limited to men (Pellerin, 2015), research on gender and trauma from military service is needed.

Much more research is necessary to better understand the needs of the veteran population as they are likely to have PTSD and in need of better social services. An effective VTC requires "the combined effort of multiple government and social service agencies, mental health treatment providers, court administration, and Veterans Service Organizations" (Yerramsetti et al., 2017, p. 517). In addition to drug and veteran treatment courts, homeless courts have become established to help the homeless individuals who are involved in the criminal justice system.

Currently, the American Bar Association identified 32 homeless courts operating across the United States, but most of them are in California. Homeless courts are special sessions that allow homeless defendants to resolve outstanding minor criminal offenses. Homeless individuals most commonly accrue tickets for ordinance violations, but some also suffer from substance use disorder and mental illness. Generally, homeless courts provide court access for "homeless defendants, working with homeless service agencies, holding proceedings in community rooms, and recognizing individual accomplishments to reconcile and resolve their cases" (Binder, 2012, p. 34). Moreover, Burns (2010) recommended that judges of homeless courts addressing "persistent societal and personal problems of homelessness requires a better understanding of policing practices in particular cities, learning about prosecutorial charging patterns, and considering alternatives" (p. 83).

While a plethora of research exists on drug courts, research is still limited for both veteran and homeless courts. The lack of employment opportunities and the decline in public assistance allows for individuals with substance use disorders who may be homeless or veterans to become involved in the criminal justice system unnecessarily. Looking forward, improved relations between research and practice is critical, particularly with declining public funds to correctly implement programs. Innovative procedures should be explored to improve the delivery of treatment and reduce recidivism through specialty courts.

The Future of Specialty Courts

Researchers on specialty courts have found evidence of success over the past 30 years, which supports courts shifting their focus from prescribing punishments to addressing defendants' underlying problems. In addition to the need for continued research on drug courts, it is critical to explore innovative procedures as resources are curtailed due to budget cuts. Some strategies are as simple as providing individualized visual aids to supplement judicial hearings to utilization of modern technology. A more traditional recommendation is to develop a community justice center, a one-stop shop for social services and treatment (Burns, 2010); however, technology may be a more cost-effective option with flexibility in creating accessible treatment for more individuals. The assistance of technology in the criminal justice system is inevitable as new devices and software are constantly introduced. Howard (2017) explored the use of virtual reality rehabilitation (VRR) programs for physical therapy, but similar programs can be created for other types of therapy. Virtual reality is a "computer-simulation of an environment that can imitate a physical presence in real or imagined worlds" (Howard, 2017, p. 319). Development of a program to simulate behavioral therapy, treatment, and counseling services will allow more individuals to receive care and progress may be recorded with virtual reality devices.

Moreover, the use of health information technology has become popular in recent years with features such as tracking physical activity and food intake (Klasnja & Pratt, 2012; Johnson et al., 2016). For individuals receiving treatment for substance use disorders (SUD) or maintaining sobriety, some may have more challenges in finding time off from work, scheduling transportation, and/or arranging for child care to participate in treatment or related appointments. There are some applications that have been created for "behavior tracking, social support, goal setting, and access to suggestions on improving performance, which may be effective for addressing SUDs" (Klasnja & Pratt, 2012, p. 1). Also, participants who were highly motivated during treatment with regular appearances before judges may lose their momentum after completion of treatment due to the lack of supervision, resulting in potential relapse (Johnson et al., 2016).

To address the common challenges of drug court participants, Johnson and colleagues (2016) conducted a pilot study with a smartphone app called A-CHESS which was "developed specifically to help people with SUDs achieve and maintain recovery" (p. 2). A-CHESS was created based on motivation theory by incorporating tools to maintain sobriety, interrupt relapse, and prevent further harm:

> A-CHESS tools include information services, such as recovery information, a self-help meetings list news about substance use and recovery, activities such as games, guided relaxation recordings and podcasts about recovery, interactive communication such as messaging and discussion boards, and assessment and feedback tools, such as the high-risk locator and the weekly survey based on the brief addiction monitor.
>
> *(Johnson et al., 2016, p. 2)*

The study found that drug court participants are likely to use the recovery support app, but further research is needed on the effectiveness of the tool in changing behaviors (Johnson et al., 2016).

One recommendation that may be more easily implemented is for courts to use visual aids to assist defendants in understanding what judges are ordering and requiring. People who are unfamiliar with the legal system may be ill-prepared to retain complex information provided during court appearances. To improve drug court completion rates, Festinger, Dugosh, and Della Porta (2018) explored the use of visual performance feedback (VPF) to improve communication between judges and defendants. An example of a VPF includes showing defendants a graph of their urinalysis results and treatment attendance over time. Festinger and colleagues (2018) found that the VPF procedure were helpful to drug court participants, but "may be more effective in drug courts that serve individuals with more severe substance use disorders and criminal histories" (Festinger et al., 2018, p. 92). Although efficacy of improving completion rates was inconclusive, further research on VPF is needed.

To connect research to practice, it is also important to inform policymakers on findings that recommend best practices. In August 2016, nine states (KY, IL, IN, MI, OH. PA, TN, VA, & WA) joined as the Regional Judicial Opioid Initiative (RJOI) Summit to develop an action plan to combat the opioid epidemic. The action plan included recommendations for the participating states to implement: (a) diversion programs through law enforcement agencies or prosecution, (b) court diversion or sentencing options for treatment as incarceration alternative, and (c) a revised screening process to focus on high-risk individuals for overdose (White & Kunkel, 2017). Continuing to bridge research and informed policy is imperative to moving forward.

In addition to the innovative procedures that may improve treatment delivery and reduce recidivism, more research on specialty courts is necessary. As an example, veteran courts research should include "comprehensive long-term data collection and an assessment of effectiveness" (Yerramsetti et al., 2017, p. 519) and research that "identif[ies] best practices, and ideally, assist[s] in the identification of those veterans most at risk and most likely to benefit from this specialized jail diversion program" (Yerramsetti et al., 2017, p. 519).

As the future of specialty courts are in jeopardy due to dwindling public funding, it is imperative to identify that researchers identify effective procedures, standardize delivery, set performance measures that assist policy makers and other researchers in establishing and evaluating specialty courts (Henry, 2018). Additional research should focus on the complexity of these issues within a broader, or more general social context:

> Should the central responsibility for these problems be attributed to individual defendants or, alternatively, is it more useful to acknowledge that substance abuse, homelessness, and mental illness are symptoms of much larger social problems, such as poverty, unemployment, lack of access to health care, housing, or education, which manifest themselves in the misconduct of individual defendants who become involved in the criminal justice system?.
>
> *(Burns, 2010, p. 86)*

As such, there are multiple perspectives that must be considered when discussing the future of specialty courts, both in research and practice.

Conclusion

The success of drug courts has led to thousands of drug courts and other specialty courts being established across the United States. While there are challenges to overcome in formally institutionalizing specialty courts, researchers should continue exploring more about the populations served by specialty courts, the treatments that best address their needs, and mechanisms that allow courts and communities to work together. The future of specialty courts relies on continued research on both the micro- and macro-level. Descriptive and in-depth observational studies on each specialty court similar to Burns (2010) is as necessary as evaluating procedures and measuring performance of its participants. The future also requires multiple collaborations with courts, social services, community organization, and behavioral treatment centers. To respond to the opioid epidemic, White and Kunkel (2017) insisted that "state courts must partner with other organizations to confront this epidemic" (p. 1).

Exploring the use of innovative techniques in specialty courts that may better accommodate participants, the need to standardize procedures, and determine efficacy of these programs is essential. Although research on specialty courts has shown them to be effective in reducing recidivism and implementing successful treatments, there remains a gap between research and practice with many populations frequently trapped in the criminal justice system. Continuing a collaborative justice model with revised admissions' criteria and cooperative agreements between the courts, community, researchers, and policymakers is recommended to improve implementation and treatment of vulnerable populations through specialty courts.

References

Alm, S. S. (2015). HOPE Probation and the new drug court: A powerful combination. *Minnesota Law Review, 99*, 1665–1696.

Atkin-Plunk, C. A., & Armstrong, G. S. (2016). An examination of the impact of drug court clients' perceptions of procedural justice on graduation rates and recidivism. *Journal of Offender Rehabilitation, 55*(8), 525–547.

Baughman, M., Tossone, K., Singer, M. I., & Flannery, D. J. (2018). Evaluation of treatment and other factors that lead to drug court success, substance use reduction, and mental health symptomatology reduction over time. *International Journal of Offender Therapy and Comparative Criminology, 63*, 1–19.

Belenko, S. (1998). Research on drug courts: A critical review. *National Drug Court Institute Review, 1*(1), 1–42.

Belenko, S. (2001). Research on drug courts: A critical review 2001 update. *National Center on Addiction and Substance Abuse at Columbia University (CASA)*, 5–60.

Berman, G., & Feinblatt, J. (2001). Problem-solving courts: A brief primer. *Law & Policy, 23*(2), 125–140.

Binder, S. (2012). Homeless court program: Taking the court to the streets. *Judges' Journal, 51*(2), 29–35.

Brown, R. (2010). Associations with substance abuse treatment completion among drug court participants. *Substance Use and Misuse, 45*, 1874–1891.

Burns, S. L. (2010). The future of problem-solving courts: Inside the courts and beyond. *University of Maryland Law Journal of Race, Religion, Gender and Class, 10*, 73–88.

Butzin, C. A., Saum, C. A., & Scarpitti, F. R. (2002). Factors associated with completion of a drug treatment court diversion program. *Substance Use and Misuse, 37*(12–13), 1615–1633.

Cissner, A. B., & Rempel, M. (2005). *The state of drug court research: Moving beyond do they work?* Center for Court Innovation, Retrieved from www.courtinnovation.org/sites/default/files/state%20of%20dc%20research.pdf

Cosden, M., & Koch, L.M. (2015). Changes in adult, child, and family functioning among participants in a family treatment drug court. *Child Welfare, 94*(5), 89–106.

Douds, A. S., Ahlin, E. M., Howard, D., & Stigerwalt, S. (2017). Varieties of veterans' courts: A statewide assessment of veterans' treatment court components. *Criminal Justice Policy Review, 28*(8), 740–769.

Driscoll, D. T. (2018). Solving the problem of problem-solving justice: Rebalancing federal court investment in reentry and pretrial diversion programs. *Minnesota Law Review, 102*, 1381–1412.

Evans, E., Li, L., & Hser, Y. (2009). Client and program factors associated with dropout from court-mandated drug treatment. *Evaluation and Program Planning, 32*, 204–212.

Evans, E., Li, L., Urada, D., & Anglin, M.D. (2014). Comparative effectiveness of California's Proposition 36 and drug court programs before and after propensity score matching. *Crime & Delinquency, 60*(6), 909–938.

Farole, J. J., & Cissner, A. B. (2005). *Seeing eye to eye? Participant and staff perspectives on drug court.* New York, NY: Center for Court Innovation.

Festinger, D. S., Dugosh, K. L., & Della Porta, J. M. (2018). Examining the use of visual performance feedback in drug treatment court. *Experimental and Clinical Psychopharmacology, 26*(1), 85–93.

Fulkerson, A., Keena, L. D., & O'Brien, E. (2012). Understanding success and nonsuccess in drug court. *International Journal of Offender Therapy and Comparative Criminology, 57*(10), 1297–1316.

Gallagher, J. R. (2014). Predicting criminal recidivism following drug court: Implications for drug court practice and policy advocacy. *Journal of Addictions & Offender Counseling, 35*, 15–29.

Gibbs, B. R., Lytle, R., & Wakefield, W. (2018). Outcome effects on recidivism among drug court participants. *Criminal Justice and Behavior, 45*, 1–12.

Goldkamp, J. S. (2003). The impact of drug courts. *Criminology & Public Policy, 2*(2), 197–206.

Goldkamp, J. S., White, M. D., & Robinson, J. B. (2002). An honest chance: Perspectives on drug courts. *Federal Sentencing Reporter, 6*, 369–372.

Gottfredson, D. C., Kearley, B. W., Najaka, S. S., & Rocha, C. M. (2007). How drug treatment courts work: An analysis of mediators. *Journal of Research in Crime and Delinquency, 44*(1), 3–35.

Gray, A. R., & Saum, C. A. (2005). Mental health, gender, and drug court completion. *American Journal of Criminal Justice, 30*, 55–69.

Griffin, O. H., Griffin, V. W., Copes, G., & Dantzler, J. A. (2018). Today was not a good day: Offender accounts of the incidents that led to their admission to drug court. *Criminal Justice Studies, 31*(4), 388–401.

Griller, G.M. (2011). *The quiet batter for problem-solving courts.* Washington DC: National Center for State Courts.

Harrell, A. (2003). Judging drug courts: Balancing the evidence. *Criminology & Public Policy, 2*(2), 207–212.

Henry, B. F. (2018). Improving the quality of drug court clinical screening: A call for performance measurement policy reform. *Criminal Justice Studies, 31*(3), 267–278.

Hickert, A. O., Boyle, S. W., & Tollefson, D. R. (2009). Factors that predict drug court completion and drop out: Findings from an evaluation of Salt Lake City's adult felony drug court. *Journal of Social Science Service Research, 35*, 149–162.

Howard, M. C. (2017). A meta-analysis and systematic literature review of virtual reality rehabilitation programs. *Computers in Human Behavior, 70*, 317–327.

Huddleston, C. W., Marlowe, D. B., & Casebolt, R. (2008). *Painting the current picture: A national report card on drug courts and other problem-solving court programs in the United States.* Washington, DC: Bureau of Justice Assistance, National Drug Court Institute.

Johnson, K., Richards, S., Chih, M., Moon, T. J., Curtis, H., & Gustafson, D. H. (2016). A pilot test of a mobile app for drug court participants. *Substance Abuse: Research and Treatment, 10*, 1–7.

Kaeble, D. (2018, April). *Probation and parole in the United States, 2016.* Retrieved from www.bjs.gov/content/pub/pdf/ppus16.pdf

Klasnja, P., & Pratt, W. (2012). Healthcare in the pocket: Mapping the space of mobile-phone health interventions. *Journal of Biomedical Informatics, 45*, 184–198.

Knudsen, K. J., & Wingenfeld, S. (2016). A specialized treatment court for veterans with trauma exposure: implications for the field. *Community Mental Health Journal, 52*(2), 127–135.

Lurigio, A. J. (2008). The first 20 years of drug treatment courts: A brief description of their history and impact. *Federal Probation, 72*(1), 13–17.

Marlowe, D. B., DeMatteo, D. S., & Festinger, D. S. (2003). A sober assessment of drug courts. *Federal Sentencing Reporter, 16*(2), 153–157.

Marlowe, D. B., Heck, C., Huddleston, C. W., & Casebolt, R. (2006). National research agenda for drug courts: Plotting the course for second-generation scientific inquiry. *Drug Court Review, 5*(2), 1–32.

Mateyoke-Scrivner, A., Webster, J. M., Stanton, M., & Leukefeld, C. (2004). Treatment retention predictors of drug court participants in a rural state. *The American Journal of Drug Alcohol Abuse, 30*, 605–625.

Miller, J. M., & Shutt, J. E. (2001). Considering the need for empirically grounded drug court screening mechanisms. *Journal of Drug Issues, 31*(1), 91–106.

Mitchell, O., Wilson, D. B., Eggers, A., & MacKenzie, D. L. (2012). Assessing the effectiveness of drug courts on recidivism: A meta analytic review of traditional and non-traditional drug courts. *Journal of Criminal Justice, 40*, 60–71.

National Association for Drug Court Professionals. (1997, January). *Defining drug courts: The key components*. Washington, DC: Bureau of Justice Assistance.

National Resource Center on Justice Involved Women. (2013). *Responding to the needs of women veterans involved in the criminal justice system*. Retrieved from http://cjinvolvedwomen.org/wp-content/uploads/2015/09/WomenVeteransREV1-21-14.pdf

Patten, R., Messer, S., & Candela, K. (2015). "I don't see myself as prison material": Motivations for entering a rural drug court. *International Journal of Offender Therapy and Comparative Criminology, 59*(11), 1188–1202.

Pellerin, C. (2015, December 3). Carter opens all military occupations, positions to women. *DoD News, Defense Media Activity*. Retrieved from https://dod.defense.gov/News/Article/Article/632536/carter-opens-all-military-occupations-positions-to-women/

Peters, R. H., Haas, A. L., & Murrin, M. R. (1999). Predictors of retention and arrest in drug courts. *National Drug Court Institute Review, 2*, 33–60.

Peters, R. H., Wezler, H. K., & Lurigio, A. J. (2015). Co-occurring substance use and mental disorders in the criminal justice system. A new frontier of clinical practice and research. *Psychiatric Rehabilitation Journal, 38*(1), 1–6.

Rempel, M., & DeStefano, C. D. (2001). Predictors of engagement in court-mandated treatment: Findings at the Brooklyn treatment court 1996–2000. *Journal of Offender Rehabilitation, 33*, 87–124.

Rodi, M. S., Killian, C. M., Britenbucher, P., Young, N. K., Amatetti, S., Bermejo, R., & Hall, E. (2015). New approaches for working with children and families involved in family treatment drug courts: Findings from the children affected by methamphetamine program. *Child Welfare, 94*(4), 205–232.

Roll, J. M., Predergast, M., Richardson, K., Burdon, W., & Ramirez, A. (2005). Identifying predictors of treatment outcome in a drug court program. *The American Journal of Drug and Alcohol Abuse, 31*, 641–656.

Roman, J., Townsend, W., & Bhati, A. S. (2003). *Recidivism rates for drug court grates: Nationally based estimates, final report*. Washington, DC: The Urban Institute.

Rossman, S. B., & Zweig J. M. (2012, May). *What have we learned from the multisite adult drug court evaluation? Implications for practice and policy*. Alexandria, VA: National Association of Drug Court Professionals.

Rubio, D. M. (2008). *Performance measurement of drug courts: The state of the art*. Williamsburg, VA: National Center for State Courts Statewide Technical Assistance Bulletin Volume 6.

Schiff, M., & Terry, W. C. (1997). Predicting graduation from Broward County's dedicated drug treatment court. *The Justice System Journal, 19*, 291–310.

Sechrest, D. K., & Shicor, D. (2001). Determinants of graduation from a day treatment drug court in California: A preliminary study. *Journal of Drug Issues, 31*(1), 129–148.

Senjo, S. R., & Leip, L. A. (2001). Testing and developing theory in drug court: A four-part logit model to predict program completion. *Criminal Justice Policy Review, 12*, 66–87.

Shaffer, D. K. (2011). Looking inside the black box of drug courts: A meta-analytic review. *Justice Quarterly, 28*, 493–521.

Shannon, L. M., Birdwhistell, S., Hulbig, S. K., Jones, A. J., Newell, J., & Payne, C. (2017). Examining implementation and preliminary performance indicators of veterans treatment courts: The Kentucky experience. *Evaluation and Program Planning, 63*, 54–66.

Shannon, L. M., Jones, A. J., Newell, J., & Neal, C. (2018). Examining the impact of prior criminal justice history on 20 year recidivism rates: A comparison of drug court participants and program referrals. *International Journal of Offender Therapy and Comparative Criminology, 62*(2), 291–312.

Slobogin, C. (1995). Therapeutic jurisprudence: Five dilemmas to ponder. *Psychology Public Policy and Law, 1*(1), 193–219.

Tsai, J., & Rosenheck, R. A. (2015). Risk factors for homelessness among US veterans. *Epidemiologic Reviews, 37*(1), 177–195.

U.S. Department of Defense, Secretary of Defense. (2015). *Implementation guidance for the full integration of women in the armed forces.* Retrieved from https://dod.defense.gov/Portals/1/Documents/pubs/OSD014303-15.pdf

U.S. Department of Veterans Affairs (2012). *Military sexual trauma fact sheet.* Retrieved from www.mentalhealth.va.gov/docs/mst_general_factsheet.pdf

White, M., & Kunkel, T. (2017). *Opioid epidemic and the courts.* Williamsburg, VA: National Center for State Courts.

Wilson, D.B., Mitchell, O., & Mackenzie, D. L. (2006). A systematic review of drug court effects on recidivism. *Journal of Experimental Criminology, 2*, 458–487.

Wolf, E. M., Sowards, K. A., & Wolf, D. A. (2003). Predicting retention of drug court participants using event history analysis. *Journal of Offender Rehabilitation, 37*, 139–162.

Yerramsetti, A. P., Simons, D. D., Coonan, L., & Stolar, A. (2017). Veteran treatment courts: A promising solution. *Behavioral Sciences and the Law, 35*, 512–522.

Young, D., & Belenko, S. (2002). Program retention and perceived coercion in three models of mandatory drug treatment. *Journal of Drug Issues, 32*, 297–328.

Zettler, H. R. (2018). Exploring the relationship between dual diagnosis and recidivism in drug court participants. *Crime & Delinquency, 64*(3), 363–397.

Zinzow, H., Grubaugh, A., Monnier, J., Suffoletta-Maierle, S., & Frueh, B. (2007). Trauma among female veterans: A critical review. *Trauma, Violence, & Abuse*, 8, 384–400.

15
CONCLUSION

Sean Maddan

Ten million misdemeanor cases are filed annually compared to just over two million felonies (Natapoff, 2015). Misdemeanors make up the vast majority of arrests and cases processed through the criminal justice system every year. Yet, due to their less serious nature, misdemeanor crimes are almost completely ignored by scholars and practitioners. The lack of emphasis and scrutiny from criminal justice personnel, judicial system operators, academics, and society at large, on misdemeanors criminal cases borders on neglect. This book has illuminated the myriad problems concerning the misdemeanor courts and the processing of misdemeanor defendants. Police, prosecutors, defense attorneys, and judges contribute to the problems inherent in the lower courts.

As Primus (2012) noted, there is an "unequal and arbitrary nature of 'justice' in the misdemeanor courts" (p. 82). Further,

> [a] justice system that fails to adhere to the rule of law, ceases to care about the accuracy of its convictions, and fails to ensure fair and equal treatment is illegitimate not just because it results in the conviction of the innocent and the unequal treatment of racial minorities. It is illegitimate on its face.
>
> *(Primus, 2012, p. 82)*

Since most citizens' primary interactions with the criminal justice system occur in misdemeanor courts, problems with the lower courts may de-legitimize the courts and compromise respect for the law, police, and justice (Primus, 2012). Likewise, Simon (2012) argued that

> misdemeanor justice has a corrosive effect on dignity far in excess of its apparent penal severity ... [t]he exposure to constant petty (as well as not so petty) degradation and domination by the police, and the absence of an advocate, or protective judicial role, produces a constitutive lesson on the lack of accord for dignity.
>
> *(Simon, 2012, p. 116)*

The preceding chapters provides an overview of the history and research along with the potential for reform of misdemeanor courts, which may benefit defendants and society. This final conclusory chapter summarizes and suggests future directions on policy and research. In particular, this chapter provides an evaluative review of the policy suggestions on improving the operation of the misdemeanor courts, the future directions for researchers in providing an accurate picture of the state of misdemeanor courts, and the potential for reforming the lower courts and cultivating efficacy. While these policy and empirical suggestions may not be readily adopted, these suggestions could greatly enhance the cause of justice in the lower courts.

Policy Directions

This first section focuses on what can be done inside the courts and the criminal justice system to enhance case processing in the misdemeanor courts. In particular, policies that promote the reform of quality-of-life policing, fully affording due process rights to defendants, providing easier access to quality legal representation, seating better quality judges, restructuring the bail system, implementing a more robust plea process, reducing the financial consequences associated with misdemeanors, and expanding and enhancing the use of specialty courts can positively impact misdemeanor court processing and case outcomes.

Quality-of-Life Law Enforcement

The first policy suggestion for misdemeanor courts focuses on policing practices. In the wake of the lowest crime rates in history in the United States, law enforcement agencies across the country have been changing their approach to law enforcement. As discussed in Chapter 4, Gau and Paul outline the impact, oftentimes negative, of quality-of-life policing (broken windows) and law enforcement decision-making on misdemeanor court processing. Aggressive quality-of-life policing can result in a massive increase in misdemeanor arrests. Such policing practices can overwhelm the lower courts with more cases. Gau and Paul suggest that heavy-handed policing practices may decrease the deterrent effect of law enforcement efforts; additionally, Natapoff (2015) intimated that police may be more likely to arrest those who have been arrested before. Based partially on police practices, Natapoff (2015) argued that misdemeanor cases are major sources of overcriminalization, racial skews in criminal populations, and increased burdens of public defenders.

One primary approach to dealing with such policing strategies is decriminalization. There are two forms of decriminalization: full and partial. Full decriminalization means the behavior is no longer a crime. Partial decriminalization reduces the sanctions for the offenses, but the behavior remains illegal. Other decriminalization reforms include providing non-arrest options, issuing citations in lieu of arrest, or eliminating jail as a penalty. Another benefit of decriminalization is the lessened impact on offenders' criminal histories.

Gau and Paul suggested that informal or reduced sanctions are equally as or even more powerful than formal punishments in deterring crime. This result is clearly positive for defendants, but also benefits society. Reducing recidivism, according to Natapoff (2015), may save the state and the defense bar millions of dollars per year. Decriminalization or reduced sanctions may return the notion of "justice" to the criminal justice system by easing some of the racial disparity in the system as well (Natapoff, 2015).

Decriminalization, however, is not a panacea. First, there are differences across states in defining decriminalization (full and partial). This leads to non-standardization across the states and the federal government on decriminalization efforts (an example is varied treatment of marijuana). Second, those who cannot pay, may still end up in jail. States have one primary mechanism to circumvent decriminalization: civil contempt proceedings. Courts view civil contempt as a non-punitive measure, merely forcing defendants to comply with court orders. In many states, defendants are not entitled to counsel for contempt proceedings. Third, decriminalization does not halt immigrant deportations for misdemeanor charges.

Due Process in the Misdemeanor Courts

The lack of due process in misdemeanor courts has been highlighted by a number of researchers and authored chapters of this textbook. Smith and Maddan (2011) found that most misdemeanor cases in Florida were resolved at arraignment, on average, in three minutes. No research has found the average misdemeanor hearing time to be more than five minutes. It takes longer to get fast food than to be processed on misdemeanor charges in the lower criminal courts. Additionally, Smith and colleagues (2011; 2017) found that most defendants appeared without counsel (more on this in the next section) and few defendants were not questioned or informed of their rights before the hearing or during plea colloquies. This, in combination with other sources and anecdotes, points to a lack of procedural justice in the misdemeanor system.

In Chapter 13, Adler, Swaner, and Rampel evaluated the apparent lack of procedural justice in the misdemeanor court system. Misdemeanor defendants' perceptions should not be completely discounted. Misdemeanor defendants, who view courts and court actors as illegitimate, are more likely to recidivate. Improving the perceptions of defendants about the courts, judges, and lawyers is difficult to accomplish in three to five minutes. Since due process and fairness are essential to ensuring compliance with court orders by defendants, improving procedural justice is critical to any reform efforts in the misdemeanor court system.

Easier Access to Quality Legal Representation

While the Sixth Amendment guarantees the right to the assistance of counsel, the right to counsel does not extend to all misdemeanor cases. The lack of access to counsel in misdemeanor cases raises major concerns as counsel is necessary to ensure justice and serves as a check on arbitrary judicial decision-making. In emphasizing the importance of counsel, Roberts (2011) observed that "an overburdened or incompetent misdemeanor lawyer could get the same result as a committed, well-resourced public defender or high-quality private counsel" (p. 309). But, not all misdemeanor cases are simple, and in "a significant number of cases with quality private representation, counsel might uncover something that will make a difference" (p. 309).

Davies and Morgan addressed the lack of access to quality counsel in Chapter 5. They suggest that counsel is important to guide defendants through the "baffling process of prosecution." Yet, in many misdemeanor cases, defendants either have no counsel or low-quality counsel. Primus (2012) urged that this was especially essential at the trial stage; defendants need "to be afforded meaningful access to counsel" (p. 86). The concept of "meaningful counsel" is key. According to Joe (2017), it is typically newer, less experienced attorneys, who are assigned to misdemeanor cases. The new attorneys often work misdemeanor cases until they "graduate" to felony casework (Joe, 2017).

Across all the misdemeanor policy suggestions listed in this chapter, easier access to and better-quality legal representation is an underlying theme. Those without counsel have worse case outcomes than those who elected to hire counsel. This is especially true for indigent defendants who cannot afford counsel. Defense counsel should be more effective and this effectiveness should be ensured (see Natapoff, 2012). Joe (2017) suggests directing experienced attorneys toward misdemeanor cases; automatic policies that migrate public defenders to felony cases only after they have reached a certain level of experience should be eliminated. As a corollary, public defenders should be given reasonable caseloads, capped if necessary, where they have adequate time to devote to all of their clients.

In making counsel more readily available, funding becomes an issue. First, there must be increased resources for public defender offices. This will allow these offices to hire more lawyers, and lower caseloads, which theoretically allows for better quality assistance of counsel. Second, application fees associated with obtaining public counsel in some states needs to be abolished. Application fees pose an added financial impediment for indigent misdemeanor defendants accessing counsel. This is problematic as there is a disconnect between the right to counsel, indigent defendants' ability to afford counsel, and the payment of application fees for the legal services by the poor.

Better Quality Judges

In addition to improved quality legal representation, misdemeanor courts require higher quality judges (Primus, 2012). Primus (2012) found that misdemeanor judges' knowledge of the law and their receptivity to legal arguments was poor; additionally, judges tended to interpret the "rules of evidence to aid the prosecution" (p. 81). This issue is particularly problematic in the 22 states that allow nonlawyer judges to preside over misdemeanor cases. As Smith, Maddan, Price, and Tvedt (2017) illustrated in South Carolina, one-third of the judges in magistrate and municipal courts were not attorneys, and this observation was compounded by the fact that in most proceedings the prosecuting authorities were law enforcement officers. As such, in nearly 90% of court proceedings, outside of the capital of South Carolina, cases were processed without any lawyers in the courtroom

Without oversight and few appeals to higher courts, Primus (2012) suggested that expanded use of writs of mandamus and habeas corpus could ensure judges "correctly and routinely apply the law in misdemeanor cases" (p. 86). Misdemeanor courts in the vast majority of jurisdictions do not keep records of case proceedings. As such, a concomitant recommendation is to keep such records, which would allow for review of cases and the potential for a more robust appeal process for convicted misdemeanants (Primus, 2012). Finally, state judiciary and state bar associations need to create mechanisms whereby attorneys can "report systematic legal mistakes by misdemeanor court judges" and any mistakes identified can be fixed (Primus, 2012).

Reforming the Bail System

Bail has been viewed as a critical right since the founding of the republic. It was so important that it was included as the first clause in the Eighth Amendment: "Excessive bail shall not be required...." Thus, the history of bail is a long one in America. Baughman (2018) reviewed that long history and contended that though misdemeanors were punished less harshly, misdemeanors are "typically as consequential for a defendant's life as a felony" (p. 872). Those who cannot afford bail may stay in jail for months; in fact, this is the primary reason misdemeanor defendants are in jail (Baughman, 2018). Lack of bail infringes on defendants' ability to prepare for trial, and as noted by Luna, Dezember, and Redlich, in Chapter 7, increase the likelihood that defendants will enter a plea.

In Chapter 12, Shteynberg and Worden focused on the current state of bail for misdemeanor crimes and suggested that several mechanisms to nullify the harmful impact of denial of bail. At the local level, early access to counsel, the use of pretrial risk assessment instruments, the use of video arraignments, notification systems for defendants to appear, and an increased use of pretrial services for release under supervision and diversion opportunities are potential reform measures. Of these local strategies, and as noted earlier by Davies and Morgan, early access to legal counsel is paramount as public defenders typically only meet with clients for a few minutes prior to any misdemeanor hearing. This early access to counsel is especially important at bail hearings. The second most important reform, which is gaining traction nationwide, is the reduction or elimination of cash bail. Eliminating cash bail reduces the incarceration of individuals because they are poor, rather than due to their being flight or safety risks.

Reforming the Plea Process

Contrary to popular belief, most cases, including misdemeanor cases, are resolved by plea, not trial. Misdemeanor defendants are likely to enter a plea because they do not realize they have a choice, they succumb to prosecutorial pressure, or they lack the funds to bond out of jail and plea to get released (Natapoff, 2012). In Chapter 7, Luna, Dezember, and Redlich discussed the validity of pleas, generally, and the limited research on misdemeanor plea bargaining. As observed by Luna and colleagues, before entering a plea, judges must determine the defendants waive their rights and enter pleas, knowingly, intelligently, and voluntarily. Trial judges are required to adequately inform defendants of their rights, and the many rights forfeited by entering a plea. By and large, trial judges accomplish this task through oral plea colloquies and written tender-of-plea forms.

Despite these constitutional requirements, little research has focused on the validity of misdemeanor plea agreements. The research that does exist demonstrates that there is wide variation in the due process afforded misdemeanor defendants (see Luna et al.; Smith & Maddan, 2011; Smith et al., 2017). As such, the plea process in misdemeanor courts must be standardized, so that all defendants are subject to similar oral and written advisements of rights and a thorough understanding of the consequences of entering a plea. Judges should not be allowed to implement individualized versions of plea procedures, advisements of rights, and colloquies. Additionally, the language used by judges in conducting oral colloquies or the printed waiver-of-rights forms must be complete and accessible. Defendants must understand their rights to "knowingly" enter plea agreements. Additionally, and no less important, trial judges must ensure that defendants enter their pleas voluntarily. Blatant and subtle coerciveness must be removed from the plea process in misdemeanor courts. The primary way to shepherd voluntary pleas would be access to counsel and nonmonetary release pending disposition.

Reduction of Financial Consequences

Financial obligations have a great impact on misdemeanor defendants. In Chapter 9, Maddan and Bell elaborated on a of myriad financial obligations imposed on misdemeanor defendants, which coupled with pretrial detention potentially result in defendants who "lose their jobs, apartments, and sometimes children and family stability" (Baughman, 2018, p. 872). Additionally, misdemeanor sanctions and financial obligations directly impact misdemeanor defendants' financial stability through imposed debt, but these obligations and misdemeanor convictions also indirectly affect job prospects, future criminal sentencing, educational attainment, and defendants' ability to acquire particular loans. Both direct and indirect costs of misdemeanor convictions profoundly burden low-level offenders.

Not only have fines, restitution, and court costs become widely used in the United States, these sanctions are likely to increase in the future. Several avenues exist to stem their growth. First, court systems should be fully funded, so that they do not rely on financial penalties to generate income to support their operation. Second, reliance on fines, court costs, and restitution should be eliminated for misdemeanor crimes provoked by poverty, or at a minimum, the penalties for these minor crimes substantially reduced. By reducing the economic burden on the poor, the courts will reduce recidivism and the costs associated with collecting these financial obligations. Third, and alternatively, monetary sanctions may be linked to defendants' ability to pay. Currently, those who are more impoverished are disproportionately impacted by monetary sanctions. Fourth, misdemeanor defendants must be informed of the potential indirect costs associated with entering a plea, so that their decisions are adequately informed. As noted previously, standardized plea colloquies and forms must provide adequate notice of rights forfeited and the consequences of entering pleas. Finally, courtroom personnel should receive continuing education and training on the importance of the misdemeanor courts, processing, and their impact on defendants' financial wellbeing. All of these reforms could lead to greater fairness and equity in misdemeanor case outcomes.

Expanded Emphasis/Use of Specialty Courts

Hartley and Naito, in Chapters 10 and 14, reviewed the current state of specialty courts, including drug courts, homeless courts, and veterans' courts. These courts operate as a type of diversion from the traditional courts. By decreasing offenders' exposure to the more punitive aspects of the legal system and focusing on therapeutic or rehabilitative measures, they are intended to reduce recidivism among low-level and first-time offenders.

Of the specialty courts discussed, drug courts are the longest in operation, and therefore the courts subject to the most study. Research has generally indicated that drug courts are successful with first-time offenders. Defendants routed through drug courts tend to recidivate at lower rates than those who are traditionally prosecuted by the criminal justice system. Lower recidivism means lower costs of operating the courts and the correctional systems. While homeless and veterans' courts are relatively new, the extant research shows some support for the effectiveness of these courts for lower-level offenders from special populations. The use of specialty courts shows promise in assisting these populations, and more jurisdictions should adopt these alternative courts. As reflected later, more research should be conducted to continue to evaluate their effectiveness.

Future Empiricism

While the policy suggestions for misdemeanor courts in the previous section are important, academics and scholars in criminology, legal studies, political science, social work, psychology, public administration and other disciplines should emphasize the empirical study of the lower courts. Although we know a great deal about the nature of felony court processing and there has been growing interest in the study of misdemeanor courts, particularly over the last decade, much remains unknown about the lower courts. This section explores two avenues that merge this divide: Conducting more research and improving data collection.

More Research

More research on misdemeanor courts is necessary and essential. Although there is an abundance of empirical, quantitative data collected by federal and states organizations, agencies, and governments on felony courts and offenders, there has been little, systemic gathering or analysis of data on the misdemeanor courts and offenders (Stevenson & Mayson, 2018). Without systemic data collection, far little research—as compared to felony research—has been conducted on misdemeanor courts, case processing, and offenders. The availability of secondary data for analysis (discussed more later) is essential to understand, compare, and improve the processing of misdemeanors. The research and analyses should be quantitative (see studies on the misdemeanor courts in New York), qualitative (Kohler-Hausmann, 2013), and mixed methods (Smith & Maddan, 2011; Smith et al., 2017).

Felony court research emphasizes case outcomes. In particular, felony court researchers evaluate whether defendants were found guilty, if defendants were given prison sentences, and the length of prison sentences. Some researchers have attempted to similarly evaluate misdemeanor outcomes. Unfortunately, data constraints do not allow for full testing of case outcomes in the misdemeanor courts (more on this limitation later). When this data becomes available, or collected by researchers, it is paramount that researchers analyze this data so that this area of study can assess the similarities and differences between felony and misdemeanor courts, case processing, and offender outcomes.

In addition to replicating the research of felony-court researchers, scholars should adopt other avenues of study in the misdemeanor courts. For instance, Smith and Maddan (2011) conducted an observational study of misdemeanor courts in the State of Florida and evaluated the due process afforded defendants, finding variations across large and small counties. This research also lends to an understanding that misdemeanor courts do not conduct business similarly to felony courts. They are different. As such, to gain a full understanding of misdemeanor court processing, these studies must move beyond a replication of felony court research and, as noted by Worden and Clark in Chapter 6, evaluate the nuances and diversity of misdemeanor courts.

Additionally, researchers should continue their work on evaluating disparities in misdemeanor case outcomes across race, ethnicity, sex, and age. As Amanda Cook has highlighted, in Chapter 8, there is limited research that has focused on these disparities in the misdemeanor courts. The research that does exists suggests that disparities exist. Research should explore the nature of the disparity in the lower courts, and whether these disparities are rooted in individual or systemic discrimination.

Finally, scholars should subject their work to peer review. While there is a growing body of study of the misdemeanor courts, this research has predominantly been published in law reviews and journals or in the form of white-papers and government and organization reports. Peer-review provides more rigorous evaluation and ensures that research is subjected to necessary scientific scrutiny. One place to start is using the research published as white papers and reports as the foundation for peer-reviewed publications, so this area can build a substantive body of knowledge.

Increased Data Collection Efforts

As referenced, there is a great deal of missing data and information about crime and criminal justice system processing, particularly in the area of misdemeanors. With little available secondary, governmental data, large scale studies are impossible. Each of the available data sources are plagued by difficulties (Stevenson & Mayson, 2018), and some of these weaknesses impact felony research as well. For instance, in the Uniform Crime Report, a collection of crimes reported to the police and compiled by the Federal Bureau of Investigation (FBI), is predicated on individuals reporting crimes to the police. In reality, many crimes are not reported. This aggregated number of unknown crimes is referred to as the dark figure of crime. Additionally, police discretion, prosecutorial decision-making, and judicial decisions influence the data collected from the criminal justice system. Thus, even the best data collected in criminal justice is missing information. Tracking offenders as they traverse the criminal justice system is almost an impossibility as the variety of data sources are produced by a particular criminal justice organization with its own organizational needs and demands. Thus, across the criminal justice system, data is lacking in one respect, or another.

This information gap is most profoundly observed in the lower courts. For example, most felony case proceedings are recorded. Whereas this is not the case in many lower courts, and as observed by Worden and Clark in Chapter 6, this is particularly true in rural areas. Without recordings or transcriptions, it is more difficult to examine the processing of cases in the lower courts. As noted by Smith and Maddan (2011) and Smith et al. (2017), oftentimes misdemeanor proceedings are conducted on average in three minutes, or less. Without recorded proceedings or accurate record collection, gathering information in these fast-paced environments is difficult.

Another difficulty with observational research is that plea bargaining and other, important decisions may be handled outside the hearing of observers. Conversations may be held at the bench or cases resolved before hearings in courthouse hallways. Some researchers found it difficult to identify or verify information due to inaccessibility of information. It is also difficult for researchers to conduct qualitative data collection when information is lacking on websites or dockets are not available until shortly before hearings (Smith et. al., 2017). No matter the type of data collection effort, data in misdemeanor courts is greatly lacking, even more so than in any other component of the criminal justice system.

It is critical that all governments require collection of misdemeanor court data and allocate funding for this data collection at a rate commensurate with felony courts. As noted throughout this book, misdemeanor criminal outcomes carry short- and long-term consequences. Requiring data collection by misdemeanor courts ensures oversight of the proceedings and outcomes with the goal of approximating actual justice. Gathering this data would require funding to hire courthouse staff and administrators, who would manage, collect, and make accessible the data.

Although necessary, this data collection effort is likely decades away. As such, individual scholars and academics should collect data on the courts in a variety of settings (Smith & Maddan, 2011; Smith et al., 2017). Doing so, would provide snapshots of the diversity of the lower courts highlighted throughout this text. In addition to cross-sectional data, long-term trend research should be gathered and analyzed. One interesting, longitudinal effort to collect data on the misdemeanor courts is Amy Bach's Measures for Justice. Since 2010, the Measures for Justice organization has been collecting official data from agencies across the criminal justice system in an effort to bring transparency to the processing of cases, including data on misdemeanor case processing. These efforts are in the early stages of capturing data in six states: Florida, North Carolina, Pennsylvania, Utah, Washington, and Wisconsin. This work is laudable, but must be funded and extended.

References

Baughman, S. B. (2018). The history of misdemeanor bail. *Boston University Law Review, 98*, 837–883.

Joe, I. O. (2017). Rethinking misdemeanor neglect. *UCLA Law Review, 64*, 738–793.

Kohler-Hausmann, I. (2013). Misdemeanor justice: Control without conviction. *American Journal of Sociology, 119*, 351–393.

Natapoff, A. (2012). Misdemeanors. *Southern California Law Review, 85*, 101–163.

Natapoff, A. (2015). Misdemeanor decriminalization. *Vanderbilt Law Review, 68*, 1055–1115.

Primus, E. B. (2012). Our broken misdemeanor justice system: Its problems and some potential solutions. *Southern California Law Review, 85*, 80–87.

Roberts, J. (2011). Why misdemeanors matter: Defining effective advocacy in lower criminal courts. *University of California, Davis Law Review, 45*, 277–372.

Simon, J. (2012). Misdemeanor justice and the crisis of mass incarceration. *Southern California Law Review, 85*, 113–117.

Smith, A., & Maddan, S. (2011). *Three-minute justice: Haste and waste in Florida's misdemeanor courts.* Washington, DC: National Association of Criminal Defense Lawyers.

Smith, A., Maddan, S., Price, D.D., & Tvedt, C. (2017). *Rush to judgment: How South Carolina's summary courts fail to protect constitutional rights.* Washington, DC: National Association of Criminal Defense Lawyers.

Stevenson, M. & Mayson, S. (2018). The scale of misdemeanor justice. *Boston University Law Review, 98*, 731–777.

INDEX

Note: Page numbers followed by "n" denote endnotes.